YOUTH MINISTRY CARGO

by
Joani Schultz
and dozens of
contributors

Loveland, Colorado

YOUTH MINISTRY CARGO

Copyright ©1986 by Thom Schultz Publications, Inc.

Third Printing

Edited by Cindy S. Hansen
Designed by Judy Atwood
Cover Designed by Jean Bruns
Illustrated by Michael Streff

Library of Congress Cataloging-In-Publication Data

Schultz, Joani, date
    Youth ministry cargo.

    1. Church work with youth.   I. Title.
BV4447.S34   1986   259'.23   86-14836
ISBN 0-931529-14-X

Printed in the United States of America

FOREWORD

From Dennis C. Benson

"**R**mmm, Rmmm, Rumm, Rumm!" I hear the echoes of my five-year-old voice. My mind replays the sights and sounds as I push two empty thread spools along the caverns and highways formed by the crumpled sheets of my sickbed. My imagination transforms ordinary objects into wonderful and exciting heroes and villains carrying on a desperate game of pursuit.

My mind slowly relinquishes this memory and focuses back on the present. I realize that God gives Christians a special gift—childlike hearts and minds; the ability to look at life with wonder and awe. As we are time and again reborn as new "children" by Jesus Christ, the common, ordinary moments and details of life are transformed.

Christ Makes All Things New

Youth Ministry Cargo celebrates the creative possibilities for youth ministry. It shares my view that God's creations are not junky or trivial. Through the life, death and resurrection of Jesus Christ, we are empowered to transform the common elements around us into lively activities, studies and fellowship with young people. The junk in the audio-visual closet, the stack of old magazines, the weeds in the church lawn, as well as the untapped human resources surrounding us—all offer unique opportunities to help young people not only **understand the content** of the faith, but also **experience the vibrancy** of the faith.

The transformation of every experience, object and occasion is a liberating force in Christ's ministry with young people. God calls us to draw richly and consistently from the very setting and community of young people in our midst, in order to create meaningful youth programming.

I am convinced God does not want us to settle for "the way we've always done things." God calls us to meet the needs of our youth in our specific setting by blending the practical and the theological. Youth workers who handle the cargo of life from this perspective discover teaching, sharing and evangelistic opportunities in every situation. The scope of such youth ministry becomes boundless.

Our Role in Youth Work

The bench mark for the authentic Christian handling of this book's creative cargo is the view of our role in youth ministry. Something special happens when we respond to God's call to work with young people. We bring with us many resources from our pasts; learning, experience, faith and wisdom. We see our youth as special. And they need us like no other person in their world.

But our role as creative developer is not to force youth to become like us, but rather to offer ourselves, implementing the spiritual gifts God has given us, to our young people. Sometimes it is difficult to believe in the ministry of young people when chaos seems to rule the 20 young people on a retreat. Keep the faith. If we believe that God uses every situation or object to transform us into his image, he will provide us with hope in times of confusion or frustration. Perhaps the chaotic retreat can help us focus on the energy, the emotional needs and the confusion about love that are indicative of young people. Hopefully, as youth workers, we can gently channel these troublesome situations into opportunities for ministry.

You are indispensable. Your authority rests in your call from God. Nothing can shake this discipleship. Although you are challenged to read, study and grow, your primary role is to enable others to know Jesus Christ. For example, you need not have an answer for a tragic death in the family of a young woman in the youth group. Perhaps 16-year-old Bill can offer his insight by sharing what he experienced in his own grandmother's death. Thank God for allowing you to provide the climate in which God is revealed through others.

This style of ministry is different than most. Instead of the parroting methods used in many public school settings and churches, **Youth Ministry Cargo** requires growth and change in young people. By involving youth in creative learning activities, they are required to respond, and in the process come to new understandings of their faith.

A Cast of Thousands

Youth Ministry Cargo demonstrates another facet of creative youth ministry: No one is creative in isolation. Creativity is a gift from the Holy Spirit to the community of faith. The most creative people in the world are those who draw intelligently from the "idea well" of others. Somewhere, at some time, someone provided the seeds for our creativity. Perhaps some ideas will seem familiar. You might come up with creative cargo all your own. Wonderful! Welcome to the family of faith.

While most ideas are never new, how they are applied is never old. *Application* is key among creative developers. We are required to use existing resources and adapt them to each individual situation. That is why **Youth Ministry Cargo** includes hundreds of variations for the ideas supplied. And there is space allowed for you to jot down your own ideas and variations, realizing that you bring your own gifts and experience to ship with the cargo. Joani Schultz and the many contributors have done a wonderful job demonstrating how ideas can become contagious streams of ministry possibilities. In this book you will find much more than ideas: Joani and her crew have given us *methods* for thinking creatively.

Isn't it wonderful to hold **Youth Ministry Cargo** and realize you are not alone after all? This collection of ideas is a living witness to the imagination and creativity that exists within Christ's church.

Keeping a Childlike View

It has been several decades since I played with my mother's empty thread spools on the sheets of my bed. But the spiritual child of God still works within me, helping me to discover and use the cargo around me. God still leads me to places and to cargo which others may overlook or disregard. In these unexpected places, my faith imagination permits me to see what others often miss. A flower, a piece of wood, a castaway mood ring or a tea bag, become vivid means to know God's presence and love. My life is fuller for having reflected on and communicated through the inanimate cargo of life.

May God bless you in special ways as you sift through the precious resources in **Youth Ministry Cargo**. And let us thank God for the community of faith that created this unusual book.

CARGO PACKING LIST

Contents

YOUTH MINISTRY CARGO PERSONNEL

CHAPTER 1

The Value of Youth Ministry Cargo

When you enter these pages, you'll take a leap into fun, creative, faith-filled possibilities. **Youth Ministry Cargo** brings you a mountain of tried-and-true ideas submitted by dozens of youth leaders across the country. Before you jump into the ideas (and I know you can't wait), here's what **Youth Ministry Cargo** can do for you and your youth group:

1. Youth Ministry Cargo will help young people experience faith and community in fresh and exciting ways. Linda confided she finally understood, or at least was beginning to grasp, the concept of the Holy Spirit after our Bible study. Our study involved more than just sitting and discussing; it involved blowing up balloons and using them as vessels of "breath," symbolizing our being filled with the Spirit. God used that experience for Linda to stretch her faith. Balloons may, at first, seem to be an odd learning tool, but not really. When you use a balloon to teach about the Holy Spirit, it's somehow no longer just a balloon.

Toothpicks, cotton balls, shoe boxes, flashlights and plungers are other learning tools presented in this book. Take a sneak peek at the learnings, adventure and fun that await you and your group:

● A piece of string loses its commonness when wrapped around a group to show the oppression of being bound by negative habits and sin. Then, when the tightly tied string is cut and the group breaks free, a new understanding of freedom in Christ occurs.

● Baking and decorating cupcakes may sound trite, until you transform "extra-fancy" ones into a teaching tool. Do this: Carve out the center of a few cupcakes and place cotton balls in them. Place the cupcakes back in the holders and decorate them with fancy toppings. Let the kids choose which cupcakes they want to gobble up. Chances are they'll go for the "fancies." But when they sink their teeth into the treat, they'll discover it's hollow—filled with cotton. Can't you just taste the point of this unforgettable lesson? Don't be fooled by what's on the outside. Look for the good on the inside.

Herb Brokering, in his book **Wholly Holy**, said this about experiential learning: "As these elements are experienced learning becomes more particular, extraordinary, joyful, holy. The specific becomes universal, the ordinary more wonderful, the physical more spiritual, the abstract more concrete, the profane more sacred, the old more new, and whole more holy."

2. Youth Ministry Cargo uses God's world of stuff to make faith-connections. Admit it. Faith sometimes feels intangible, is hard to describe, difficult to put into words. Faith-connections with tangible, everyday objects help make sense out of nonsense.

At a youth group devotional, kids were asked to take off their shoes and place them in the center of the circle. After a few giggles and some fun, the question emerged: Which shoe best describes your relationship with God right now? The kids glanced around. Michelle picked up a brand-new tennis shoe. "I feel like my relationship with God is really new right now. I don't have any scuffs or holes yet because we've just begun." Joel chose another shoe. "This grungy, dirty loafer reminds me that God and I have been through a lot together these past few months." As the kids each continued, a spiritual experience occurred. The depth and ease of sharing wouldn't have happened if the question was simply, "How would you describe your relationship with God right now?" Common, ordinary shoes helped the kids make meaningful faith-connections.

Using ordinary stuff to make extraordinary faith-connections is nothing new. Almost 2,000 years ago Jesus demonstrated the power of taking objects and relating them to faith. Herb Brokering explained: "Much of the Gospel is in parable form. The parable creates *space* for personal opinion. It evokes original images. It can be elusive and fascinating. It invites us into its meaning. It reveals in us personal and collective images. It points beyond itself. A parable is a symbol and stirs the unconscious. It has a united force, and binds us together in its intriguing Message."

Here are just a few parables—cargo stories to jog your memory:

● **Sheep**—Jesus wanted people to know the power of forgiveness (Luke 15:4-6).

● **A mustard seed**—so what's the kingdom of heaven like? (Mark 4:30-32).

● **New cloth on an old coat/new wine and old wineskins**—items clarified questions about fasting (Matthew 9:16-17).

● **A house built on rocks and another built on sand**—these construction efforts vividly show the difference a solid faith can make (Luke 6:46-49).

● **Seeds and the sower**—what happens with the Word of God? (Luke 8:5-8).

● **A lamp under a bushel**—two objects combine to teach about sharing faith (Matthew 5:14-15).

● **A lost coin**—Jesus wants us to know his joy when someone repents (Luke 15:8-10).

● **A pearl**—it's another way to describe the kingdom of heaven (Matthew 13:45-46).

● **A fish net**—one more example of the difficult-to-explain kingdom of heaven (Matthew 13:47-50).

Jesus captured people's attention and challenged them to see faith and life in refreshing ways. But even before Jesus, Old Testament characters taught lessons with their available cargo:

● **Vineyard and grapes**—displays a picture of the people of Israel (Isaiah 5:1-7).

● **Eagles and the vine**—reflects God's power in their lives (Ezekiel 17:3-10).

● **Lion's cries**—expresses loss for two princes of Israel (Ezekiel 19:2-9).

● **A boiling pot**—presents a dismal look at Jerusalem's siege (Ezekiel 24:3-14).

So you see, using stuff to teach isn't new. Ordinary objects can stretch our imagination and bring us to new understanding.

It's sad, but some people think using objects for youth ministry programming smacks of mere gimmickry. Well, it doesn't. Jesus and the prophets used objects to clarify and bring meaning. Our Lord referred to himself as bread (John 6:35), a lamb (John 1:29), the vine (John 15:1), the gate (John 10:9), and other common objects of his day. Gimmicks? I don't think so. Common objects cement our ideas of God and the Christian life.

The goal in using stuff for faith-connections always points to Jesus. That doesn't mean the name "Jesus" has to be spoken all the time. But it does mean that Jesus' qualities, characteristics, and hope for the body of believers must shine through. Jesus is the essence of the Gospel; he is the salvation message, the way to life, and the example for who we are and how we relate to others.

3. Youth Ministry Cargo celebrates creativity as an explosion of

possibilities. Imagine this book as a launching pad. Its pages will blast you into new ways to see life and to learn. Innovative adventures in building faith and community will stretch you and your young people's thought-and-feeling patterns.

With God as our author of creativity, our Creator, it's only fitting we hunt for ways to celebrate creativity in youth ministry. Can you imagine our Maker taking a clump of dirt and transforming it into a living being? Amazing. Out of the ordinary. Extraordinary. Simple. Creative!

So why not see what lessons can be learned, what "breath of life" can be breathed into common "clods" such as index cards, leftovers and cardboard boxes. Challenge your group to tread on risky ground, to build community and to strengthen faith through experiences. Enjoy creativity's spark. Bask in the light creativity shines on past traditions and routines.

Creativity does make a difference. The youth group's topic one night was "success"—being a star. The kids who planned the evening's learning experience went far beyond the typical. When group members arrived, they walked into a sparkling, glittery, sky-like place. The room glistened with stars: the old dug-from-the-closet Christmas tree star sparkled in one corner and colored-paper stars hung from the ceiling. Small groups made star-shaped patterns by tossing a ball of yarn from person to person. Kids divided into groups by using Starburst candy colors. They filled in five answers on a five-point star to tell what success meant to them. The whole evening wove in and out of the scripture, "You must shine among them like stars lighting up the sky, as you offer them the message of life" (Philippians 2:15b). The star bombardment sunk in: We are God's stars. We are the ones who must shine God's love to those around us.

The best "ah-ha" of the night was Brenda. When we stuck a foil star on her forehead, she beamed, "I'm a star! Hey, I'm a star!" Through the stuff of stars, Brenda saw the light. She heard God's words: "You're special; you count; you make a difference; I love you."

I wonder if the learning would've been so clear if all the star stuff had been left out. I doubt it. For whenever youth leaders can bring the Gospel alive—miracles happen. Kids grow.

For starters in creativity, enter these "risky" phrases into you and your young people's vocabulary:

"Let's try it!"

"Why not?"

"We've never done this before, but . . ."

"What do we have to lose?"

4. Youth Ministry Cargo is unique. This book invites you to participate in the creative process. And that's fun! Chapter 2 probes what's inside this cargo of creativity. From there, each page offers an idea, ready and waiting for you to adapt and make your own.

Lots of people get scared when they think they might have to be "creative." But **Youth Ministry Cargo** wants you to dig inside yourself and let out the gifts God has given you. Freight out your fears; freight in God's gifts. Then you, too, can capture life in all its fullness. Take to heart what Jesus said, "I have come in order that you might have life—life in all its fullness" (John 10:10). Being aware of the collection of cargo around you and how it connects with faith and relationships can help you begin the quest for abundant life. And that's exciting!

The jampacked idea pages break down your wall of boredom; they keep you from always doing the "expected"; they challenge you to imagine yourself as elastic, ready to stretch and bend in ways never dreamed possible. **Youth Ministry Cargo** believes you can do it!

Creating with cargo also begs you to risk. You can't imagine yourself clothed in newspapers? or tossing a bathroom plunger at a target? Don't be too quick to eliminate these suggestions. Take a risk. Stretch beyond what you "normally" do. Start becoming unpredictable. Then let that risk-taking quality rub off on the kids you work with. Young people bubble with creativity and enthusiasm when given the chance. If you're willing to "try it," your group members will try it too. And they'll witness in you a more Jesus-like person, one who's willing to serve in unexpected and living ways.

5. Youth Ministry Cargo showcases God's gifts. This book symbolizes what happens when you corral dozens of innovative risk-takers—youth leaders who use common, ordinary stuff all the time. Not only will you smile at some of the objects people have used to illustrate learning or fellowship, but you'll give thanks for the gift of creativity God has dished out among the contributors.

For each idea you use—crazy crowdbreaker or serious Bible teaching—give God the glory. Thank him for the splendid array of gifts he's given us to use. For through him, kids grow. Lives change. And God becomes real.

CHAPTER 2

What's Inside the Cargo of Creativity

When it comes to creativity, some people sizzle; others fizzle. The difference between a creative sizzler and a creative fizzler isn't the ability to be creative, but rather knowing you can be creative.

Human beings each hold within themselves pieces of creativity simply waiting to be freed. It's true. Some people seem to ooze with creativity—musicians, artists, actors, writers, dynamic youth leaders. But that doesn't mean those who don't ooze as much, don't have it. We just aren't always in touch with our creativity.

Everybody is creative in his or her own way. And the body of Christ illustrates that beautifully: "Each one of you has received a special gift in proportion to what Christ has given . . . Under his control all the different parts of the body fit together, and the whole body is held together by every joint with which it is provided. So when each separate part works as it should, the whole body grows and builds itself up through love" (Ephesians 4:7, 16).

Designing a spectacular youth program, painting, singing, writing—all shout the label "creativity." But what about the person who can cook and bake, fix a motor or figure out a math problem? Those talents are equally creative. And we need each other.

So whether you consider yourself a sizzler or a fizzler, the next pages lead you through a creative process you can have fun with.

The process contains three basic ingredients that open the window to creativity. They are:
- Letting go
- Making connections
- Putting it all together

Imagine the creative process is a cave and you're a spelunker. If you're apprehensive about cave exploration, the idea is pretty frightening. But if you know and love cave adventures, a fascinating, new discovery awaits around every bend. So, on with spelunking! Explore the cargo of creativity!

Letting Go

You must begin any creative process by "letting go." That is, seeing beyond the walls, busting out of the box, breaking away from boundaries. You must take on the qualities of a rubber band. You work at being stretchable. Expandable. Elastic. Willing to take on new shapes.

Letting go is an attitude. William C. Schutz, in his book, **Joy**, calls letting go the process of "freeing, or acquisition." And to let go, people "must be open to experience, able to perceive and sense their environment, and be aware of their own internal feelings."

To show you how attitudes play into the creative game, here are three things that let you go and three things that hold you back.

● **What lets you go**—*taking a risk.* Taking a risk means you're willing to break away from the old habits and chance a new beginning. Being a Christian is risky business; being a youth leader is risky business too. For example, suggesting kids decorate the church yard for Easter with balloons, banners and kites; or focusing a learning experience around a ratty, old address book.

Check your risk-ability by answering this:
The last time I took a risk with my youth group was . . .

today _____

yesterday _____

a week ago _____

a month ago _____

a year ago _____

I can't remember _____

What'd you learn about yourself? How often do you take risks? Maybe something is holding you back . . .

● **What holds you back**—*fearing failure.* Being afraid to fail is the strongest blockade in the risk-taking category of creativity. Nobody likes to fail. Nobody. But if people never make mistakes, they'll never learn or grow. In his book, **Lateral Thinking**, Edward de Bono says, "The need to be right all the time is the biggest bar there is to new ideas. It is better to have enough ideas for some of them to be wrong than to be always right by having no ideas at all."

Maybe you think kids will laugh at you if you suggest a miniature snowball fight with cotton balls. Or making a movie screen ad to publicize your youth group. Or studying the Bible through the mail by sending cake mix boxes around the country. Or worse. What if you try one of the hundreds of ideas in **Youth Ministry Cargo** and it bombs?

God eggs us on. He wants us to risk and forget about failing. He challenges us to be foolish now and then: "For what seems to be God's foolishness is wiser than human wisdom, and what seems to be God's weakness is stronger than human strength" (1 Corinthians 1:25).

But there's more to letting go.

● **What lets you go**—*seeing outside the box*. People give birth to innovative ideas because they look at life and the stuff around them in unusual, unexpected, out-of-the-box ways. Instead of being locked into boundaries—a pipe cleaner suddenly becomes more than a tool for cleaning pipes. It bends into a moldable, shapable object for teaching Christian truths; it becomes a link in a chain of many pipe-cleaner links; it becomes a coil, a springy, spongy, bouncy toy.

But seeing outside the box isn't always easy.

● **What holds you back**—*being locked in*. There's nothing worse than being chained to ideas, feelings and ways of doing things. In his book, **A Whack on the Side of the Head**, Roger von Oech explains, "Most of us have certain attitudes which lock our thinking into the status quo and keep us thinking 'more of the same.' These attitudes are necessary for most of what we do, but they can get in the way when we're trying to be creative." Roger von Oech calls these attitudes *mental blocks*. "As you can well imagine, it's difficult to get your creative juices flowing if you're always being practical, following rules, afraid to make mistakes, not looking into outside areas, or under the influence of any of the other mental locks."

To demonstrate the problem of being locked in, look at the following nine dots. Without lifting your pencil, draw four straight lines through all nine dots. Remember: Look outside the box!

The answer is on the next page. Get the point? We have to look outside the box to stretch our creativity and to get answers to puzzles!

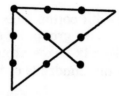

But there's more to letting go.

● **What lets you go**—*believing anything goes*. That's right. Pursue your wildest ideas and imaginations. Instead of thinking that theaters only advertise popcorn, candy and a few local businesses, make a movie ad to promote your youth group. Instead of thinking needles are simply instruments for sewing, use them in unusual ways. At a youth group meeting, stick needles in strategic places such as ceiling tiles and erasers. Ask the kids to search for them. Compare the experience to God: He is always present—even in difficult times when we think he is hard to find.

Let your youth group brainstorm ways to build closer friendships among the members. Allow ideas to pop like popcorn. Don't hold back. Anticipate sporadic popping! Think of ideas like a secret-friend system; games to mix old friends with new friends; drawing names for partners at each meeting; a trip to Hawaii—don't forget, anything goes!

After the brainstorming session, when all the ideas (even the outrageous ones) are accepted, have the kids decide what they'll do. Because you believe any idea is possible, the kids may choose to host a Hawaiian beach party in the winter for friends to come and share the "Son"!

● **What holds you back**—*making judgments*. I remember a psychology class in college. One day the professor brought in examples of the Rorschach inkblot test. Seated in the front of the class, I clearly could see each blob and was delighted when he asked us to shout out what we saw. Most of the class yelled out butterflies and other "obvious" shapes. But I was intrigued. I started voicing my perceptions—a sideways sailboat sloshing in a storm and a couple of other unpredictable (but obvious to me) answers. The teacher stopped. He looked at me and said, "You need help." I knew he was kidding because the class chortled. But I quit responding. The professor's judgments on my creative observations stifled me—even though it was in fun. All I was doing was trying to look at inkblots in a new way. Yet I felt put down for it. I learned more than psychology testing that day. I learned the danger of making judgments and that we should never put down creativity—even if it seems wacky and far out. How else do people look outside the box?

Judging ideas as right or wrong, or good or bad, kills creativity. So, put a moratorium on judging while you and your group move on to making connections.

Making Connections

Letting go is a creative process ingredient you'll always need to work at. The next ingredient is "making connections." Now the fun begins! This step is the idea-generating time, the opportunity to really think big, small and somewhere between the two.

If you think creativity stales or only happens once in a while or to the "gifted," look around you. Make connections. Life helps us see creativity at its peak. Always fresh, revitalizing, new, fascinating, remarkable, profound. Focus on God's example. Frederick Buechner said it so well in **Wishful Thinking**: "Using the same old materials of earth, air, fire, and water, every twenty-four hours God creates something new out of them. If you think you're seeing the same show all over again seven times a week, you're crazy. Every morning you wake up to something that in all eternity never was before and never will be again. And the you that wakes up was never the same before and will never be the same again either."

Making connections means you're ready to transform common objects; you're ready to get into the action. But remember—God started it all; he's the great transformer. If God can transform common clay pots like us into his image, think what we can do with a regular old pot: plant seeds in it, collect offering in it, decorate it with bright-colored paint and decoupaged letters and pictures, fill it with warm water and have a foot-washing service! Read and rejoice in these words about God's creativity:

● "When anyone is joined to Christ, he is a new being; the old is gone, the new has come" (2 Corinthians 5:17).

● "So then, you Gentiles are not foreigners or strangers any longer; you are now fellow citizens with God's people and members of the family of God" (Ephesians 2:19).

So, we're ready to begin the next leg of our journey into creativity—making connections. Here's where to start:

1. Make the ordinary extraordinary. Making something extraordinary isn't magic, it simply means your imagination is nudged into seeing a familiar object in a new way. A basketball hoop suddenly becomes a means of teaching a truth about shooting blindly. With a blindfold around each person's eyes and a basketball being flung at the hoop, kids soon learn how hard it is to make it on their own. But with the aid of a coach, someone telling them where to stand and from where to shoot, the chances are greater that the blindfolded person will score. Likewise, with God's help we have direction. An ordinary hoop and net make the point. And it's fun too.

Something "regular," that's always used in a particular way, transforms into something new. Here's an exercise you can do alone or with your youth group. It's one I like to do with a group—especially when we're traveling, camping or just feeling like being spontaneous. We call the game "This could be a . . ." We use any object nearby and transform it into whatever our imaginations can create. For instance, a banana. Our circle of "creators" pass it from one person to the next, acting out the idea as they fill in the blank, "This could be a . . . telephone receiver. Hello, anybody home?" ". . . a pistol. Stick-em up!" ". . . a microphone. Feelings, whoa, whoa, whoa, feelings." ". . . a smiling pair of lips. Smile, you're on **Candid Camera!**" ". . . a frowning face. Whaa, I want my mommy!"

You'll be surprised how much fun you can have with an ordinary object turned extraordinary. The game gives permission to be crazy, let go and give your imagination a workout.

2. Thinking metaphorically: "This is like . . ." In another sense, creativity takes on a metaphorical mind-set. The thinking process is one of comparing a word, phrase or object with something else. For example, a flashlight is like our faith. A gift-wrapped box is like us.

In **A Whack on the Side of the Head**, Roger von Oech says, "The key to metaphorical thinking is similarity. In fact, this is how our thinking grows; we understand the unfamiliar by means of the similarities it has with what is familiar to us. For example, what were the first automobiles called? That's right, 'horseless carriages.' And the first locomotives were called 'iron horses.' We refer to resemblances between things all of the time. We say that hammers have 'heads,' tables have 'legs,' roads have 'shoulders,' and beds have 'feet.' " We go from the familiar to understand that which might be unfamiliar.

Jesus spoke in parables because he knew people would grasp great truths through simple explanations. God created us to think by "making connections."

Sometimes these connections surprise and delight us. Here's another parable. What do you connect from this?

> "Once there was a class
> who wanted to sculpture Jesus.
> They had no clay or wood or marble,
> so they took pumpkins
> and they had their art premier
> at night with candles.
> One person looked at a pumpkin
> until she saw it as a pumpkin pie.
> She took it to a park
> and ate it with her friends
> on Halloween night.
> Everyone who was there
> thought it was a very good way
> to see Jesus in a pumpkin.
> Someone started the song
> 'Blessed be the pie that binds.'
> When they quit laughing, they agreed
> that a pie can do it and can be a tie."
>
> (From **"I" Opener** by Herb Brokering)

What connections did you make? Did the parable seem like a bunch of nonsense? Or did it make sense? One connection I've made with that parable is to use it for a "pumpkin youth night" in the fall. The kids come with pumpkins, carving knives and old candles. We carve religious symbols in the pumpkins and decorate the worship area with the carved masterpieces each containing a lighted candle. That leads into a worship service planned by the kids, using the pumpkin parable. We build community, worship and turn an ordinary pumpkin into a honey-glowing worship tool.

Since we're into making connections, try this. Beside each word or picture on the next page, jot down all the connections you can think of. For example, connections for the word "secret" could be: secret pals; secret gifts (deliver, ring the doorbell, run away); secret trip (surprise the kids with a "mystery" bus ride), etc.

Remember to let go first, then make connections.

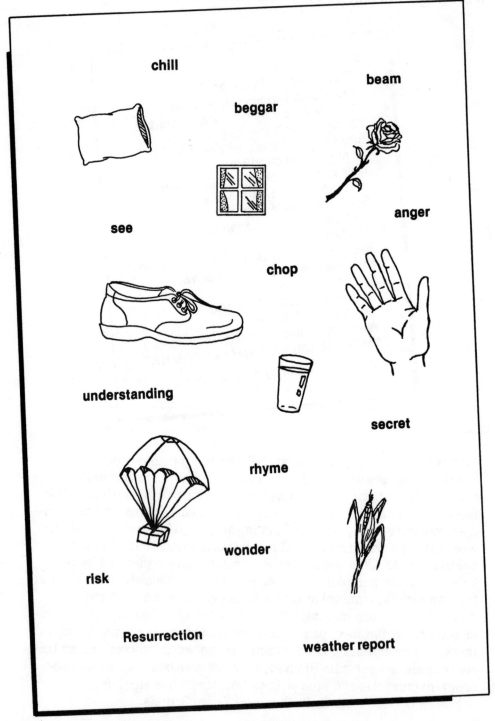

chill

beam

beggar

anger

see

chop

understanding

secret

rhyme

wonder

risk

Resurrection

weather report

3. Generating ideas. Lots of people call this stage brainstorming. That's when you dream up as many possibilities as you can. This chain of ideas is linked together by your imagination. One comes after the other, with no judgments passed. Here are some generating "rules of the game" to help you along:

● **Use more than one brain.** Get together with a bunch of others. You can brainstorm alone, but when you add other people, you're adding other possibilities. And it's fun. How about asking a few youth group members to help you think of ideas? your peers? the church staff? your co-workers? a conglomeration of older and younger people? Ask people you'd normally never "lump" together: truck driver, school teacher, sixth-grader, disabled person, grandparent, banker, organist. Imagine the combination of ideas these people can generate.

● **Create an atmosphere of trust.** When you're generating ideas yourself, usually you don't have to worry about what other people will think. But when you gather a group of thinkers, make sure they feel okay about each other. Ideas die when someone is afraid to voice an opinion for fear of what the others will think. A hint: Create common ground before you start. For example, if you're going to generate ideas for the big autumn kick-off event, ask people to each share their favorite fall activity. Get acquainted a bit. Even if you've met many times before, it does no harm to initiate a fresh bond of trust.

● **Promote a cross-pollination of ideas.** This follows an aura of trust. Let everybody know that any idea is allowed. Even if the brainstormers think it won't work, even if they're trying to be funny, even if they think it's dumb. Let the ideas fly! This helps the pollination process. When ideas flow freely, you'll generate more ideas. That's because one idea illuminates somebody else's thought process, and so on.

So set an agreement from the start: No judging. All ideas are fair game.

● **Use a just-right-size group.** When you're involving others in brainstorming, use small groups. No less than two; no more than eight. I know that sounds small, but large groups often inhibit sharing. Four to six people works best. That means if you have a small youth group of four, great! Everybody gets in on the act all at once. If your group is larger than eight, break it into smaller groups. Then pool the best of the ideas.

● **Write down all ideas.** If you're generating ideas alone, write them all down. Have a pile of scratch paper handy. Keep the left-over ideas. They might ignite your creativity another dry-idea time.

When you're working with a group, record all the ideas given. It's best to have one person designated as the recorder. Have the recorder jot down everything—and I mean everything—that's generated. This person carries great responsibility. Watch that the recorder doesn't fall into the I'll-edit-my-way trap or I'll-just-write-down-what-I-think-will-work trap. That's dangerous for the idea-generating process. The I'll-edit-my-way trap involves a recorder who thinks he or she can reword the idea better—but the idea usually loses its original intent. It's okay for a recorder to reword what's been said as long as he or she listens carefully and *asks* if that's what is meant. The I'll-just-write-down-what-I-think-will-work trap censors most of the group's ideas. Every idea—even if it's meant to be a joke—should be written down. This gives credibility to the important rules: no judging and *everything* is possible.

● **Have fun with it.** Generating ideas can be hard work, but it's fun too. Help yourself and others to see it as a time to let loose and be crazy. Get rid of inhibitions and judging what's right and what's wrong. You can't have fun when you're afraid to make a mistake. So erase these phrases from your vocabulary:

Other phrases you know that kill creativity's fun: _____

Got them erased? Okay, now on to the next step.

4. Jump-start your generating process. All this sounds great, you say. But sometimes I feel like my idea fuel supply is on empty. I'm in a desert and there is no sign of life. When it's hard to get those creative sparks flying, it's good to have a handful of "jump-starters." I call them jump-starters because you've got the ideas inside you, but they need to come out. Jump-starts are other sources, avenues of thought or jolts that get you thinking.

When my creativity seems at a standstill, I jump-start it by running through the five senses. For example, if I'm trying to think of a way to illustrate a Bible story, I'd ask: Can it come alive through the sense of smell? Perfume could be used to illustrate Mary dousing Jesus' feet; or the aroma of baking bread could be used to illustrate Jesus' words, "I am the Bread of Life." Could a Bible story come alive through the sense of touch? Perhaps by playing a game of Hug Tag and then talking about how Jesus reached out and touched people. Or closing with "peace of the Lord" handshakes and hugs. Or could a passage speak by using sound? How about accompanying Psalm 150 with cymbals, drums and flutes? Or would whispering a passage while reading it be more effective? How about the use of taste buds? Tasting a Passover meal would have more impact than simply reading the story. Passing around an apple while reading the story of Adam and Eve would be interesting. Who will take the first bite? Could a passage come alive through the sense of sight? Would acting out a story with the group members make a greater impact? Would a visual presentation of a movie or music video open up a world of discussion?

Using the five senses is just one jump-starter I use. Here's a list of other ideas; you add to it:

● Think through the newspaper bits—who, what, when, where, why.

● Remember the four seasons.

● Thumb through a thesaurus.

● Rummage through a junk drawer.

● Keep an "ideas" file that holds anything you find exceptionally interesting.

● Journey to new places.

● Imagine other people other ages.

● Browse through a dime store or flea market.

● Play a word-association game.

●Scavenge a junkyard.

Add your own: _____

_____

_____

_____

Now would be a great time to start your own idea file. Collect a potpourri of clippings, a seed of a thought, a game or activity you find interesting, anything that seems adaptable. Even if you never use the idea "as is" it's great for kicking off new innovation.

Putting It Together

After letting go and making connections, it's time to put it all together. Here's where thoughts become actions. This stage of the creative process makes your already-done work worthwhile, not just a frivolous exercise in idea-birthing.

1. Shop for the best. As you wade through your (huge, gigantic, overwhelming) list of (incredible, super, great) ideas, it's time to shop for the best. Imagine you're going to the supermarket to buy next week's groceries. Chances are you'll select foods that meet your needs for the upcoming seven days. If your cupboards bulge with 25 full cereal boxes, you probably won't buy cereal. Or if your 10 pounds of flour will last a while longer, you won't spend your money on more flour.

Get the picture? In spite of all the tantalizing ideas (or aisles of groceries), you can't possibly try them all. So go for what best meets your group's needs at this time. There will be opportunities to use the other appetizing ideas—so save them for later.

What's your group's greatest need? Is it to experience a burst of creative worship? Do group members need to get to know each other better? Does your group need a boost in biblical knowledge? Or do you just want to have a good time?

You've got to be in touch with your group's needs. Chapter 3 explores a number of ways to determine your group's needs. Once you have that information, your shopping task becomes easier. Let's say your kids generated creative ways to learn about and experience the body of Christ. Here's their list of ideas:

●meet on a masking-tape body shape while reading 1 Corinthians 12:12-27

●solve a mystery game that needs each person's clues

- use a string of Christmas tree lights to show everybody is necessary—if one bulb is missing, the string won't shine
- interview church board members to find out what they do
- create a clay sculpture representing all ages and types of people in the church
- write a special reading to be shared with the entire congregation

It's tough to pick only one idea. They're all good ones. But what meets your group's needs *right now*?

You know your teenagers need cohesiveness—a bond. They need ways to say each person is valuable. To best meet that need, the mystery game or the tree lights might rank as top possibilities.

2. Assign "do it" duties. This putting-it-all-together step is where many leaders fall short in providing the best creative experiences. Remember, people learn best by doing; the more you involve people in owning the project, the more they'll give *and* receive.

Lots of youth group leaders let certain thoughts or feelings interfere with their ability to assign young people and other adults "do it" duties. They say:

- "It's just easier if I do it myself."
- "I can't trust the kids to follow through."
- "If it's gonna be done right, I better do it myself."
- "What if they fail?"
- Add your own: _____

Of course, there's a bundle of risks that come with assigning others "do it" duties. You're right—they might fail. Or they might forget. And maybe you could do it better. But if you're a true promoter of the creative process and growth in young people, you'll want others to join in the fun.

I remember weekly planning meetings with two different young people each week. We'd meet to decide an opening devotion for the weekly instruction class. The pairs of teenagers came in all shapes and sizes of abilities. Some were painfully shy; others were comfortably extroverted. Some had never planned or led anything, anywhere. It was a challenge. But each week, we'd explore new creative worship possibilities according to their abilities and comfort levels. One week, a puppet play; another, a clown skit. Responsive readings. Group games. Skits. Game shows. Sharing activities. Each week the kids helped plan and lead. And each week I watched them grow in confidence and self-worth.

Don't simply dump a duty on another person's shoulders and expect him or her to "do it." That's a big mistake. As a leader, nurturer and creative-growth helper, make sure teenagers or other adults aren't abandoned in their creative endeavors. They need your guidance; they need your assurance and presence to nudge them along.

Start by thinking of youth group members who would feel comfortable assisting, organizing or leading the idea. Make assignments: "Heidi, can you find the scripture readings? Kim, do you have a string of tree lights that won't work unless every bulb is in it? Rick, will you choose an appropriate song and play your guitar to lead group singing?"

There. You've assigned your "do it" duties. Kids will feel valuable, they'll stretch themselves into creative leadership and new possibilities. I've seen shy, afraid-to-speak-to-more-than-one-other-person kids transformed into confident leaders when given the opportunity. I marvel at the growth that occurs when young people are given responsibility in the creative process.

3. Make it happen. The creative experience happens *now*. All your plotting and planning may have looked like a skeleton, but now it's matured into an activity, an idea with flesh. Do it now. Involve others. Enjoy.

Present the idea with enthusiasm. Let people know you're willing to take a creative risk; you're willing to experience a "new."

4. Look into the rear-view mirror. Most youth groups foster a bad habit of never looking in the rear-view mirror. That is, they preoccupy themselves with what's ahead and don't evaluate what's been. Chapter 3 contains helpful evaluation tools you can use.

Without learning from what was great about an idea or what was not so great, groups don't move ahead with clarity of purpose.

Don't be afraid to ask: "What did you like? What would you have changed? How did you feel when we did . . .?" Without proper feedback, your next creative adventure can't be refined.

In his book, **Joy**, William Schutz says: "Many products may be generated in the course of creative activity, but the evaluation as to which of these satisfy the situation, and which are worthless, is essential. This phase distinguishes the bizarre from the creative, and the productive from the mundane."

Evaluation. It's necessary to grow. So don't forget to look in the rear-view mirror.

Letting go, making connections, putting it together. Three vital steps to breathing life into creativity. Let these be your stepping stones to a delightful adventure of seeing life, learning and experiencing our Lord in new and refreshing ways.

CHAPTER 3

How to Unpack
And Use Cargo

These step-by-step guidelines will help you put ideas into action. Apply these eight tips and your experience with **Youth Ministry Cargo** will be a rich one! Don't hesitate to use the hints for other areas of your youth ministry too.

1. Collect your group's needs. Kids' emotional, social, physical and spiritual needs help dictate what they're receptive to learning and doing. If they're worrying about next Friday's dance or whether or not their parents will divorce—a youth group meeting on the historical confessions of the church won't cut it. Not that a lesson on historic confession is bad. It just won't meet kids' present needs.

Focusing on needs helps you choose appropriate activities for your group. For example, if a group of teenagers has never been together before, you shouldn't plan an in-depth, personal sharing session on inadequacies and inabilities. The meeting would probably be a failure. A more appropriate, need-meeting activity would be a non-threatening mixer that focuses on building friendships. You could use the interview questions in Getting to Know You on page 336. Kids could ask each other questions such as, "How would you describe a perfect vacation?" Or, "How did you feel on your first day of junior high school?"

Need-collecting should be done every three to six months—but no less than once a year. That's because kids' needs are always changing. Here are a few ways to go about need-collecting.

● **Anonymous cards**—Ask young people to each write on a 3×5 card: their age, their sex, the greatest need in their life right now, and their friends' greatest needs right now. This simple device can identify some immediate needs.

● **Random phone calls**—Ask other adults and young people to survey several youth group members. Develop a brief phone survey so all the calls are similar. Make sure the callers record each answer. Include questions such as:

- What do you like about the youth group?
- What would you change about the youth group?
- If you could have a youth meeting on any topic, what would it be?
- If you could choose any topic to help plan, explore, or lead, what would it be?
- What kind of group would you feel comfortable bringing your friends to?
- **Mail survey**—Together with one or two young people, write a needs survey, make copies and mail to all your youth group members. Include a return date for the survey to be mailed or brought to the church. The following example includes a wide selection of needs and concerns:

Choose five concerns from this list and rank them. Make "1" your highest concern, "5" your lowest concern.

_____ family problems	_____ communication
_____ how to talk with parents	_____ independence
	_____ drinking
_____ making choices	_____ sex
_____ smoking	_____ the future
_____ money	_____ anger
_____ school	_____ shyness
_____ loneliness	_____ happiness
_____ joy	_____ guilt
_____ forgiveness	_____ world hunger
_____ peace	_____ community
_____ service	_____ outreach
_____ how to share my faith	_____ making friends
	_____ dating
_____ breaking up	_____ suicide
_____ death and dying	_____ other: _____
_____ worship	_____

- **At-event surveys**—Select one of the need-collecting methods and do it anywhere kids have gathered: worship services, retreats, youth group meetings or lock-ins.

Offer treats such as cupcakes, coupons, back rubs or bookmarks to all the people who complete the survey.

●**Needs "pool party"**—Gather a number of young people and adults who represent a spectrum of "types" of people; for example, athletic, musical, shy, outgoing, etc. Pool their ideas. Write down everything your thinkers say about needs.

●**Needs "show time"**—During a youth group meeting ask partners to think of two specific needs they have in their lives right now. Ask pairs to act out their needs without using words. Have other group members guess the needs. Make sure someone records all the needs acted out.

●**Needs mosaic**—Distribute scissors, tape, old magazines and newspapers. Give kids each a sheet of construction paper to fill with words or pictures that reflect their greatest needs right now. Then have kids tell about their needs mosaics.

These need-collecting ideas will get you started. Now let's travel with a typical youth group through the steps for using **Youth Ministry Cargo**.

Imagine that your church's teenagers have been actively involved in the youth group for the past few years. They've built friendships and feel comfortable sharing their faith with each other. After taking a group needs survey, you discover one of their needs is "service and servanthood." The following steps help you meet this expressed need.

2. Get acquainted with Youth Ministry Cargo. If you've got any threads of explorer in you, you won't be able to put this book down! That's because so many fun, new ideas are just waiting to be discovered—and used!

Begin by looking at the topical index on page 57. Skim the list and underline the topics that jump out at you as need-meeters. For example:

ROCK MUSIC—150, 151, 154
RULES—197
SCHOOLS—197
SELF-IMAGE—7, 10, 18, 47, 113, 131, 152, 161, 195, 217
SERVANTHOOD—36, 143, 207, 214
SERVICE PROJECT—45, 59, 67, 143, 204, 215
SHAVING CREAM—213

Next, investigate the Contents on page 7. Star the cargo you have on hand. Circle the cargo you want to acquire. For example:

ROLLER SKATES
   204) Outreach on Wheels
★ **ROPES**
   205) Bound for Glory
(**SEEDS**)
   206) A Spring Worship
★ **SHOES**
   207) Shoe Renew
   208) Shoes-and-Jacket Scramble
SHOWER CURTAIN
   209) Rear-Projection Screen

Both lists are like sticks of unlighted dynamite waiting to be ignited. You and your group will explode with new, exciting challenges. To get acquainted with these lists, you can:
- browse through the pages alone.
- check things out with a dreamer-type person.
- bounce around ideas with the church staff.
- discuss possibilities with one or two young people.
- grab a team of adult volunteers to work with you.

Together, evaluate and scrutinize what will work best for you. And that's where the "Variations" sections come in. Most ideas aren't done *exactly* the way they're written. You might use smaller groups, or focus on a different object, or rearrange the theme to better meet your needs. To consciously push you into that process, each idea offers a few adaptations and space for your own great ideas. If you need energizing, read the section in Chapter 2 titled "Jump-Start Your Generating Process."

If your youth group's need is to reach out in service, check out the topical index under "Servanthood." You might choose the following idea:

Shoe Renew

How would your group members react to a foot washing service? Would they take it seriously, or would they make fun of the whole idea? Young people are sometimes so self-conscious about their feet that a foot washing service does not always convey the message of servanthood that you want them to receive. One way to convey the same point in a contemporary way is to have a Shoe Renew. Here's how it's done.

For the next meeting, ask each young person to wear a pair of shoes that needs renewing—either dress shoes which need a shine or tennis shoes in need of new laces. Ask the group members to wear shoes they don't mind having "touched up." Have on hand different kinds and colors of shoe polish, rags and brushes, as well as several pairs of brightly colored shoelaces.

Begin by reading the story of Jesus washing the feet of the disciples (John 13:1-17). Tell the kids that, in Jesus' day, when guests entered a home after walking about on dusty paths, they would have their feet washed by the servants of that house. Jesus washed his disciples' feet to show them that they should be servants to one another.

After dicussing the meaning of servanthood, let the kids serve one another by renewing the shoes of a partner, either with a glowing shoeshine or with a new pair of colorful laces. Not only the shoes, but the whole group will feel renewed through serving one another.

—Mark Killingsworth

Variations

1. Renew old shoes, then sell them at a garage sale or donate them to a mission.

2. During the Christmas season, renew old mittens and hats as well as shoes. Hang the mittens and hats on a tree and place the shoes at the base. Encourage congregation members to add to the collection. Give the items to a children's home, nursing home, or agency that assists needy people in the community.

Now think about how you can adapt, change, vary, alter and modify that idea. Here are some starters.

● Have one young person portray Jesus and renew all the shoes.

● Use a mime or clown to begin the Shoe Renew and involve other kids as followers.

● Decorate the room with footprints or hanging shoes.

● Serve shoestring potato chips for a snack.

● Challenge the kids to renew someone else's shoes during the next week.

● Use the Shoe Renew as a "kick-off" for choosing a service project.

● Do the Shoe Renew with the whole congregation.

● Do the Shoe Renew with the Sunday school children.

Wow, there are seven more variations on one idea. Your job involved taking the cargo idea presented and molding it to fit your unique situation.

If you're still having trouble thinking of variations and mumbling, "I can't do that," use these bonus "jump-starters."
- Adapt the idea to a different time of the year.
- Change one rule or action.
- Invite different age groups to participate.
- Blindfold participants.
- Link the idea to the season or theme of worship.
- Change the time of the day it can be done.
- Plan a unique meeting place.
- Refocus the theme or thrust and change why it's being done.
- Use a different set of cargo.

3. Select the best Youth Ministry Cargo ideas for you and your youth group. This step isn't easy. Narrowing down all the possibilities can be a chore. But it's challenging and fun. The experience itself is getting closer.
- Decide why you're going to do the idea. Designate a clear purpose, a goal.
- Make certain the idea fills a need.
- Decide when you'll do it: next year? next month? next week?

4. Share leadership. Go through the **Youth Ministry Cargo** idea line by line noting tasks that need to be done. For example:
- Arrange for announcement and publicity that kids should wear old shoes.
- Ask kids to collect supplies: shoe polish, rags, brushes, brightly colored shoelaces.
- Find a young person to read John 13:1-17 and explain the significance of foot washing.
- Recruit someone to give instructions for the Shoe Renew experience.

Many leaders choose to organize ideas by themselves. But this step challenges you to involve others. Helping out and making it happen enriches the whole experience and gives the others a sense of ownership in the idea.

5. Get your "cargo" together. This means making sure everything happens. "Cargo" becomes the essential ingredient for most ideas (after the people). Be a scavenger when it comes to collecting supplies. Go for the inexpensive, ask for donations, collect junk, contact congregational members.

For a while, some of my favorite cargo-items were paper sacks. Thanks to a church member who worked in a paper sack factory, our group was supplied with all the sacks we'd ever need! Because of the surplus of sacks, using paper bags was high on my list of fun. Sacks became masks, they held surprise decoration kits, we played sack games, we made puppets and name tag bags, etc.

6. Enjoy the activity. That's right. All your planning and preparation pays off now! Take the Shoe Renew: It's a fun, touching, experience for the group. The kids gain a deeper understanding of servanthood and explore how they feel being givers and receivers of love—they just plain enjoy themselves.

Make memories. When you put creative ideas into action, you're stretching faith and friendship memories for each person.

I'll never forget a particular retreat worship experience. Remember when McDonald's sold hamburgers in red cardboard boxes? Each time we met for worship, the brilliant worship leader used those boxes. One time we used the boxes to build walls of sin that blocked our view of each other and kept us apart. The next time we flattened the boxes to form a red cross on which we wrote our confessions of faith. Then came my favorite—the grand finale! The boxes were filled with confetti, balloons and bread to celebrate communion. After the retreat, every time I went to a McDonald's I thought about that unique, meaningful, unforgettable worship experience with the boxes!

Just think. If you do a Shoe Renew with your group members, each time your kids look at a pair of shoes they'll be reminded of servanthood.

7. Look for learnings. The McDonald's boxes held an obvious impact for me. Sometimes learnings and unforgettables might not be so obvious. Simply because group members aren't ooohing and aaahing with profound statements, that doesn't mean they haven't grown. After an activity, encourage kids to verbalize their discoveries. Ask:
- What did you learn or re-learn about yourself?
- How will you be different after this?
- What's one thing you'll do differently now because of this ex-

perience?

Or have them complete:
- Because of this experience, my faith . . .
- Because of this experience, I feel . . .
- Because of this experience, I think . . .
- Because of this experience, I hope . . .
- Because of this experience, I will . . .

And learning doesn't always come in giant leaps. Sometimes learning sneaks up and surprises people—even yourself! Sometimes insights come to those who won't participate.

I recall an intergenerational worship in which we asked small groups of eight to build newspaper walls around themselves. The whole group numbered around 250 people. That's a lot of wall-builders. Being the leader, I was especially conscious of what was going on. I continued to stress, "If you're not in a group, join a group. Or if you see people without a group, invite them into yours. Then build your walls."

But one woman, arms crossed, refused to participate. I encouraged her. She ignored me. I thought, "Well, not everyone can be reached in the same way."

After the experience, we all talked about what it felt like to build walls. Everyone chimed in with personal revelations of sin, barriers in relationships and other good insights.

The next day, I'd almost forgotten about the woman who didn't join in. To my surprise, she sought me out. With misty eyes she took my arm and said, "Yesterday I was afraid no group wanted me. I was scared they'd reject me. But I didn't want to reach out, even though some had invited me to join their group. I had built a huge wall around myself."

The woman learned something about herself—even though I thought the experience had failed for her. So be cautioned: Don't judge too quickly whether or not an idea has succeeded or bombed.

Teenagers might not be so apt to corner you and verbalize their learnings. But in building an atmosphere of trust and approachability, you'll be surprised how kids will grow—and let you know!

8. Evaluate the activity. Here are several practical suggestions for monitoring **Youth Ministry Cargo** (and any other) program's strengths and weaknesses.
- Meet with a small group for verbal feedback. Ask: "What did you like about the stuff we did? What would you change? What

would you do again? What can we learn from this for future ideas?"

● Prepare an evaluation form for participants to fill out. Add fill-in-the-blank statements such as: I really liked . . . If we did this again, I'd change . . . One thing I learned from this . . .

● Give kids each a paper plate and marker. Have them write evaluations on the paper plates and toss them back like Frisbees to you.

● Give the youth group members each a piece of paper and a pencil. Have them write evaluations on the paper and fold it into a paper airplane—for a flying assessment.

● Make traffic signs from posterboard: stop, yield, speed limit, soft shoulder, kids' crossing, etc. Post the signs in the meeting room; then ask youth group members to gather by the sign that best describes their assessment of the activity. Allow time for discussion.

● Gather stuff such as scouring pads, plastic fruit, flowers and ribbons. Ask kids to compare the experience to the stuff. For instance, "This experience was most like a scouring pad for me because I felt uncomfortable with myself, but I decided to clean up my act."

● Plan a traffic light evaluation. Hand out paper, pencils, and green, yellow and red circle stickers. (You can get the stickers from any office supply store.) Have kids list their feelings, thoughts and reactions to the experience. For example, in the Shoe Renew, someone might write:

> uncomfortable   unsure
> excited!   happy!
> ready to serve   challenged
> embarrassed

Then have each person evaluate the feelings, thoughts and reactions with the stickers. Imagine each color represents a traffic light color:

● **Use red for stop.** This wasn't good ("embarrassed").

● **Use yellow for caution.** This could go either way. (For example, "uncomfortable" could be bad if you felt awful about the experience, or it could be good if it prodded you to change or take action.)

● **Use green for go.** This was great! (For example, "excited," "ready to serve," "happy," "challenged.") It means all systems go!

Get the most out of **Youth Ministry Cargo** by following these eight tips step by step. Proper planning, preparation and follow-through ensure super experiences for you and your group. It's worth the time and effort.

CHAPTER 4

Using Your Own Cargo of Creativity

Before you plunge into these pages, take time to evaluate where you are in the "creativity stream." Take this self-quiz:

Cargo Creativity Quiz

Circle the exclamation point (!) if your answer is yes; circle the period (.) if your answer is no; and circle the ellipsis (. . .) if you're not sure. The scoring is at the end of the self-quiz.

	Yes	No	Not sure
1. Seeing something unusual in the ordinary comes easy for me.	!	.	. . .
2. I need to work at thinking outside the box.	!	.	. . .
3. I think more creatively when I'm around other people.	!	.	. . .
4. I think I'm creative.	!	.	. . .
5. People tell me I have good ideas.	!	.	. . .
6. I'm uncomfortable trying something I don't think will work.	!	.	. . .
7. I see the church as a creative outlet for me.	!	.	. . .
8. I usually make judgments on ideas before giving them a try.	!	.	. . .
9. Creativity scares me.	!	.	. . .
10. Creative youth group programs usually go over the kids' heads.	!	.	. . .
11. Young people would rather be told what to believe than question it for themselves.	!	.	. . .
12. Creative youth ministry is just gimmickry.	!	.	. . .
13. If Jesus could use cargo to teach with, so can I.	!	.	. . .
14. I'm afraid nobody will understand me if I try something new.	!	.	. . .
15. The kids in my youth group just laugh if I attempt to do anything creative.	!	.	. . .
16. I involve young people in the creative process.	!	.	. . .
17. I cling to traditional, non-threatening approaches.	!	.	. . .
18. I feel uncomfortable with creativity.	!	.	. . .
19. The people in my church feel uncomfortable with my creativity.	!	.	. . .
20. The kids in my group feel uncomfortable with my creativity.	!	.	. . .

---

21. Being creative is someone else's business, not mine. ! . ...
22. I buy books with ideas, because I don't have any. ! . ...
23. When you're too creative, nobody understands you. ! . ...
24. God is the author of creativity and challenges us to do the same. ! . ...
25. I see newness in almost everything around me. ! . ...

Total your score by giving yourself these points for each answer:

	My Score				My Score
1.	!=5 .=0 ...=2		14.	.=5 !=0 ...=2	
2.	.=5 !=0 ...=2		15.	.=5 !=0 ...=2	
3.	!=5 .=0 ...=2		16.	!=5 .=0 ...=2	
4.	!=5 .=0 ...=2		17.	.=5 !=0 ...=2	
5.	!=5 .=0 ...=2		18.	.=5 !=0 ...=2	
6.	.=5 !=0 ...=2		19.	.=5 !=0 ...=2	
7.	!=5 .=0 ...=2		20.	.=5 !=0 ...=2	
8.	.=5 !=0 ...=2		21.	.=5 !=0 ...=2	
9.	.=5 !=0 ...=2		22.	.=5 !=0 ...=2	
10.	.=5 !=0 ...=2		23.	.=5 !=0 ...=2	
11.	.=5 !=0 ...=2		24.	!=5 .=0 ...=2	
12.	.=5 !=0 ...=2		25.	!=5 .=0 ...=2	
13.	!=5 .=0 ...=2			Total:	

Scoring

100-125: Great! You're on the creative edge of youth ministry. Keep up the good work!

75-99: Okay. You're standing on the horizon of some fun possibilities. With more encouragement and assurance that it's okay to be out of the ordinary now and then, you can do it!

74 and below: Find some creative people to hang around with. Don't be afraid to risk. Trust God's gifts of creativity and let yourself go. Everybody has a spark of creativity just waiting to be ignited.

You can be creative and you can help others stretch to be creative. Don't forget—God loves you, and he's blessed you with sprinklings of his creative genius:

- "Each one of us has received a special gift in proportion to what Christ has given" (Ephesians 4:7).
- "The Spirit's presence is shown in some way in each person for the good of all" (1 Corinthians 12:7).

1. Use your gifts. Because God entrusts us with his Spirit and his special gifts—we must use them the best we can. In Matthew 25:14-30, Jesus tells the tale of a master and three servants. "He gave to each one according to his ability: to one he gave five thousand silver coins, to another he gave two thousand, and to another he gave one thousand" (Matthew 25:15). God gives us each a number of gifts, abilities and talents and he wants us to use them. So what if we all can't be Michelangelos, Bachs or Edisons. We can be the best possible people—wisely, creatively managing our blessings.

Remember the rest of the story? The servant with the most money invested and doubled it. The other servant doubled his money too. But the servant who "had received one thousand coins went off, dug a hole in the ground, and hid his master's money" (Matthew 25:18). Of course the master wasn't pleased with the miser.

How does this apply to our own creative gifts and abilities? What lesson can we learn from the miser's mistake? Did he fear failure? Couldn't he see any other use for the money? Did he think investing wasn't worth chancing? In all of this, God says, "Take a chance! Use what I've given to you."

And this book invites you to take a chance with new ideas and your own innovative capabilities. Take a closer look at the risk-taking times of your life:

- Think of a time you took a risk and failed:
  What happened?
  How did you feel?
  Did the world end? Were there new beginnings?
- Think of a time you risked and succeeded:
  What happened?
  How did you feel?
- Compare the two times. What did you learn?

2. You're not alone. In spite of the risks involved and twinges of scariness in trying something new, God stretches us to take risks, but he doesn't leave it at that. He surrounds us with other people.

Scripture reminds us again and again that we're connected. One of the most vivid and well-known passages of connectedness can be found in 1 Corinthians 12: "For the body itself is not made up of only one part, but of many parts ... God put every different part in the body just as he wanted it to be. There would not be a body if it were only one part! As it is, there are many parts but one body ... If one part of the body suffers, all the other parts suffer with it; if one part is praised, all the other parts share its happiness. All of you are Christ's body, and each one is a part of it" (1 Corinthians 12:12, 18-19, 26-27).

Take a closer look at the encouraging, supportive, positive people in your life:

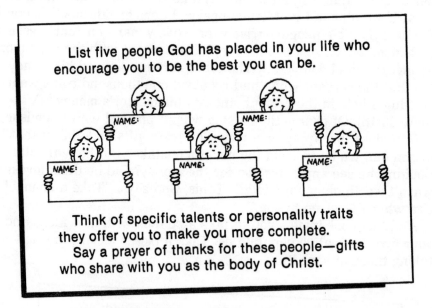

List five people God has placed in your life who encourage you to be the best you can be.

NAME: NAME: NAME: NAME: NAME:

Think of specific talents or personality traits they offer you to make you more complete.

Say a prayer of thanks for these people—gifts who share with you as the body of Christ.

3. You're free to fail. God uses people like you and me. Definitely not "perfect" types. But if you'll browse through your Bible, you'll soon find that God didn't choose people because of their flawlessness. Yet in spite of their blunders and bloopers, God used them in incredible ways. Just like he uses us today. So don't be afraid if you blow it once in a while. God's forgiveness glues the pieces back together again.

Take a closer look at these well-known Bible characters. Notice their humanness. See how God used their strengths as well as their weaknesses. Use these Bible references:

Abraham—strengths: Genesis 15:1-6; weaknesses: Genesis 16:1-4; 17:15-19; God used: Genesis 12:1-3; 22:15-18.

David—strengths: 1 Samuel 16:11-13; 17:48-50; weaknesses: 2 Samuel 11:2-5, 14-17; 12:13-14; God used: 2 Samuel 7:8-16.

Jacob—strengths: Genesis 32:7-12, 22-30; weaknesses: Genesis 25:27-34; 27:1-29, 34-36; God used: Genesis 28:10-22; 35:9-12.

Martha—strengths: Luke 10:38; John 12:1-2; weaknesses: Luke 10:39-42; John 11:20-22; God used: John 11:5, 23-27.

Moses—strengths: Exodus 14:13-14, 21-25; 19:1-7; weaknesses: Exodus 3:11; 4:1-17; 5:22-23; 6:1-13; God used: Exodus 3:7-10; 6:2-8.

Noah—strengths: Genesis 6:9-22; 7:1, 17-23; 8:1; weaknesses: Genesis 9:20-29; God used: Genesis 8:1, 15-19; 9:1-3, 8-17.

Paul—strengths: Acts 19:4-8; Philippians 4:11-13; weaknesses: Acts 8:1-3; Romans 7:15-20; God used: Acts 9:20-22; Colossians 1:25-26.

Peter—strengths: Matthew 16:13-19; John 21:15-19; weaknesses: Matthew 26:31-35, 69-75; God used: Matthew 28:19-20.

Rahab—strengths: Joshua 2:8-20; weaknesses: Joshua 2:1-7; God used: Joshua 2:21-24; 6:22-25; Matthew 1:1-17.

Thomas—strengths: John 20:28; weaknesses: John 20:24-25; God used: John 20:29-30.

4. You're free to succeed. Even though you're free to make mistakes and goofs now and then, remember you're free to succeed too!

"Your life in Christ makes you strong, and his love comforts you" (Philippians 2:1). And remember: "God is always at work in you to make you willing and able to obey his own purpose" (Philippians 2:13).

If those verses don't bolster your courage and belief in success, how about these?

" . . . And how very great is his power at work in us who believe. This power working in us is the same as the mighty strength which he used when he raised Christ from death and seated him at his right side in the heavenly world" (Ephesians 1:19-20).

And all the glory of our success goes to God, who gives everything to us in the first place:

"To him who by means of his power working in us is able to do so much more than we can ever ask for, or even think of: to God be the glory in the church and in Christ Jesus for all time, forever and ever! Amen" (Ephesians 3:20-21).

Let these words shine as encouragement for you. Enjoy **Youth Ministry Cargo**, which is stuffed with extraordinary ideas that use ordinary objects. Use your God-given gift of creativity, and stretch others to be creative along with you. You *can* do it!

CARGO TOPIC LISTING

The Index

The purpose of this index is to help you find entries according to theme, issues and happenings in youth ministry. **Each activity is listed by entry number, not page number.**

CARGO FREIGHT LISTING

The Activities

ADDRESS BOOK

An Apostle's Address Book
TOPIC: FRIENDSHIP

In this Bible study, group members will examine Paul's list of friends and co-workers in Romans 16; discover new insights into Paul's friendships and relationships; discuss reasons for building strong friendships; and determine to build deeper friendships with other Christians.

For each person, gather a Bible, pencil, piece of paper and envelope. You also will need an address book and a Bible commentary.

Ask the youth group members to form a circle. Pass around the address book, and ask these questions:

● Have you ever seen an address book? Have you ever used an address book? Why did you use it?

● What is the purpose of an address book?

● What information can be recorded in an address book?

● Is an address book ever like a diary? If so, how?

Say, "Romans 16 shows us the 'address book' of the apostle

Paul. As he closes his letter to the Christians in Rome, he mentions a number of individuals to whom he wishes to send greetings. A study of these individuals is both interesting and challenging. Let's examine them.

"Who is the first person listed? What do you notice about this individual? Phoebe carried this letter to the Christians in Rome. What does that tell you about her? Some people have accused Paul of having a low opinion of women. After reading what he wrote about Phoebe, how would you answer that charge? The words 'has been a great help' literally mean 'protectress.' What do you think this means? How could Phoebe have done this? Do you think women in the church today have been placed in the lesser roles of service? Why or why not? What ministries do women in your church perform? What ministries, if any, are they excluded from? Why? What can be done to expand the role of women in ministry today?

"Who is mentioned in verses 3 and 4? How are these individuals described? Why do you think the Gentile churches were grateful to them? According to Romans 16:5, how were Priscilla and Aquila serving the church in Rome? What would be the benefits and disadvantages of meeting in a house-church?

"Read verses 6-15. How many women are listed? What does Paul say about these women? The words Paul uses for 'work very hard' literally mean 'to toil to the point of exhaustion.' What does this tell you?

"Look at verse 7. Another couple is named by Paul. What do they have in common with Paul? What do you think 'relative' means? What experiences have they shared with Paul? What advantage did they have over Paul? Since Paul became a Christian shortly after the stoning of Stephen (Acts 7), this couple must have had a direct link with the original church in Jerusalem. What advantages did that present? Notice they are called 'apostles.' The word 'apostle' literally means 'messenger.' Understanding this, how were these two apostles?

"What is special about Epaenetus (verse 5)? What advantages and disadvantages are there in being the first convert? Imagine you were the first convert in your school. What would you do to win others to Christ?

"In verse 10 Apelles is said to have been 'tested and approved.' What are ways Paul might have tested him? What are some ways God does this in our lives? What is the purpose of testing? What does it mean to be 'approved'?

"Look at verse 13. Who is

named? How is he described? It is possible Rufus is the same person mentioned in Mark 15:21. Thus, he would be the son of Simon of Cyrene. What did Simon do? If this relationship is true, what influence do you think it had on Rufus? Recognize that the mother of Rufus was not literally Paul's mother, but she performed the role of a mother to him. Who in the church has done that for you? Why is this 'mothering' so important? What does this 'mothering' include?

"Read verses 21-23. Which individuals are listed in these verses? Whom are you familiar with? What are they now doing with Paul or for Paul?

"Look back through the 'address book' of Paul. Why do you think these people are so important to Paul? How effective would Paul have been without them? Who do you think can accomplish more, an individual working for Christ, or a team working for Christ? Why? Who has more problems, a team or an individual? Why? What are some problems an individual faces? a team?

"As we close this study there are some principles I want to point out. These principles are important to us as we live for Christ and together serve him.

"Paul was a friend-maker as well as a soul-winner. He did not live an isolated life. He made friends as he won people to the Lord. He appreciated his friends and developed friendships.

"God uses people who can make friends. Read any biography of a famous and successful Christian and you will find an individual who made friends. The people who are used mightily by God have time for friends.

"We need friends. We cannot exist without them. Jesus called us sheep. Sheep flock together for a number of reasons such as comfort, safety, feeding and protection.

"The church is the perfect place for friendships to develop. There should be no strangers in the body of Christ. Scripture clearly teaches we are members of the same family. After an in-

itial welcome and introduction, friendship-building with others in the church must begin.

"Now, I challenge each of you to pick a person in our group and start building a friendship with him or her. Choose someone you do not know or hardly know. Once you've selected someone, decide how you will build your friendship. How about a telephone call? a letter? a snack after church?"

Distribute paper, pencil and envelope to each person. Have the kids write down the name of their future friend and place it in their envelope. On the envelope, have them write "future friend." Ask them to take the envelopes home as a reminder to make contact with the friend during the week. Have the kids tell about their fellowshiping activities at the next meeting. Have the kids write the name, address and phone number of their new friend in their address book at home.

—Doug Newhouse

Variations

1. Ask the young people each to go through their address book and choose a friend or a relative they haven't communicated with for a long time. Have them contact the friend or relative through a letter or phone call.

2. Give each person a pencil and enough pieces of paper for

each group member. Instruct the young people to write a "telegram" (a short note) to each person in the group telling what they appreciate about him or her. Encourage the writers to sign their names. However, if it is an extremely shy group, give the students the option to leave the notes unsigned.

Instruct the students to take off one of their shoes and place the shoes along the wall. Use the shoes as "mailboxes" in which fellow group members may deliver their telegrams (**Building Community in Youth Groups,** by Denny Rydberg, Group Books).

Your Ideas and Variations

_____
_____
_____
_____
_____
_____
_____
_____

ADVERTISEMENTS

2

Advertisements in School Newspapers
TOPIC: PUBLICITY

Have you ever noticed the as-

tronomical costs of advertising? Very seldom do I advertise in the city newspaper because of the skyrocketing prices. I have found the school newspaper to be an affordable alternative.

I create my own ad copy about youth group events, make it print-ready, and take it to the school. (I like to make my own ad copy so I'll know exactly how the advertisement will appear.)

Advertising in school newspapers is a great way to communicate with young people—and it's inexpensive.

—J.B. Collingsworth

Variations

1. Place special holiday greetings in the school newspapers.

2. In the school papers, run pictures and stories of your youth group members who attend that school.

Your Ideas and Variations

_____
_____
_____
_____
_____
_____
_____
_____
_____
_____
_____
_____
_____
_____

Commercial Camouflage
TOPIC: BIBLE STUDY METHODS

Commercial Camouflage is a unique Bible study that uses advertisements.

We are saturated with sales pitches for products or services that supposedly will improve our current situations—whatever they may be. Most commercials contain a key phrase that, when heard by itself, identifies the company to us. These phrases, can and do, remain in our minds long after the commercial is over. Many have even become part of everyday vocabulary.

In some commercials, there are significant parallels to Christian life, thought and practice. For example, AT&T's phrase, "Reach out and touch someone" may be a reference to the healing ministry of Jesus or the compassion Christ asks us to show toward one another.

Ask your youth group members each to choose a familiar phrase from a commercial. They should consider two things when choosing: first, how can the phrase be applied to Christian principles; second, what Bible story or stories relate to the phrase? Ask that kids be ready to present several of the commercial phrases at the next

meeting, and discuss them as time permits.

Your youth group will find this approach interesting because they can easily relate to the commercial messages. The group members also will experience a sense of ownership in choosing the phrases and helping to prepare the studies.

—Steve Roberts

Variations

1. Illustrate the commercials by cutting out ads and letters from magazines. Glue them on construction paper or posterboard. Display the signs during the meeting.

2. For another effective approach, use one commercial each week and develop a Bible study around its theme. Ask one person to contact you with his or her commercial phrase. Get together and prepare the lesson for the next meeting. This step is imperative in order to develop a biblical viewpoint and choose appropriate Bible verses. You could plan a Bible study around the phrase "Reach out and touch someone" and the theme of loving others. Use these verses: Matthew 5:43; 19:19; 1 John 4:7-8.

Your Ideas and Variations

_____

_____

_____

_____
_____
_____
_____
_____
_____

4

A Pile of Ads
TOPIC: VALUES

Using a pile of old magazines, your youth group members can compare Christian values with secular values.

Gather everyone around a pile of magazines. Ask the kids to randomly tear out advertisements.

Next have them sort the ads into piles according to what really is being sold to the consumer (aside from the product). For example, an ad for antiperspirant could be selling "acceptance." Certain food ads could be selling "love." A shampoo ad could be selling "popularity." These themes are stressed in ads the young people see every day but, perhaps, never look at closely.

Ask the kids to discuss whether these statements ads make are true. Can they become more popular simply by using a certain shampoo? Can they win their family's love by cooking a particular brand of ham?

Ask the youth group members to write advertisements for some of their favorite products—or for the group itself. First write an exaggerated ad; then be absolutely truthful. For example, "Our youth group is packed with enthusiastic, caring, loving teenagers who welcome strangers with open arms. _Everybody_ is welcome to join in the fun and sharing. _Every_ visitor feels accepted and a part of the group."

A more truthful ad could be, "Our youth group is packed with enthusiastic, caring, loving teenagers who try to welcome strangers with open arms. Although we sometimes feel as shy as the visitors, we try to make them feel comfortable by talking with them. God loves us and forgives us all—thank goodness!"

—Mardie H.C. MacDonald

Variations

1. Ask the young people to sing their commercial to the tune of a familiar song such as "Twinkle, Twinkle, Little Star" or "Mary Had a Little Lamb."

2. Rather than magazine ads, use videotaped television commercials.

Your Ideas and Variations

_____
_____
_____

5

Promoting Youth Ministry
TOPIC: PUBLICITY

I was trying to come up with a unique idea to promote my church's youth ministry program. I wanted other young people to know what our church could offer them. One night, I was in a movie theater. As I sat there eating popcorn and drinking a soft drink, ads began to appear on the screen. As I looked at the ads for local car lots, pizza places, barber shops and beauty salons, a thought popped into my mind! We could put a youth ministry ad on that theater screen and every young

person could see what was going on in our church. So this is what I did.

I called the theater and found out who produced the ads. I had some quality slides of our youth group activities made by a professional photographer. I bought a sound track of a Christian song and put together a script that went something like this: "Great things are happening at Grand Avenue Baptist Church—in everything from Bible study on Sunday mornings to fun meetings on Wednesday evenings. More than 200 young people gather for fellowship, sharing and games. Our young people say: (I recorded youth group members) 'It's exciting,' 'Challenging,' 'A place to be me,'

'Jesus is changing my life,' 'I see my friends being touched,' 'I feel loved and accepted,' 'People really reach other people')."

The movie ads really made a difference. Many times I would go to the theater and watch as the ad was being seen by a rather captive audience. I noticed that when our ad appeared there was silence in the large room, because it was different. We were sharing the excitement of our youth group with people in our city.

—J.B. Collingsworth

Variations

1. Ask the youth group members to help create new movie ads.

2. Make a billboard or a marquee for your church property. Advertise current youth group activities and church events.

Your Ideas and Variations

_____
_____
_____
_____
_____
_____
_____
_____
_____
_____
_____
_____
_____
_____

Daring to Dream
TOPIC: HOPE/FUTURE

Our lives are sealed with dreams and wishes. We aim for certain goals from the time we are small children until the day we die. Here is an activity to help your group share their hopes and dreams.

Before the meeting, make two sets of stars, one set out of aluminum foil and the other set out of construction paper. Use as many colors of paper as the number of small groups (eight to 10 people) your group will form. Glue the dull side of the foil to the construction paper star. Prepare a prayer space for the end of the meeting. Choose a room that can be darkened well. Place matches and a number of candles in the center of the room. You also will need string, tape and copies of the handout.

Break into smaller groups of eight to 10 people. Hand each person a star. Form groups according to the color of the stars. Give a set of the following questions to each group. Give them 20 minutes to discuss the questions.

Our Dreams

1. If you had three wishes, what would you wish?

2. When you were a child, what did you want to be when you grew up?

3. What was something you dreamed or wanted as a child that you find funny now?

4. How will you know when your dream has become a reality?

5. How do your dreams compare to your needs?

6. What non-material things do you wish, hope or dream for right now?

7. Envision yourself five or 10 years from now. What dreams do you have?

8. Name someone who has influenced you. How has that person made you see some of the hopes you have for yourself?

9. What are some gifts, talents or qualities that you have as a result of your experiences so far in your life?

10. What has your experience of God been like?

11. What good do you bring to the world right now?

12. What good do you expect to bring to the world?

13. Share some dreams that have become realities for you.

14. What kinds of things do you need to change before you can accomplish your dreams?

15. What are some dreams you once had that you no longer want? Why?

Gather as a large group. Ask the young people to think of the many dreams or wishes they've had. Then have the participants write on the back of their stars a "dream come true" that God has granted. Suggest things such as a good family, great friends, a fun summer vacation, success in school, etc.

Have the group move into the prayer space. Light the candles. Begin with a moment of silence and ask each person to read his or her "dream come true" on the back of his or her star. Close with this prayer, "Thank you God for the many things you give us: our hopes, dreams, gifts and talents. Continue to guide our dreams and desires. Help us to want what you want, and use the gifts you give us. Amen."

Give everyone some string and tape. Hang the stars on the meeting room ceiling as a sparkling reminder of God's blessings.

—Mary Kay Fitzpatrick

Variations

1. Gather the teenagers in a circle. Ask them each to describe the following:

● A dream that didn't come true.

● A dream that did come true.

● A dream they hope will come true in the future.

2. Make a giant star out of cardboard. Cover it with aluminum foil and place it in the center of the room. Gather the kids in a circle around the star and ask one person to stand on it. Have the others affirm the person by saying why he or she is "a dream come true." For example, "You help out all of the time when I need it." Or, "I like your funny sense of humor. You lift me up when I feel sad."

Your Ideas and Variations

_____
_____
_____
_____
_____
_____
_____
_____
_____
_____
_____
_____
_____
_____
_____

7

Foiled Again
TOPIC: FRIENDSHIP/SELF-IMAGE

Here's a great crowdbreaker for your group when it meets for the first time or when your topic is self-image, friendship or building trust.

Divide the group into pairs and ask them to sit facing each other. Give each person a 14-inch-long piece of foil. Say that each person will make a mask of his or her partner. Ask anyone who wears glasses to remove them for this exercise. Demonstrate the process by holding the foil to your partner's forehead and molding the foil around his or her face. Encourage everyone to apply a little pressure while molding the mask. (People are not very comfortable touching each other's faces.) Ask the kids to remove the mask, show it to their partner and tape it on the wall.

This exercise will encourage the kids to take an active role in the remaining activities. They will have nothing left to fear and will be open to sharing the things that make them special.

—Mary Kay Fitzpatrick

Variations

1. Give each of the young people a piece of foil and ask them

to form a symbol of their hobby; for example a "book" for someone who enjoys reading, a round ball for a person who enjoys sports, a "pencil" for a person who enjoys writing. Share the symbols in a large group.

Your Ideas and Variations

_____
_____
_____
_____
_____
_____
_____
_____
_____

God's Vessels
TOPIC: GROUP BUILDING

Aluminum foil can be used for more than wrapping leftovers. It can be great stuff to use for a significant Bible study.

Divide 2 Corinthians 4 into six sections (three verses per section). Assign volunteers to read the sections. Ask how our bodies are like "earthen vessels." How does God use our human weaknesses to fulfill his work?

Give each young person a large square of aluminum foil,

and instruct the kids to fashion pots or "vessels" out of the foil. Let each one "show and tell" his or her original creation.

Ask the young people to think of different things they would like to put in their vessels; ask them what they think God would like to put in their vessels. Then discuss how Christians are containers for the Good News. Ask what it feels like to be filled with God's love.

Close the session by saying, "Each individual, though important, is only a small portion of the bigger picture. We need to join together and work together in Christian groups. We need to love and help each other." Ask the young people to fashion their individual foil vessels into one large vessel, a vessel large enough to contain even more good things from God.

—Denise Turner

Variations

1. Form vessels from clay instead of from aluminum foil.

2. Use the following study to help the young people understand that human weakness is not a reflection of spiritual strength, but rather an opportunity for greater faith. Distribute pencils and copies of the handout in the next column.

Discuss the doubts and fears, then read 2 Corinthians 4:7-18. One at a time, read the con-

---

Doubts

Rank the following troubles and doubts from 1 to 8. One is the most troublesome, 8 the least:

——— serious illness of a relative or friend

——— a relationship with a friend that is hurting or breaking

——— lack of money

——— problems with parents

——— feeling left out or lonely

——— concern about the future

——— fear of failing in school

——— other

(A copyrighted resource from **Youth Ministry Cargo.** Permission granted to copy this handout for local church use only.)

---

cerns raised in the handout.

Encourage the group to make helpful comments and suggestions on each item. Specifically try to find words or ideas from 2 Corinthians 4:7-18 that might be helpful to the person with the problem. Allow adequate time for the youth to respond to each of the doubts or concerns (**The Youth Group Meeting Guide,** by Rich Bimler, Group Books).

Your Ideas and Variations

_____

_____

_____

_____

_____

_____

_____

_____

_____

_____

_____

_____

_____

APPLES

9

Apples and Repentance
TOPIC: REPENTANCE/ADVENT

Use apples, as they relate to the story of Adam and Eve, to help young people focus on repentance. The following worship experience can be used any time, but is especially appropriate during the month of December. If your denomination does not observe Advent as such, simply omit Reader One and substitute the words "this time before Christmas" for the word "Advent."

Ask young people to volunteer to read the parts. Sit in a circle with lighted candles or an Advent wreath. Place a bowl of apples in the center. Dim the lights.

● **Reader One:** "Tonight we light the candles of our Advent wreath. Advent is a time when we think of repentance and meditate on the promise of the coming of the Savior."

● **Reader Two:** "To repent means to turn away from something—to move in a different direction. According to the biblical story, Adam and Eve were the first human beings who had the opportunity to repent. The early church remembered their story during Advent."

● **Reader Three:** "In the earliest days of the Christian church, few people could read or write. Dramas were performed to enable the people to learn the stories of the Bible. These became known as 'miracle' and 'mystery' plays. The Paradise Play portrayed the creation and sin of Adam and Eve and their expulsion from the Garden of Eden. Since this play often concluded with the promise of the coming of the Savior, it was performed during Advent. A tree, hung with apples, was used to symbolize the Garden of Eden. Christians began to erect this 'Paradise Tree' in their homes on December 24, the feast day of Adam and Eve."

● **Reader Four:** "You are invited to take an apple, a symbol for the first sin of human beings. Look at it and think of sins or things in your life that you wish to turn away from this night."

(Pass the bowl of apples around the circle. An adult leader invites the young people to share aloud, making it clear that it is all right to say "pass." First, the adult leader shares something he or she would like to turn away from.)

● **Reader Five:** (Read Matthew 1:18-23.)

● **Reader Six:** "One of the names for Jesus is Emmanuel which means 'God with us.' God *is* with us and loves us and will help us turn away from the negative and guide us in the best directions for our lives. Let us use this Advent season to be quiet, listening for God's direction."

● **Reader Seven:** "Let us pray. Dear God, this night we thank you for the birth of your son, Emmanuel. We celebrate your presence with us! We know that your love will give us the power we need to turn away from the things in our lives that hurt us and to turn toward all that is good and helpful for our growth. Amen."

—Kathi B. Finnell

Variations

1. Let your youth group make Advent logs. Saw a log into 1-foot sections, then saw each section in half (one for each youth group member). On the rounded side of the log halves, drill five holes for five candles. Decorate the logs with evergreen branches and red ribbon.

Your Ideas and Variations

_____
_____
_____
_____
_____
_____
_____
_____
_____
_____
_____
_____
_____
_____
_____
_____
_____
_____

10

Apples of God's Eye
TOPIC: SELF-IMAGE/CREATION

Here's an idea to help your group members study Psalm 138:8 and celebrate in their uniqueness as children of God. They are "the apples of God's eye."

Bring enough apples for everyone in your group, plus a few extra. Place them in the center of the room.

Ask everyone to sit in a circle around the apples. Once everyone is together, have them each select one apple and study it carefully. Ask the following questions:

● What is the purpose for that apple?

● Who created your apple?

● How was it able to grow?

Have the members return their apples to the center of the circle. Mix them up and see if the kids can find their original apple. When everyone has an apple, ask the following questions:

● Are you sure it is the same apple?

● How can you tell?

● What special markings or colors does your apple have?

● Who has the best apple? Why?

Say to the group, "Whether we realize it or not, we are a lot like these apples. We are created by God. And even though there are no two of us alike, we all have the same purpose for our lives—to glorify God.

"Once you take the skin off of several apples, they all look the same. How often do we place our values and judgments on what can be seen on the surface? We must realize that it takes time to get under the skin to really know one another."

Ask a volunteer to read Psalm 138:8. Discuss the following questions:

● Whose purpose is the Lord trying to fulfill?

● In fulfilling his purpose, will God abandon the work of his hands? Explain.

● What then is the purpose for your life?

● Will God abandon you? Why or why not?

● On a scale of 1 to 10, with 10 being the highest, how open is your life to God's purpose?

● What is one thing you can do to help God fulfill his purpose in your life?

● When do you plan to start?

Say to the young people, "It doesn't matter who you are, what color you are, what situation you are in, or what sins you have committed in the past—you are still God's creation in whom he desires to fulfill his purposes."

Divide the group into pairs and have each pray for the other. Pray that God will begin, now, to fulfill his purpose in their lives. Thank the Lord for his love that endures forever.

—Tommy Baker

Variations

1. Study other verses that celebrate our uniqueness as children of God: 1 Corinthians 3:16-17; 2 Corinthians 5:17; 1 Peter 1:18-19; 2:9; 1 John 3:1.

2. Divide into teams and have an apple-eating relay race. Place an apple in the mouth of the first person on each team. Instruct the members to pass the apple from mouth to mouth, taking a bite as they go. (Don't use hands.) First team finished eating its apple wins.

Your Ideas and Variations

_____
_____
_____
_____
_____
_____
_____
_____
_____
_____
_____
_____
_____
_____
_____

11

Good Luck Apples
TOPIC: EXAMS/CARING

Teenagers need support and encouragement with their school work. Giving "good luck apples" has become one of our youth group rituals.

During the Sunday evening meeting prior to final exams, I place a bowl of apples in the center of our circle. After a prayer asking God to help each person to do his or her best on the upcoming tests, I pass the bowl and ask each person to take an apple.

This is one way our group ministers to our young people in

their daily activities. We really do care.

—Kathi B. Finnell

Variations

1. Give everyone a 3x5 card, pencil and string. Ask the kids to write on their card a prayer request concerning their upcoming tests. Attach one end of the string to the card and the other end to the apple stem. Have the young people keep these "prayer apples" in sight daily. Every time they see their apple, have them pray their prayer. After the tests, they can eat their apples and note that God answers prayers.

Your Ideas and Variations

_____
_____
_____
_____
_____
_____
_____
_____
_____
_____
_____
_____
_____
_____
_____
_____
_____
_____

12

Identification Badges

TOPIC: GROUP BUILDING/CROWD-
BREAKERS

Make identification badges by using a relatively inexpensive assembly machine. This type of machine opens up all sorts of possibilities when working with young people who don't know each other.

Two suppliers of badge-making machinery and badge parts are: Badge a Minit, Box 800 Civic Industrial Park, LaSalle, IL 61301, (309) 224-2090. If you're just getting started making badges, you'll probably want their "Starter Kit," item no. 1000. Buying a starter kit will enter your subscription to The Bright Idea, a quarterly idea-journal to keep you up on their latest developments. The other supplier is Mr. Button Products, Box 68355, Indianapolis, IN 46268, (317) 872-7000.

Spend the least amount of preparation time by using plain-paper disks of any color, marked with a circle corresponding with the badge size. Distribute these circles to the participants. Ask them each to

decorate a badge using colored markers, crayons or stickers. Cut out the circles and assemble the badges according to the instructions which come with the machinery.

Use different badge colors to distinguish your youth group from other churches, cities or conferences. Or, colors can be used to divide young people into discussion groups, work groups or whatever.

Let's say you use a badge color to identify different church groups at a regional event. Later, you want to mix participants up for a get-acquainted session. Offer a predetermined number of colored pens for drawing and

writing their names on the badges. Let nature take its course, then shout, "All who signed their name in red, in the northeast corner!" And so on, and your get-acquainted session has begun.

The previous suggestions require very little pre-event work on your part; the following ideas need more "homework."

Often a design or phrase will need to be on every badge. You can select from a wide variety of pre-printed designs in catalogs, or you can ask someone to design a custom badge from a sketch you submit. Each option has advantages.

There is, however, a third alternative involving transfer letters, artists in your group, and a trusty copy machine. Personalization during the event allows free expression from everyone. When we've done this, it has been a great community time of cooperation, sharing, competition and fun. Disadvantages include some people's self-perception as "non-artists," loss of control over the finished product, and the necessity to have enough assembly machines to get all the badges finished in a timely fashion.

If you have preregistration for an event, designate small groups by using symbols, color combinations, type-style variations, etc. to effect such divisions.

For example: You're having a large group for a weekend retreat, and on Friday you're serving ice cream at midnight. How many servers do you need? Seven? Great! Simply draw ice cream cones on seven buttons before they are assembled. Then when you need the seven ice cream servers, they will know immediately who they are.

There are so many ways you can use badge-making machines. Have a great time coming up with your own ideas!

—Walter H. Mees Jr.

Variations

1. Design name badges for the members of your church. Ask them to wear their badge each Sunday for easy identification!

2. Let each group in your church design badges for its members. For example, adult choir could design a badge with a large, black music note; children's Sunday school could design a badge with a Bible on it; youth group could design a badge with their group name (for example, "LYF" which stands for Lutheran Youth Fellowship); the wedding committee could design a badge with bells on it, etc.

Your Ideas and Variations

_____
_____
_____

_____
_____
_____
_____
_____
_____
_____
_____
_____
_____
_____
_____

BAGS

13

Throwing Away Sin
TOPIC: CONFESSION

Philippians 4:8 is a section on mental health—a listing of virtues: true—able to face reality; honest—worthy of reverence; just—in accordance with the highest ideals of right and wrong; pure—not polluted with elements that stain the soul; lovely—inspiring love; of good report—possessing more than a few virtues.

For a lesson focusing on these virtues, gather large squares of newsprint, black markers and one small trash bag for each youth group member.

Read and discuss Philippians 4:8. Ask group members what it

means to be true, honest, just, etc. Ask if they can be all of these things at school, with their families and with their friends. Why or why not?

Tell group members, "If you've ever been angry, take one of the large squares of newsprint and write the word 'anger' on it. Put it into your trash bag."

Do the same with feelings of jealousy, dishonesty, hate, etc. until the trash bags are full.

Then say, "Now you have to carry this trash around with you. Try to think of ways to eliminate some of the garbage in your life."

Take the trash bags outside to the church dumpster. Close with a prayer asking God for forgiveness. Ask for his help as you exercise love, honesty and truth. Throw away the bags of sin!
—E. Jane Mall

Variations

1. Give everyone a piece of newspaper and a marker. Have the participants each write on their newspaper a sin they want to confess. Have them "get rid" of the sin by wadding up the paper and tossing it to the center of the room. Ask one person to gather all of the paper in a plastic garbage bag. This can lead to a discussion on servanthood; it also can lead to a discussion on Jesus taking on all of our sins.

Your Ideas and Variations

_____
_____
_____
_____
_____
_____
_____
_____
_____
_____
_____
_____
_____
_____
_____
_____

14

Trick or Treat
TOPIC: HALLOWEEN

Top off a Halloween party with this bag of goodies. On a brown paper bag, use a black marker to write the words "Trick or Treat." Open the bag so that it stands by itself. Fill the bag with "tricks" and "treats." To each item, tie orange and black ribbons and arrange the ribbons so that they come up out of the bag and hang over the edges. You will need two items for each youth group member. Half of the objects should be "tricks" and the other half should be "treats."

● **Tricks:** These items should be funny things like a pen that has run out of ink, a piece of paper with instructions to do something silly such as "howl like a coyote," and other gag gifts.

● **Treats:** These items should be small gifts such as chewing gum or miniature candy bars.

Have the youth group members sit in a circle. Walk around the circle with the trick-or-treat bag and have each member pick one of the ribbons. He or she gets to keep the chosen item. Share all of the goodies. Next, go around the circle again and have the kids choose another item. If the youth group members chose a "trick" the first

time, have them keep choosing until they get a "treat" the second time.

Who says trick or treats are only for little kids?

—Karen Musitano

Variations

1. Divide your youth group into trios. Give each team a pumpkin and a sharp knife. Give each team only one minute to cut up the pumpkin into no more than 10 pieces.

Have the teams rotate to a different pumpkin. (Supply round wooden toothpicks.) Give each team two minutes to put its "jigsaw puzzle" pumpkin back together, using the toothpicks to hold the pieces in place.

The first team done or the team with the most "together" pumpkin after the time limit is the winner. Pumpkins must be able to stand up alone to be considered a winner (**Try This One ... Strikes Again**, Group Books).

2. On Halloween, Katherine Smithberger and her youth group give out treats and friendship for older and shut-in people. She says, "We ask people in the congregation to bring candy and baked goods to the church the Sunday before Halloween. We compile a list of people in our church and community who might benefit from a friendly visit on Halloween night. Then, on Halloween, we canvass the

area, visiting people, singing to them and leaving goodies. A party back at church finishes off a fun Halloween."

Your Ideas and Variations

_____
_____
_____
_____
_____
_____
_____
_____
_____
_____
_____
_____
_____

BALLOONS

15

Easter Balloon Hunt
TOPIC: EASTER/CROWDBREAKER

Here's an Easter idea that will get your youth group members hopping with enthusiasm!

Before the group meeting, hide deflated balloons in the room or outside. With each balloon, place a long piece of string.

Divide the kids into groups of five; have the groups choose

names such as "Egg Raiders." Ask each team to line up. Have the members place their hands on the waist of the person in front of them. The last person in line will give verbal instructions to the team, trying to get them to hop in unison. The first person is the only one who can touch the balloons.

The object of the game is to hop around the room in a connected line and find the balloons. The first person blows up the balloon, ties the string to it, and places the balloon between the teeth of the second person. This process continues until everyone has a balloon in his or her teeth or until time is called.

Play songs such as the "Bunny Hop" or "Peter Cottontail." After five minutes, call time and award 100 points for each balloon; 500 points for each yellow balloon. Award prizes such as chocolate Easter bunnies and color-dyed, hard-boiled eggs. You also can make awards by blowing up balloons and using a marker to write titles such as "Most unique hopper" or " 'Hoppiest' group member."

—Tim Smith

Variations

1. Plan an Easter egg hunt for the young children in your church. Have your youth group members boil eggs, decorate them, then hide them around the

churchyard or in the building. Cover one of the eggs with aluminum foil. Award a special prize for the person who finds it; for example, an Easter basket full of candy or fruit.

2. Buy a bag of regular-size marshmallows, a bag of miniature marshmallows, a box of toothpicks, and a can of cake-decorating frosting. Have the youth group members make Easter bunnies out of the marshmallows. For the rabbit head and body, stick a toothpick through two large marshmallows. For each ear, stick a toothpick through three miniature marshmallows. Break a toothpick in half and stick it through a miniature marshmallow for a tail. Design the eyes, nose and mouth with the frosting.

Your Ideas and Variations

_____
_____
_____
_____
_____
_____
_____
_____
_____
_____

16

Hot Air Balloons
TOPIC: CROWDBREAKERS

This activity involves balloons, hot air and people. This is a game that can be played just about anywhere and can last as long as the supply of hot air does. If you have an overly-active group, this lung-expansion exercise will help take the wind out of their sails.

Use masking tape to mark start and finish lines approximately 20 feet apart. Divide into teams of four. Explain the rules of the game and give each team an inflated 12-inch balloon. Have some extra inflated balloons in case some pop during the game.

The goal of this game is for each team to _blow_ its balloon to the finish line without touching it or letting it touch the ground. Each team should start simultaneously and try to reach the finish line before the last group crosses. If the balloon touches a team member, or the ground, the team must begin again at the starting line.

Be sure to give each team enough room to maneuver. Don't establish boundaries—that's part of the fun!

—Steve Roberts

Variations

1. Divide the young people into two teams. Ask the first two people in each team to stand side by side. Place an inflated balloon between their hips. Stand 10 feet away from the teams. Instruct the pairs to walk up to you, walk back to their team, and pass the balloon to the next pair. No hands allowed at any time. If the balloon falls, the pair must begin again; if the balloon bursts, they must get another balloon and begin again.

2. Here's another idea for a fun relay. Place Vaseline on the tip of each person's nose. Then place an inflated balloon on the nose of the first person in each line. The participants each have to balance the balloon on their nose, walk to a chair (which is placed 10 feet away), sit down, stand up, walk back to the line, then use their hands to place the balloon on the next person's nose. Supply plenty of tissue for nose clean-up at the end of the relay.

Your Ideas and Variations

_____
_____
_____
_____
_____
_____
_____
_____
_____

_____
_____
_____

17

Imagine That
TOPIC: CREATIVITY

Help your youth group members learn to use their imaginations and not to take things for granted. All you'll need are oblong balloons, markers, a tin can and newspaper.

Inflate an oblong balloon. Pass it around the group, asking each person to pantomime the use of some similarly shaped object using the balloon. One could decide it's a clarinet, another could pretend to brush his or her teeth, another could rock it like a baby, still another might conduct an orchestra.

Then divide the group into two teams. Take an ordinary object such as an empty tin can or a newspaper and ask the kids to list all the possible uses for that object. The team with the most ideas wins. Award prizes such as a packet of balloons for each team member. Discuss these questions:

● Why is it easy to take certain things for granted?

● How can we use our imaginations and be creative with

85

the gifts God gives to us?

● How can we appreciate the "familiar" aspects of our lives?

Give everybody a balloon and marker. On their balloons, have the members draw two eyes and the words, "Appreciate the things you see." Have the kids take the balloons home as reminders to use their imaginations and not take things for granted.

—Mardie H.C. MacDonald

Variations

1. Another game that uses the kids' imaginations as well as memories is Cinderella Shoe Match. As each girl arrives to a youth group meeting, ask her to remove her right shoe. (This in itself is rather unusual and should provoke curiosity right away.) After you've collected all the shoes, send the girls into another room. Then give each shoe to a boy to hold.

In the other room, have the girls step behind a sheet that is hanging from the ceiling. Only the girls' feet should show under the sheet curtain.

Then call in the boys and have them find their partner by matching the shoe they're holding with the shoe under the curtain. Or, to add some difficulty, have the girls remove the other shoe so the guys have to try to fit the shoes, Cinderella-style (**More . . . Try This One**, Group

Books).

2. Knee Feelers is a game that gets the kids thinking and "feeling."

Take a person out of the room and blindfold him or her. At the same time, have five to eight people form a line facing the same way in the meeting room. The blindfolded person is brought back into the room and must guess the identities of the people in the line—by touching them from the knees down. It is often difficult to guess correctly since everyone often wears similar pants and shoes (**Try This One . . . Too**, Group Books).

Your Ideas and Variations

_____
_____
_____
_____
_____
_____
_____
_____
_____
_____
_____

18

Self-Portrait Balloons
TOPIC: SELF-IMAGE

All of us are unique creations:

tall, short, quiet, or outgoing. The youth group members will use balloons and other fun stuff to create self-portraits representative of their colorful selves.

Gather 13-inch balloons of various colors, streamers, ribbons, construction paper, tape, markers, string and scissors.

Tell the kids they are going to create a self-portrait using these materials. Have each choose a balloon. Ask them to choose a color that symbolizes something about their personality (red—enthusiastic; blue—quiet; green—

loves nature, etc.). Then, have the teenagers blow up the balloons and use the markers to draw faces. Use the other supplies to create hair, eyes, hats or whatever.

When everyone is finished, have a self-portrait pageant. Ask each youth group member to explain his or her creation. Make sure the balloons have strings tied to them. Bunch balloons together and attach a sign that says, "Our youth group. What a colorful bunch!"

—Lissa Pressley

Variations

1. Gather a roll of butcher paper and several markers. Roll out the paper and have a young person lay on it. Trace around his or her body, then have him or her design a life-size portrait. Let each youth group member try this art project.

2. Give paper and pencils to the youth group members, then divide them into pairs. Have them set the paper on top of their heads and tell them to draw their partner. Don't let them remove the paper from their heads until they're finished. Collect and display the masterpieces; judges should determine which is best, funniest, etc. Award your winners with colored pencils to encourage further development of their talent (**Try This One . . . Strikes Again**, Group Books).

Your Ideas and Variations

_____
_____
_____
_____
_____
_____
_____
_____
_____
_____
_____
_____
_____
_____
_____

BALLS

19

Blinded Basketball
TOPIC: GOD'S WILL

Have you heard of the phrase "shooting blindly"? It means not knowing what you are doing or why, yet you do it anyway. In this activity, the youth group members get to "shoot blindly" and compare it to leading a life without direction from God.

You'll need a basketball and a blindfold. Ask the kids to wear comfortable clothes and meet at a nearby basketball court.

One at a time, blindfold the kids, bring them to the foul line, and ask them to shoot as many baskets as they can in 60 seconds. Have several take turns.

Allow a few minutes to compare this activity to life: A lot of people try to go through life "shooting blindly." They don't know where they're going or why.

Blindfold more kids, giving them 60 seconds each to shoot. However, this time have someone stand next to the blindfolded kids to guide them, help them, and direct their shots.

Again discuss the implications. The Holy Spirit gives guidance and help, but some people insist on doing things their own way. Even though the Spirit is in their life, his effects are limited by the people's stubbornness to do things their own way.

The third time around, ask people to take shots from the foul line, unblindfolded, and with a coach to assist them. Give 60 seconds to each.

Relate this to life. If you let the Spirit help you live life the way it was intended to be lived, the change will be dramatic and the game will actually be enjoyable.

—James D. Walton

Variations

1. Make use of the court by playing basketball. Play guys against girls, sponsors against kids, or January through June birthdays against July through December birthdays!

2. Gather one blindfold for each young person and one 10-foot cord for every 10 people. Give the group members the long piece of cord. Ask them to grasp the cord with both hands; blindfold all of the students.

Tell the group a letter of the alphabet to create with the cord. Have the group members decide when they have com-

pleted the task. (Don't tell them.)
Repeat the exercise several
times, having the group create
different letters or shapes
(**Building Community in Youth
Groups**, by Denny Rydberg,
Group Books).

Your Ideas and Variations

_____

_____

_____

_____

_____

_____

_____

_____

_____

_____

_____

_____

20

Freeze Play
TOPIC: GAMES

Freeze Play is a hilarious
game. Have fun with it!

Place a basket at each side of
the room. Divide your group into
two equal teams and assign
each one a basket. The object is
for each team to score by putting a 7-inch Nerf ball into their
basket.

The only catch is this: When
the ball is in the hands of a

player, no one can move, even
the player with the ball (unless
he or she is throwing it to a
teammate). A person can hold
the ball for only five seconds. If
he or she holds it longer, the
ball is forfeited to the other
team. The player with the ball
may throw it to himself or herself only once, and then must
throw it to another teammate.
Once the ball is in midair, everyone may move. If a team
moves when it is not supposed
to, it forfeits the ball to the
other team.

This game requires coordina-
tion and thought. The fun comes
with remembering when to run
and when not to run.

—Bob Hicks

Variations

1. Vary the height of the
goals. For one game place the
baskets on the floor; for another
game place the baskets on
chairs; for another game place
the baskets on the tops of two
ladders.

2. Use a beach ball and two
clothes baskets. Then switch to
a tennis ball and two coffee
cans. You even could play
Freeze Play on a basketball
court—using a basketball.

Your Ideas and Variations

_____

_____

_____

_____
_____
_____
_____
_____
_____
_____
_____
_____
_____
_____

2. Have everyone bring a pillow and kneel throughout the game.

3. Ask all team members to lay flat on their backs throughout the game—watch the crazy results!

Your Ideas and Variations

_____
_____
_____
_____
_____
_____
_____
_____
_____
_____
_____
_____
_____

21

Low-Clearance Volleyball
TOPIC: GAMES

Here's an idea for the volleyball enthusiast who is plagued with low ceilings and no gym.

When you want to play volleyball, add one new rule: All players must sit on the floor. Their behinds cannot be raised more than one inch off the ground during the game. Use a small beach ball since it is lighter than a volleyball and it won't destroy your room. All other volleyball rules remain the same. Now you can play volleyball any place—any time!

—Jeffrey A. Collins

Variations

1. Use these same rules, allowing one bounce between each hit.

BEANBAGS

22

Hitting the Target
TOPIC: CHRISTIAN LIVING

Scripture tells us that Christians have certain expectations. "Just as I am," Jesus died for me. But he did it to free me to pursue a higher degree of living. This higher degree of living doesn't save me, but it is impor-

tant for two reasons: First, it is better for a person to live the kind of life exemplified by Jesus; second, living a Godly life is the least I can do to repay Christ for my salvation.

Besides paper, pencils and a few beanbags, you'll need a plastic laundry basket for a target, and a strip of cloth for a blindfold.

Place the "target" about 6 feet from a given spot; allow each young person to have a turn throwing the beanbags into it. It's easy, right? Next, add some difficulty by blindfolding a few volunteers and letting them try to hit the target. After a couple try it, spin the next few people and point them in the direction of the target; then spin a few other kids and point them away from the target. Finally, blindfold one participant, spin him or her, then remove the target altogether. Allow him or her to see how bad the "miss" was, enjoy the reaction, and gather the group for the lesson.

Discuss the experience. Note

the ease of hitting a well-identified target, even when blindfolded, if you know what direction to aim for. Then talk about the misdirectioned experiences and finally what happened when the target was removed altogether.

Now read these Bible verses: 1 Corinthians 4:16; Philippians 3:17; Hebrews 6:11-12; 3 John 11.

Allow a time for discussion. Ask how these verses help to guide us when we make decisions about friendship, drugs, money, everyday behavior. Then say, "Obviously, behavioral targets are easier to hit when they are clearly visible to us—either through definite direction given us at home, church or school, or by the example of people we respect.

"The implication of the Bible passages we just read is that there is a standard of living that pleases God. It can be discovered by looking at the lives of Jesus and Paul as recorded in scripture, and then imitating them."

Have each young person set a goal for the following week. For example, cleaning up his or her bedroom, making friends with someone from another "group," or relating better with parents.

Distribute paper and pencils, then ask each young person to write down the goal, leave it with you, and then report back at the next meeting.

Close with a circle prayer asking God to help them reach their goals.

—Walter Mees

Variations

1. Plan a Beanbag Bonanza fun night. Center the entire evening around Beanbags. Use these ideas:

● **Clapping Contest:** Give the contestants each a beanbag. Have them practice tossing up the beanbags and catching them. Then add the "tricky" part. Have the kids clap as many times as they can between the toss and the catch. The winner is the one who claps the most before catching the bag.

● **Head-to-Head Relay:** Divide the teenagers into two teams of equal numbers; give a beanbag to the first two people in each team. Have them stand close together and place the beanbag between their foreheads. They can't use their hands to keep the bag in place; they only can use

their heads! Stand 10 feet away from the teams and say, "On the word 'go,' race up to me, then back to your team, and pass the beanbag to the next pair. If the beanbag drops from your foreheads, you must go back to the starting line and begin again. When all of your team members finish, sit down and yell, 'We're done!' "

● **Bag Toss:** This activity is similar to an egg toss. Form two lines of kids and have them face each other. Give each of the kids in one line a beanbag. Have them toss the bag to the person directly opposite them. Then have each team take one step backward. Continue this process: toss, catch, step back, etc. If a pair of kids drop their beanbag, they have to sit down. Toss away until one pair remains!

Your Ideas and Variations

_____
_____
_____
_____
_____
_____
_____
_____
_____
_____
_____
_____
_____
_____

BELLS

23

Sharing Christianity
TOPIC: CHRISTIAN LIVING

Christ's love keeps the believer from following the crazy ways of the world. His love makes people new. This is the heart of the Gospel.

For this meeting, you'll need three bells to tie on three kids. On a table, place a button, piece of clay, confetti, candle and crayon.

Give three students a bell to hang on their neck, wrist or waist. When all are seated, explain that the bells are to signify that the people wearing them are Christians. Even though everyone in the room is a Christian, you don't have enough bells to go around.

So ask the others to take one item (button, clay, etc.) from the table and explain how the item signifies they are Christian. You might be surprised at their answers. For example, "This button signifies that my faith holds me together." "This piece of clay signifies that I am formed by God." "This confetti reminds me that God showers

his blessings on me," etc.

Say, "Just because a person wears a bell does not mean that he or she is a Christian."

Let everyone brainstorm for things they do, say or wear that demonstrate they are Christian. Then ask, "Can a person do, say and wear all of the right things, yet still not be a Christian? If so, how do we show we are Christians?"

Gather the bells and other items and put them away. Say that Christians are identified by Christ's love shining through them. Close by singing, "They Will Know We Are Christians By Our Love" (**Songs**, by Yohann

Anderson, Songs and Creations, Inc.).

—E. Jane Mall

Variations

1. The word JOY can be used to remind us of the command to love—

Jesus
Others
Yourself

Tell the young people to reflect on their love of Jesus, others and themselves, deciding which has been most neglected Have them write a prayer asking for help in loving Jesus, others and themselves. The prayer should be as specific as possible. When everyone has written a prayer, have a period of quiet for each to silently pray. Close by praying together the Lord's Prayer.

Your Ideas and Variations

_____
_____
_____
_____
_____
_____
_____
_____
_____
_____
_____
_____
_____
_____
_____
_____

24

The Great Bicycle Race
TOPIC: GAMES

A bike race is an all-time favorite, energetic activity for a summer youth group meeting or camp.

The Great Bicycle Race consists of 100 laps around a specified course. For example: Begin at the front of the church; head toward the park; turn left between the park and pool; go back to the front of the church. The object is for eight teams to complete as many laps as they can in a specified time. The bikes start in four rows of two—position determined by the drawing of numbers.

The youth group is divided into eight teams. The teams each choose an area to be their "pit." Riders must change positions in the pits and not on the road. Every person in the group must ride at least one lap. Violations cost the team a one lap penalty.

A couple of weeks prior to the race, we obtained our bikes by bidding for unclaimed, dilapidated bikes at a police auction. Each team was given one bike to

design, paint or repair for The Great Bicycle Race.

The day of the race, we awarded prizes for the best bike, most creative design and fastest "junker." We also gave prizes to the first, second and third place teams. The prizes were appropriate for a bike race: handlebar tape, pants clips, reflectors and locks.

—Randy Gross

Variations

1. Have the bikers collect pledges from church members, neighbors and relatives; for example, one dollar per lap. After the race, have the bikers collect the money to build up the youth fund, donate to a community charity or give to a world hun-

ger organization.

2. Use tricycles instead of bicycles and scale down the course. Set up an obstacle course around the church parking lot—all rules apply! Have the kids race around barrels, through water puddles, in tunnels made from refrigerator boxes, etc. Award prizes such as "Best Three Wheeler" (give the person three wheels off of an old tricycle), "Three-Wheel Maniac" (give the person a pair of goggles to help block the wind).

Your Ideas and Variations

_____

_____

_____

_____

BILLBOARDS

25

Hunger Facts
TOPIC: HUNGER/POVERTY

The reality of world hunger staggers those of us who live in Western affluence. But simply hearing about world hunger does little to motivate us into changing our living patterns. To enlighten our young people about this enormous problem, we designed an activity that would present them with the facts and that would enable them to share these facts with others. We decided to have the kids make a billboard on world hunger.

To make a billboard, your youth group will need: a large portable surface (at least 4 feet by 6 feet, wallboard, plywood, or paneling); newsprint or other large pieces of paper to cover that surface; colored construc-

tion paper or oak tag to make flaps; markers; tape; factual information on world hunger (from denominational or interdenominational hunger organizations such as Bread for the World, 802 Rhode Island Ave. N.E., Washington, D.C. 20018, (202) 269-0200).

At a youth group meeting, ask the students to examine the information they received on world hunger and select eight to 10 key facts they want to share with the congregation. They should identify the most significant words or statistics that deserve emphasis. For example, "Many people who live in pover-

ty-stricken, Third World countries live *25 to 30 fewer years*
than Americans."

Have the students cover the
large surface with paper. Then
have them neatly letter the selected statements on the paper.
From colored paper, have the
kids cut flaps to cover the "significant words." Fasten them to
the surface with a piece of tape
across the top of each one.

Display the "billboard" for
several weeks in a central area
of the church. Station young
people by the billboard and have
them encourage church members to "lift the flaps and
learn."

—Brethren House Ministries

Variations

1. With permission, display
the board at a shopping center
or mall. Have the young people
talk with people, invite their
handling the flaps, and distribute hunger literature. At the
same time, collect money and
donate to world hunger organizations. Emphasize to the people
that not only do we need to be
aware of world hunger, we need
to do something to alleviate the
problem.

Your Ideas and Variations

_____

_____

_____

_____

_____

_____

_____

_____

_____

_____

_____

BINOCULARS

26

Perseverance
TOPIC: PERSEVERANCE

Teach the young people that
with patience and perseverance
they can do many things.

Meet at the parking lot or an
inside area where you can make
a chalk line on the floor. Ask
one of the group members to use
chalk and a yardstick to draw a
straight line about 8 feet long on
the floor. Ask two volunteers to
read Ezekiel 1:9 and Hebrews
12:13. Then have the group
members take turns looking
through the large end of binoculars while trying to walk the
chalk line—one foot in front of
the other, right on the line. This
will be difficult at first, but with
patience and perseverance, it
can be done.

After everyone has had a

chance to walk the line, discuss these questions:

● How is living the advice given in the scriptures like walking the chalk line seen through the binoculars?

● Why is it difficult to walk the chalk line?

● Why is it difficult to walk the scripture line—to live the advice given to us in the Bible?

● What do we have to do to stay on the chalk line? scripture line?

● Name some of the most difficult scripture lines to follow. Why are they difficult?

Have everybody line up single file and walk heel-to-toe to the refreshments. Serve licorice strings or peppermint sticks. Remind the kids that walking the straight line of faith—living the advice of the scriptures—can be done with patience and perseverance.

—Janet R. Balmforth

Variations

1. Once the students master walking forward on the line, have them walk backward, then sideways.

2. Try walking a straight line while blindfolded; then while blindfolded and holding a person's hand, then without the blindfold. Discuss how we sometimes need other people's help as we go through difficult times.

Your Ideas and Variations

_____
_____
_____
_____
_____
_____
_____
_____
_____
_____
_____
_____
_____

BOOK JACKETS

27

Book Jacket Publicity
TOPIC: PUBLICITY

Have you ever used book jackets to promote your youth ministry? We decided on book jackets because all the young people were required to have covers on their school books.

Our youth group designed a one-size-fits-all book jacket and printed our youth group's theme on it. We printed thousands of different-colored covers; everybody wanted them! They were sturdy, durable and very useful.

We sold them for a small profit. Soon, book jackets were everywhere on nearly everyone's books—regardless of the church they attended!

—J.B. Collingsworth

Variations

1. Sponsor a book-jacket-design contest. Invite everyone in your congregation to submit a sample design. Have a group of young people serve as judges. The winning artist can sign his or her name to the masterpiece!

2. Make bookmarks out of colored posterboard and clear Con-Tact paper. Cut the posterboard into 1-inch-by-6-inch strips. Give the youth group members each a strip. Have them write their name on it along with a verse such as, "The Lord is my strength and my song" (Psalm 118:14). To protect the bookmarks, cover them with clear Con-Tact paper.

Your Ideas and Variations

_____
_____
_____
_____
_____
_____
_____
_____
_____
_____
_____
_____

BOWLING BALLS

28

Try to Remember
TOPIC: RESPONSIBILITY/LEADERSHIP

Do your youth group members have trouble remembering assignments—who will bring refreshments next week? who will do a devotional next week? who will write an article for the church newsletter? Forget tying a string around their finger—give them a bowling ball to take home!

Most bowling alleys have old, battered bowling balls that they would be pleased to donate to your youth group. You could paint a number "8" on a black bowling ball to indicate, "You will be 'behind the eight ball' if you forget . . ."

Make sure the current "holder of the ball" remembers not only his or her specific responsibility, but also to bring the bowling ball back. The bowling ball is a hard-to-forget reminder of assigned tasks!

—Arlo R. Reichter

Variations

1. Liven up a boring, black bowling ball. Decorate it with bright-colored paints, decoupaged pictures and letters.

2. After six months of bowling-ball reminders, celebrate the group members' improved memories by going bowling.

Your Ideas and Variations

_____

_____

_____

_____

_____

_____

churches to add a photograph of their youth group and a list of activities they like to do.

Fair is fair! Your own group members must study one book of the Bible and choose symbols for it. Have the kids compose a letter explaining their book of the Bible and the objects they chose to represent it. They can make a list of their favorite activities and pose for a group photograph. Copy and send the letter, activity list and photo, along with the cake boxes, to the 65 congregations.

Response time will be slow. This Bible study will take some time to complete. But the enthusiastic response is well worth the wait.

—Mardie H.C. MacDonald

BOXES

29

Bible Study by Mail
TOPIC: BIBLE STUDY/OUTREACH

Members of your group can share this project with other youth groups across the country, while learning more about the Bible.

You'll need 66 identical, empty cake boxes. Cover each box with white contact paper. On each box, write the name of one of the books of the Bible.

Choose the names of 65 other congregations across the country and send each of their youth groups an empty box. Ask each recipient to place in the box some objects that they feel are symbolic of the book of the Bible they've been assigned. For example, objects for Luke could be a small piece of flannel, used in making baby clothes, and baby blankets (to symbolize Jesus' birth); and a rough piece of wood (to symbolize Jesus' death on the cross). Encourage the

Variations

1. Ask the churches to fill their cake box with recipes for Christian living. For example, "Read the Bible daily," "Appreciate the gifts God gives you," "Look for ways to help others," etc.

2. Make shelves for the cake boxes by decorating large cardboard boxes or wooden crates. Label the shelves "Boxes of Bible Studies."

3. Maintain the contact with your new-found friends. Send them each a copy of your youth newsletter; encourage your youth group members to write to

the church; set up a pen-pal system with the other youth group members.

Your Ideas and Variations

_____
_____
_____
_____
_____
_____
_____
_____
_____
_____
_____
_____

30

Box Creations
TOPIC: DECORATIONS/
CHRISTIAN SYMBOLS

You can do some creative stuff with common boxes and large appliance boxes that many supermarkets, appliance dealers, department stores and other businesses toss in the trash. Be sure to make arrangements for pick-up several days in advance, since many dealers tear cartons apart after unpacking.

Your group can have lots of fun decorating the boxes with Christian symbols, making collages and even large crosses. Paint the box yellow, light blue or another pale color. Over this base, decorate the box with Christian symbols—various crosses, the monograms for Christ, etc. Books with helpful illustrations of Christian symbols, can be found in your church's or pastor's library. If you would like to experiment with a medium other than paint, colored tape can be used to create the symbols. Once completed, the boxes can be stacked up, placed on tables or hung from the ceiling to create a colorful, festive atmosphere.

Box collages are also fun to create. You will need scissors, glue or paste, and lots of magazines and newspapers. Personal photographs can also be used. Each person is to create a box collage that says something about himself or herself. Hobbies, interests, Bible themes, achievements, goals and dreams can all be portrayed on the collages.

A large collage cross can be used for a special worship service. The boxes should all be the same size. They can be stacked and glued, taped or strung together to form the upright portion. The horizontal portion is made by tacking boxes on top of a board. Use poster paints and cutouts from magazines, old curriculum materials and news-

papers to decorate the cross.
Design one side to represent
death/Crucifixion/Good Friday;
the other side to represent life/
Resurrection/Easter. Direct the
Good Friday side of the cross to-
wards the congregation during
the prayer of confession. Following the absolution, have two people slowly turn the cross around
as the congregation sings.

Your group can have lots of
fun thinking of creative uses for
boxes, boxes and more boxes.
—Ed McNulty

Variations

1. Decorate a box with colorful paper. Cut a slit in the top
and add a sign that says "Suggestions." Place 3×5 cards and
a pencil by the box; encourage
the kids to give suggestions for
improvement, games, discussion
topics, etc.

2. Decorate another box and
label it "Prayer Concerns." Encourage the kids to write their
concerns on a 3×5 card and
drop it in the box. Each week,
collect the cards and pray for
the specific needs of the youth
group members.

Your Ideas and Variations

———————————————
———————————————
———————————————
———————————————
———————————————
———————————————

Counting the
Days Before Christmas
TOPIC: OUTREACH/ELDERLY

Help the youth group mem-
bers catch the spirit of giving at
Christmas. The youth group
members can make special gifts
to give to elderly members of the
congregation, nursing home residents, hospital patients, or members of the congregation without
family.

At the local grocery store, obtain several boxes that still have
the 24-square, packing dividers
in them. Decorate the outside of
the boxes with Christmas wrapping paper. In each of the sections, place a small item that
symbolizes Christmas or relates
to the Christmas story. For example: a tree ornament, a star
made from construction paper
and glitter, a Christmas poem, a
recipe for Christmas cookies, a
favorite scripture, a postage
stamp with instructions to write
someone a letter and wish them
"Merry Christmas," etc.

Wrap each of the items in tis-

BOXES

sue paper and number them one
through 24. On an index card,
type instructions to open one gift
each day before Christmas,
starting with number one.

Brighten the Christmas season
for others with this gift-packed,
holiday-wrapped idea.
—Karen Musitano

Variations

1. Use a simple paper chain
as a prayer reminder and count-
down to Christmas. Have each
person in your group make a
holiday chain to display at
home.

Begin by cutting red and
green construction paper into
1-inch-by-8-inch strips. Depending on when you begin your holi-

day chain, cut the number of
strips to equal the number of
days until Christmas. The kids
will write a name or activity on
each link. They will open a link
each day and pray for the person named, read the Bible verse
listed, or do the activity given.
Here are some ideas to write inside the links:

● **Giving thanks for youth
group members.** As a group, list
the names of youth group members—active and inactive. Don't
forget your adult sponsors. Have
each person transfer the names
to his or her chain.

● **Giving thanks for your
church family.** With your group,
list tasks—big and little—that
are accomplished by your

105

church members. Fill the chain with these tasks and the people who do them. Use the chain as an awareness tool and a way to say thank you.

● **Giving thanks for family and friends.** Have each individual fill the chain with names of personal friends and family members.

● **Using links for personal devotions.** Prepare a list of short Bible readings, one for each link, to be used as daily personal devotions.

Sprinkle these Bible verses throughout the chain links: 1 Corinthians 1:4-9; 2 Corinthians 1:3-4; Ephesians 1:3; Philippians 1:3-11; Colossians 1:3-4; 1 Thessalonians 1:2-4; 2 Thessalonians 1:3.

● **Doing nice things for others.** Create a list of quick activities (phone a friend, say "I love you" to your parents, drop a note to your grandparents, etc.) to do after opening each link.

Watch this paper chain activity "disappear" as Christmas draws closer!

Your Ideas and Variations

_____
_____
_____
_____
_____
_____
_____

_____
_____
_____
_____
_____

32

Our View of God
TOPIC: GOD/PERCEPTION

This is a unique way to illustrate our limited ability to understand the true nature of God.

Place a large appliance box in the center of your meeting room. Give each person a utility knife; ask everyone to cut a hinged flap (three-sided cut) anywhere on the surface of the box. Don't tell the kids what the box is for.

After each member has cut a peephole, ask all members to leave the room. Place a large object, or a person, in the box.

Bring group members back into the room and allow them to peek, one at a time, through a hole. Of course, inside the box it's dark, and one small hole provides very little light. As each person looks, his or her flap should be left open, allowing more light to enter for the benefit of the next person. Before long, the object, or person, will be recognizable.

This activity provides a great opportunity to talk about the ways we "peek" at God. Maybe some of the negative images come from our inability to see the whole picture. Maybe we need other people to help shed light (the need for corporate worship). Or, maybe we never will understand God until our "boxes" are removed in heaven and the full light is shining on us!

—Steve Newton

Variations

1. Have the participants make "binoculars" by taping together two empty toilet paper rolls. Give them a marker and have them write, "See what God has given me."

2. Give the young people each a 3-foot piece of colored telephone wire. Have them shape a pair of glasses to remind them to look for God in all they see and do.

Your Ideas and Variations

_____
_____
_____
_____
_____
_____
_____
_____
_____
_____
_____

33

Spiritual Building Blocks
TOPIC: SPIRITUAL GROWTH/
CHRISTIAN LIVING

In this Bible study, participants will examine Peter's list of the qualities of Christian living; determine why these qualities are necessary for Christians; discuss ways to develop the qualities; select one quality to personally work on developing.

Cover eight shoe boxes with white paper. In bold letters, write one of the qualities listed in 2 Peter 1:5-7 on each box. The qualities are: faith, goodness, knowledge, self-control, perseverance, godliness, brotherly kindness, love. Place the boxes side by side as you begin the study. Each group member will need eight pieces of paper and a pencil. You also will need newsprint and a marker.

Tell the young people you're going to examine essential qualities of Christian living. Give each group member eight pieces of paper and a pencil. Instruct them to look at the shoe box labeled "faith." On one piece of paper, have them write answers to these questions:

● How would you define this quality?

● Why is this quality important in Christian living?

● What would happen if this quality were a part of every Christian's life?

Give the young people time to write brief answers, collect the papers and place them in the corresponding box. Move on to the next quality until all eight have been analyzed.

Instruct group members to read 2 Peter 1:3-4. Ask:

● What has God in his power done for us?

● What does Peter call God's Word?

● What can the "great and precious promises" do for us?

Say, "Now, let's examine some of the teaching in God's Word. Look at verses 5-7. Notice Peter lists the qualities we've just considered. Let's see what you wrote about them." Read and discuss the contents of each box separately. As you progress, build a pyramid with the empty boxes. When you've finished, have young people look at verses 8 and 9. Ask:

● What's the first promise Peter gives? What do you think it means?

● What's the second promise Peter gives? What do you think it means?

● Which quality does our group need most? Why?

● What are some ways our group can develop this quality?

● Which quality do you need most?

● What can you do to develop this quality in your life?

As group members tell ways to develop these qualities in their lives, ask someone to take notes on the newsprint. After all have shared, form pairs. With the notes, remind young people of the commitment they've made. Have the pairs share concerns and pray together.

—Doug Newhouse

Variations

1. Divide into eight small groups. Give each group a "quality box," Bible, commentary, concordance, piece of paper and pencil. Ask the groups to check their concordance for Bible references to their quality. They also can look in the commentary for extra meaning. Share the discoveries.

2. Ask the young people to each choose one quality they would personally like to further develop. Have them write the quality on one side of a 3×5 card. On the other side, have them list two ways they can accomplish this. For example, if a person decided to improve "knowledge," he or she could list, "I will ask my pastor for a good Bible study guide, and begin a daily scripture study." "I will go to Sunday school each week." Have the kids keep the "quality commitment" cards as a reminder of their desire for

personal growth.

Your Ideas and Variations

_____

_____

_____

_____

_____

_____

_____

_____

_____

_____

_____

_____

_____

BROCHURES

34

Community Touch
TOPIC: PUBLICITY

I'm a brochure nut! Sometimes, after I have read a brochure, I will keep it because it is attractive or is filled with catchy sayings.

To make a brochure, you'll need a few pictures and some information. A brochure is more readable if it's not wordy—the more specific the better. The brochure I developed for our youth group pictured the kids posed outside the church. Above the picture were the words, "Want to be a part of a great youth group?" Below the picture were the words, "A place where every person is special." Inside the brochure were several pictures of our young people and sponsors involved in various activities, information about the church, and information about the different youth ministry activities.

A brochure exposes your youth group to the community. Non-members are introduced to your exciting group in a unique way and may want to be a part of it.

—J.B. Collingsworth

Variations

1. Distribute the brochures at schools, shopping centers, grocery stores and community events.

2. Update the brochure each year—let the youth group members help with the design and preparation.

3. Develop a brochure for your church!

Your Ideas and Variations

_____

_____

_____

_____

_____

_____

_____

_____

35

Fliers for Windshields
TOPIC: PUBLICITY

Here's a way to reach out to the community and, at the same time, advertise your church service times.

Plan a full day for this activity. Beforehand, prepare copies of a flier using information about your church. Here's what our flier looked like on the front:

> **We Have Cleaned Your Windshield So You Can See Where You Are Going!**
>
> (Compliments of the First Baptist Youth)

On the back was printed:

> **Join us for our journey together.**
> **First Baptist Church**
> Services at 8 a.m. and 10:30 a.m.
> Sunday school at 9:15 a.m.
> **See you there!**

Gather your youth group members on a Saturday morning. Give them lots of old rags, paper towels, glass cleaner and fliers. Divide them into small groups and assign an adult sponsor to each. Have them go to local shopping centers, clean all of the windshields in the parking lot, then leave a flier under a windshield wiper of each car.

This activity is a great witnessing opportunity, as well as something that creates good will and lets people know about your youth group.

—J.B. Collingsworth

Variations

1. Call a local paper or television station—let them cover your service project!

2. Sponsor a flier-design contest. See what creative ideas your church members offer.

Your Ideas and Variations

_____
_____
_____
_____
_____
_____
_____
_____
_____
_____
_____
_____
_____

BROOMS

36

Servanthood
TOPIC: SERVANTHOOD/OUTREACH

A broom and bar of soap visually underline the meaning of the non-verbal film "Oh Happy

Day." (Order this film from film companies such as Ecu-Film, 810-12th Ave. S., Nashville. TN 37203.) The film depicts a bearded street sweeper who changes the lives of some of the people he encounters as he cleans the city streets. These people include a woman trying to smuggle liquor, an officious customs agent, a young couple competing against each other by piling up more things than the other, a grieving widow and a street prostitute. They once lived isolated lives; he leaves them living in a supportive community. Only a businessman, blindly chasing a huge silver dollar, pays the sweeper no heed.

This symbolic, non-verbal film offers plenty of stimuli for thought on values, choices and the role of Christ. A broom and bar of soap can be used with the film to emphasize the cleansing role of Christ in our lives. Here's how:

Make sure the floor of your meeting room is messy. Ask someone who's not a part of your group to arrive early and begin sweeping the floor when the first member arrives. The sweeper should be dressed in work clothes and appear slightly unkempt. The person may smile but not talk, even if group members direct a question to him or her. Before starting the film,

serve a messy snack food such as popcorn so that the sweeper will have plenty to clean up after the film.

Show the film after the briefest possible introduction. Say that there will be no dialogue in the film, but don't go into "what to look for," thereby robbing them of the opportunity to discover the film's symbolism themselves. Have the sweeper stop during the screening.

After the showing, use the discussion guide that comes with the film. At this point the sweeper should commence cleaning. Watch the reaction of the group members as you go over the discussion questions. Do some of the members ignore the sweeper? Do some giggle or laugh? Do they seem puzzled by

what's going on, or even a bit upset? Do some purposely throw more trash on the floor? Does anyone help pick up the debris?

After the discussion, start the devotional service with a call to worship based on Psalm 51:1-2. On a small table, place a bar of soap, a cross, an open Bible, a pan of water, a washcloth and a long towel. Sing the gospel song, "Oh Happy Day." (If the group doesn't know it, listen and sing along with a recorded version, or read the words aloud together.) After a prayer, read 1 John 1:5-9. Pass out pencils and paper and ask the members to think about something they are sorry they did—or didn't do. It can be something that happened recently or long ago. Have the kids write their experience down—not in detail, in just a few words. When everyone is done, tell them to crumple up their papers and throw them on the floor. The sweeper quickly sweeps or picks them up and throws them in a wastebasket. As he or she does this, declare that God forgives us. You can incorporate 1 John 1:9 in the statement. Go around and wash each person's hands with the soap. If you're especially daring, wash the feet also. Have someone read John 13:1-17. (If time is short use only verses 12-15.) This is a good time to explain the role of your sweeper, if the young people haven't already commented on him or her. Use the towel to dry their hands and feet. Ask if anyone knows the ancient Latin name for towel ("stola"). Jesus took a "stola," a towel, and wiped the disciples' feet. From this we get the word stole, the cloth that ministers and choir members often wear over their shoulders. Lift up a prayer of thanksgiving for the cleansing power of Christ. Close with a hymn of service.

—Ed McNulty

Variations

1. Ask each group member to assume the role of a servant for the next meeting. A couple of kids could set up the meeting room; one could make copies of any necessary handouts; three others could supply and serve refreshments; and everybody could clean up.

2. Give each person a Handi-wipe and a marker. Have the young people each write down a goal of servanthood. For example, "I will help cook dinner once a week" or "I will offer to babysit my little brother so Mom and Dad can enjoy a free evening," etc. Ask the "servants" to keep the Handiwipes as reminders.

Your Ideas and Variations

BUBBLES

37

Creation
TOPIC: VULNERABILITY

Soap bubbles can create a special spirit in worship or in other group settings. They also can be instructional. Bubbles simulate the act of creation as our breath blows life into them. In fact, they even look like little globes or worlds. We must be gentle—blowing too hard won't work; once formed, the bubble is extremely fragile. Creation is equally vulnerable—we need to tenderly care for the earth, each other and ourselves. We can look into the bubbles and see our reflection, in the same way that we see our beauty and value reflected as children of God. Some bubbles contain rainbow colors—we can consider the rainbow to be a symbol of God's promise to care for us. Bubbles evoke a sense of wonder within us, as do all of God's miraculous creations.

—Lynn Potter

Variations

1. Buy bubble soap at discount stores—or make bubble soap by combining ½ cup liquid soap such as Ivory with ½ cup water. Create bubbles by dipping one end of an empty thread spool into the liquid and blowing out through the other end.

2. Instead of soap bubbles, use bright-colored balloons; bounce and tap them from person to person.

3. Use large, fragile weather balloons. Order these from Edmund Scientific, 1016 E. Gloucester Pike, Barrington, NJ 08007.

Your Ideas and Variations

_____
_____
_____
_____
_____
_____
_____
_____
_____
_____
_____
_____
_____
_____

BULLETIN BOARDS

38

Group Bulletin Board
TOPIC: GROUP BUILDING

As a helpful identity process for a retreat, camp or youth program, form a group collage.

Set up a bulletin board and supply lots of tacks. Ask the kids to tack on the bulletin board some items that reveal who they are individually and in relationship to the group (for example, magazine pictures, drawings, bandannas, etc.).

The process of doing this will reveal a lot about the individuals and the group dynamics—such as how well they work to-

gether, feelings about personal space and boundaries, degrees of participation, etc. After the collage is formed, ask each person to share what his or her items symbolize.

Read to the group Romans 12:4 or 1 Corinthians 12:12-26. Celebrate that we all are individuals, but together we make one great group.

—Lynn Potter

Variations

1. Title the bulletin board, "One Great Group." Tack construction paper hearts around the border; have the young people each write their name in one of the hearts.

2. Present a Bible study titled, "The Body of Christ." Use these verses: Romans 12:4-5; Ephesians 4:1-16; Colossians 1:18-20.

Your Ideas and Variations

_____
_____
_____
_____
_____
_____
_____
_____
_____
_____
_____
_____
_____
_____
_____
_____
_____
_____

39

Making Banners
TOPIC: RETREATS/BANNERS

Make burlap banners as a reminder of a special weekend retreat, focusing on the retreat's theme. Following is a description of the banner we made.

Each person was supplied with a 10-inch-by-18-inch piece of burlap, one 12-inch dowel, several pieces of brightly colored felt, string, scissors and glue.

Our theme was "Jesus"—who he is, what we think about him, what he expects of us. We made banners illustrating the early Christian symbol of the fish, affixing to the banner the Greek letters which spell "fish" and mean:

Jesus Christ God Son Savior

ΙΧΟΥΣ

To make each banner, we folded and then glued 2 inches of the burlap fabric over the dowel. We cut a large fish out of white felt and glued it on the burlap. Then, we cut each of the five Greek letters from a different color of felt and glued the letters vertically to the fish.

String was tied to each end of the dowel to make a hanger. Our finished product looked like this:

The kids took the banners home and hung them in their rooms. They were very special reminders of a very special weekend.

—Walter Mees

Variations

1. Make tassels out of yarn. Hang one on each end of the dowel or across the bottom of the banner.

2. Attach bells to the banner, which will jingle in the wind.

3. Tack streamers of ribbon to the banner, which will flutter in the breeze.

Your Ideas and Variations

_____
_____
_____
_____
_____
_____
_____
_____

_____
_____
_____
_____

CALENDARS

40

Red-Letter Day
TOPIC: HOLY SPIRIT

God reveals his wisdom through the Holy Spirit so that the believer may know of the things that God so freely gives.

Through the Holy Spirit, we are more able to understand spiritual things. You cannot accept God's truth—or know it— except through the Holy Spirit. A deaf person cannot judge a music contest; a blind person cannot judge a beauty contest or an art show; and the unsaved cannot judge spiritual things. The Christian also is unable to judge, but can understand all things with the help of the Holy Spirit.

For the meeting, gather one or two large calendars for the upcoming year. (Have enough so that each student will receive one page.) You also will need red markers, a piece of paper and a stamped envelope for each student. Place some burning incense or perfume in the middle of the room to represent the Holy Spirit.

Ask everyone to form a circle around the incense. Read and discuss 1 Corinthians 2:9-16. Concentrate on the Holy Spirit. To help the students understand who and what the Holy Spirit is, ask them these questions:

● Is the Holy Spirit with us now? Explain.

● Are we changed by the Holy Spirit? How?

● Does the Holy Spirit invade our hearts, or do we have to ask for and want the presence of the Holy Spirit?

Give each student one page (month) of a calendar for the upcoming year. Ask each to choose a "Red-Letter Day"—a day when the kids will diligently pray for the Holy Spirit to enter their hearts and guide them. Ask them to take their calendar pages home and post them so that they won't forget.

Give each person a piece of paper and a stamped envelope. Ask them to write a memo to themselves regarding their Red-Letter Day. Assure them that no one will see this letter. Ask the kids to self-address the envelope, seal the flap and write their month on the back.

Say, "This is not a magic way of getting things! For example, 'I will pray that the Holy Spirit

will help me get good grades on the test on September 19.' Your Red-Letter Day is to be a sincere, quiet, private invitation to the Holy Spirit to come into your heart. The letters are your reminders. Throughout the year, in the week before the appropriate month, I will mail the letters to you. There will be no follow-up. This is between you and the Holy Spirit. Take it very seriously."

You will probably never know how this worked. There are times when we cast a stone into the water and never know where the ensuing ripples flow. You don't have to know. God will. And you can pray each month through the coming year that your youth group members will know the sweet joy of the Holy Spirit in their hearts.

—E. Jane Mall

Variations

1. At a retreat, one youth leader read the story of Moses talking to God on holy ground (Exodus 3:1-6). The leader had the participants find a place inside or outside for their "holy ground." Throughout the retreat the kids went to their special place to think, meditate and talk to God.

The leader had his kids continue this process by finding holy ground at home—a place where they could go at any time

118

to think or to pray.

2. Have your youth group members each complete the following Spiritual Autobiography (**Spiritual Growth in Youth Ministry**, by J. David Stone, Group Books). Discuss the autobiographies in small groups.

Spiritual Autobiography

1. My earliest memory or awareness of God _____

2. The major religious events or experiences in my life (family, church, youth group, camp, etc.) _____

3. My spiritual high point (when I felt the closest to God) _____

4. My spiritual low point (when I felt most distant from God) _____

5. Special people who have played a role in my faith journey _____

6. Where I am right now in my relationship with God _____

7. Where I would like to be in my relationship with God _____

8. What's missing in my relationship with God _____

(A copyrighted resource from **Spiritual Growth in Youth Ministry**. Permission granted to copy this handout for local church use only.)

Your Ideas and Variations

_____
_____
_____
_____
_____
_____
_____
_____
_____
_____
_____
_____
_____
_____
_____
_____

41

Scripture Scramble
TOPIC: BIBLE STUDY

Here is a good way to get double use out of your verse-a-day scripture calendars. If you don't have one, order one by writing to Workman Publishing Company, 1 West 39th St., New York, NY 10018, or check with your local Christian bookstore.

Before your group arrives, place used pages from the calendar around the room. Leave some pages in plain view, some up high on shelves, some under chairs and tables, etc. Then, once the young people have arrived, have them search for, and collect as many pages as they can. When all the pages have been collected, award points in the following ways: for the November 19th page, award 19 points; for the February 3rd page, award 3 points, etc. If the youth group members can memorize the verse on the page, they receive double the points. If the verse is more than three lines

long and they memorize it, they receive triple the number of points. Award a prize for the most points won—how about a verse-a-day calendar?

—Jeffrey A. Collins

Variations

1. Calendar pages also can be used to divide your group into teams. Give out pages running from Monday to Saturday. (Pull out the Sunday pages so that you have an even number of teams. Thus, Monday through Wednesday becomes one team and Thursday through Saturday becomes the other team.) Your first team event could be a scripture-memorization contest. Give the team members two minutes to memorize the verse on their page. The team with the most verses memorized wins!

Your Ideas and Variations

_____

_____

_____

_____

_____

_____

_____

_____

_____

_____

_____

_____

42

The 28-Day Name Game
TOPIC: BIBLE STUDY

One challenge of youth ministry is creating new and exciting ways to present basic Bible knowledge. And what could be more basic than learning the books and themes of the New Testament?

The youth group sponsors and I created The 28-Day Name Game. We decided to use the month of February because it was the closest in number of days to the number of New Testament books, with the 28th day "free." However, other months could be used by designating free days throughout the month.

In order to motivate our teenagers to participate, we:

● Introduced the game and its objectives to the congregation during two Sunday morning services.

● Invited parents to play the game at home.

● Encouraged members of the congregation to "sponsor" one or more young people at 10 cents per square.

● Offered two versions—beginners and advanced.

You can make the game cards by typing the following information on an 8½×11 piece of paper. Make copies for each youth group member.

The 28-Day Name Game							1
"Books of the New Testament"							MATTHEW
Beginners—Memorize the names of the books only.				Advanced—Names and themes of each book.			
2 MARK	3 LUKE	4 JOHN	5 ACTS	6 ROMANS	7 1 CORINTHIANS	8 2 CORINTHIANS
9 GALATIANS	10 EPHESIANS	11 PHILIPPIANS	12 COLOSSIANS	13 1 THESSALONIANS	14 2 THESSALONIANS	15 1 TIMOTHY
16 2 TIMOTHY	17 TITUS	18 PHILEMON	19 HEBREWS	20 JAMES	21 1 PETER	22 2 PETER
23 1 JOHN	24 2 JOHN	25 3 JOHN	26 JUDE	27 REVELATION	28 May God Richly Bless You	Sponsored by the Fenton Lawn Youth Come on and join our adventure

Cover each square with the following information. Glue only the left side of each square covering so that the kids can open it and memorize each day's assignment.

						1 Christ, the King
2 Christ, the Servant	**3** Christ, the Man	**4** Christ In His Deity	**5** First-Century Missions	**6** Gospel of God	**7** Christian Conduct	**8** Paul's Authority
9 Salvation by Grace	**10** The Church as the Body of Christ	**11** Rejoicing In Christ	**12** Pre-Eminence of Christ	**13** Christ's Return	**14** Day of the Lord	**15** Church Order In Ephesus
16 Holding the Truth	**17** Church Order at Crete	**18** Christian Intercession	**19** Priesthood of Christ	**20** Faith That Works	**21** Suffering and Glory	**22** Warning Against False Teachers
23 Christian Fellowship	**24** Christ's Commandment	**25** Walking In Truth	**26** Contending for the Faith	**27** Things to Come	**28** All the Books of the New Testament	Sponsored by the Fenton Lawn Youth Come on and join our adventure

We found that this game generated a lot of interest among junior high kids and senior high kids alike. Our participation rate has been nearly 100 percent, and many of our teenagers have achieved the learning objectives!

Variations

1. Plan a contest for the end of the month to see who remembers the most. Award calendars, Bibles or devotion books.

2. Create calendars according to other themes such as women in the Bible, famous Bible characters, Psalms and Proverbs.

Your Ideas and Variations

_____
_____
_____
_____
_____
_____
_____
_____
_____
_____
_____
_____
_____
_____
_____
_____
_____
_____
_____

CAMERAS

43

Caught in the Act!
TOPIC: OUTREACH/
*   INTERGENERATIONAL*

This project enables young people to discover the ways church members minister to others while in the work environment.

Arrange to use several instant-print cameras and purchase film. Divide the youth group into several teams and give them each a camera and some film. The project goal is to capture working church members on film in the act of ministry. Work-place ministry takes place whenever people try to do their jobs in a Christian way. Examples are: the carpenter who is careful and accurate in his work and gives his customers good service; the friendly and helpful check-out person at the grocery store; the medical doctor who works long and hard to provide quality care for her patients; etc.

Explain to the church members that during the next several weeks, the youth group members will be taking pictures of them at their work sites. The kids will need to set up appointments with some of the church members, depending upon the members' vocations.

Label a bulletin board, "Our Church at Work" or "Our Witness—Alive and Well" or "Our Ministers at Work." Display the pictures on the church bulletin board.

—Arlo R. Reichter

Variations

1. Have the youth group members take pictures of young people ministering to others in the school environment.

2. Make a slide show of church members of all ages ministering to others. As background music play, "We Are His Hands," by White Heart. Sing songs such as, "They Will Know We Are Christians By Our Love" and "Lord, Be Glorified" (**Songs**, by Yohann Anderson, Songs and Creations, Inc.).

Your Ideas and Variations

_____
_____
_____
_____
_____
_____
_____
_____
_____
_____

44

God's Wonderful World
TOPIC: CREATION

Instant-print cameras are worth their weight in flashbulbs when it comes to youth group activities. Here is one way to use the cameras.

Divide the young people into groups of three or four; provide each group with a camera. Send them outside to snap several nature shots. Mark off a certain area that can be covered, otherwise you may have to track down the extremely ambitious (or extremely unambitious) teenagers across state lines! After a set time limit, regroup for the lesson.

Some of the photos will be funny; others will be beautiful. All of the pictures can be used as a springboard for a study of God's work in the world.

Read Psalm 121 and remind the group members that the God who made the heavens and the earth is more than able to meet their needs. Ask each group to choose one favorite photograph and compose a related skit, poem or song to present it. Instruct the teenagers to include at least one piece of information about how God is at work in our world today.

The following could be sung to the tune, "Row, Row, Row Your Boat." "This is a picture of a pretty flower. God makes these so beautiful, yet cares for us much more."

Label a bulletin board, "God's Wonderful World." Ask the young people to make a collage out of their photographs. Display the bulletin board so everyone can enjoy the pictures of God's creation.

—Denise Turner

Variations

1. Ask the youth group members to take pictures of people; then discuss the body of Christ (1 Corinthians 12:12-26).

2. Tape record various sounds of nature: chirping birds, blowing wind, dripping rain, etc. Play the recording and have the young people guess the sounds.

Your Ideas and Variations

_____
_____
_____
_____
_____
_____
_____
_____
_____
_____
_____
_____
_____
_____

CANDLES

45

A Call to Commitment
TOPIC: COMMITMENT TO CHRIST

This activity, designed for a youth group service project, meeting, or retreat, helps encourage teenagers to commit themselves publicly to Christ or a task. Since commitments can be general, the leader must direct this encounter. Using Matthew 10:32-33 as a guide, share how Jesus calls each of us to acknowledge him before others.

In the center of the room, set up a table. On the table, place a small candle for each person and one large candle (the Christ candle). You also will need several pieces of aluminum foil. Light the Christ candle and darken the room.

Encourage the young people, one at a time, to light one of the small candles with the flame of the Christ candle; express his or her commitment to Christ; make a candle holder by wrapping the base of the small candle with aluminum foil; and place the small candle on the table.

Don't expect all to participate. In an average group, about half of the members will participate. Let young people know they're not being pressured into coming forward.

Through this activity, those who come forward gain courage, and even those who don't are challenged to look deeply into their own lives.

Say, "Just as many small candles light up a dark room, we can, with each other's help, be the 'light of the world.' " As a closing prayer, read Matthew 5:13-16.

—David Olshine

Variations

1. Rather than vocally making commitments to Christ, have the young people make silent commitments. This encourages all participants (including the shy ones) to look deeply into their lives.

2. At the end of the activity, give the young people each a small candle, 3×5 card, pencil and piece of tape. Have them tape their candle to the 3×5 card and write down their commitment. Ask the participants to keep the cards and read them occasionally to refresh their memories about the commitment they made at the retreat.

Your Ideas and Variations

_____

_____

_____

46

An Illuminating Look at the Holy Spirit
TOPIC: HOLY SPIRIT

Use candles to "highlight" the work of the Holy Spirit in the life of a Christian.

Gather a candle and matches for each person.

Pass out a candle to each person. Begin by asking obvious questions: What is this? (A candle.) What does it do? (Produces light.) Ask everyone to hold his or her candle out in front; then turn out the lights. While it is dark, talk about why the candles fail to produce light. Although they look like candles, and in fact *are* candles, they do not perform the function of candles until they're lighted.

Turn on the lights. Ask how the Christian can relate his or her life to the candle. Christians have the capacity, even the responsibility, to produce light in a dark world. We cannot do it under our own power, but only as

we are empowered to do so by the fire of the Holy Spirit. Ask volunteers to read Matthew 5:14-16 and Ephesians 5:3-13.

Darken the room again. Light the candles one by one by tipping the unlighted candlewick into the flame of a burning one. After all the candles are lighted, close with a prayer that we would not quench the Holy Spirit in our lives, but we would allow him to work through us and make us beacons for others.

—Linda Ferree

Variations

1. Prepare a Bible study on light. Use these verses: Genesis 1:3; Psalms 27:1; 119:105; Isaiah 2:5; 42:6; Matthew 4:16; John 1:1-5; 3:16-21; 8:12.

2. Use this idea at night—outdoors.

Your Ideas and Variations

47

The Peace Candle
TOPIC: SELF-IMAGE

After an intense weekend youth retreat, filled with talks, small group activities, Frisbee, football, laughter, food, and very little sleep, close the event with The Peace Candle. This activity always highlights a retreat.

On the final evening, ask each young person to go somewhere alone (either inside or outdoors) to evaluate his or her life—where there need to be changes,

growth or forgiveness. Encourage each individual to listen to God, and prepare to share with the group after 15 or 20 minutes of reflection.

While the kids are having their "alone time," prepare the room. Place a large, lighted candle in the center of the room and turn out the lights.

Instruct the young people to sit quietly in a circle around the candle. Once all the kids are present, say, "Perhaps God has talked to you this weekend. I hope so. Tonight we each have a chance to share our faith with one another as this candle is passed to you by the person on your right.

"The person with the candle is the only one allowed to speak—praying out loud, sharing what God has taught, thanking a friend for something or anything else. If you don't wish to share, simply pass the candle to the next person."

After the candle has been passed around the entire circle, close by giving words of encouragement and hugs. The group will be united together in a dynamic new way.

—David Olshine

Variations

1. Pass the candle around the circle one more time. Ask each person to answer this question when he or she holds the can-

dle: "What is something you will always remember about this weekend?"

2. Pass the candle one final time. As the young people each hold the candle, have them say one thing they appreciate about the person on their right. Close this time of sharing by having the kids place their arms on each other's shoulders as you play the song "Friends," by Michael W. Smith.

Your Ideas and Variations

_____
_____
_____
_____
_____
_____
_____
_____
_____
_____

CANDY

48

Cotton Candy and Earthly Riches
TOPIC: VALUES

The next time you're at an amusement park or somewhere cotton candy is sold, buy some,

gather your youth group members, sit down and teach a lesson.

Compare the cotton candy to earthly riches—notice how appealing it is, how pretty it looks, how good and sweet it tastes, and so on. Earthly riches are also appealing, pretty and give pleasure. Have the young people taste the cotton candy and notice how quickly it dissolves.

The same is true with earthly riches—put them in a fire and watch how quickly they will be consumed. Ask the young people, "In whom are we to put our hope for the future?" Tell them that the Bible says to put our hope in God (1 Timothy 6:17).

Ask the kids to think about what earthly riches they might be putting their hopes in for happiness, gratification, etc. Discuss the topic further; then go on to enjoy the day, a little wiser.

—Gloria Menke

Variations

1. Use ice cream instead of cotton candy.

2. Develop this object lesson into a Bible study by discussing verses such as John 16:33 and 1 John 2:15-17.

Your Ideas and Variations

_____
_____
_____

_____
_____
_____
_____
_____
_____
_____
_____
_____

49

Elijah on Mount Carmel Apple
TOPIC: BIBLE STUDY

A creative way to share the story of Elijah and the prophets of Baal (1 Kings 18) is to have a hot plate, a pot, one apple for each group member, and the appropriate number of bags of caramel candies and sticks.

As you begin the lesson, turn on the hot plate, pour the candies into the pot and begin melting them. While you teach, constantly refer to Mount Carmel. For example, you could begin by saying, "So Ahab sent to all the people of Israel, and gathered the prophets together *at Mount Carmel.* And Elijah came near to all the people *at Mount Carmel,* and said, 'How long will you go limping with two different opinions? If the Lord is God, follow him; but if Baal, then follow him.' And the people *at Mount*

Carmel did not answer him a word . . ." (1 Kings 18:20-21).

Continue the story, adding Mount Carmel wherever you can. The visual stimuli will help your students remember this great story.

By the time you are finished with the lesson you will have made a delicious caramel apple for each student.

—Tom Franks

Variations

1. Every time you mention the word "Carmel" in your presentation, toss out a piece of caramel candy to the kids. At the end of the lesson ask review questions. Distribute caramel candies as rewards for correct answers.

Your Ideas and Variations

_____
_____
_____
_____
_____
_____
_____
_____
_____
_____
_____
_____
_____
_____
_____

50

Heart Candy
TOPIC: VALENTINE'S DAY

This activity involves heart candy with messages printed on them—the kind you used to pass around in elementary school on Valentine's Day!

Bring two bags of heart candy to one of your February youth meetings. Instruct the teenagers to close their eyes and pull a few candies out of one of the bags.

Divide the kids into groups of four and ask them to develop a role play using one or two of the candy messages and a scripture reference or Bible story. For ex-

ample, a group could use hearts with "Love Always" and "Forever Yours" and John 3:16, "For God so loved the world that he gave his only Son, that whoever believes in him should not perish but have eternal life." A person could role play Mary and pretend to hold baby Jesus. She could stand and offer Jesus to the audience as someone reads the candy messages and the scripture.

Allow time for all of the small groups to present their role plays. Bring out the other bag of candy and give everybody a handful. Have the kids give a piece of candy to each person along with an affirmation such as, "I appreciate your smile" or "You're a good friend." After everyone has been affirmed, eat

and enjoy the candy!
                    —Denise Turner

Variations

1. Play charades with the candy hearts. Instruct each of the youth group members to act out the messages while the others guess.

2. Give the young people each a handful of candy hearts. Ask them to read the messages, give them to other kids who fit the descriptions, and explain their reasons for the gift. For example, a person could give a heart inscribed with "Truly Fine" to another and say, "You are one of my best friends." A person can give a heart inscribed with "Outstanding" to another and say, "Your outstanding sense of humor and personality add life to our meetings."

Your Ideas and Variations

_____
_____
_____
_____
_____
_____
_____
_____
_____
_____
_____
_____
_____

51

**Helping a Friend
With a Drug Problem**
TOPIC: SUBSTANCE ABUSE/WORSHIP

The pressure to abuse drugs is ever-present in the lives of young people today. Use Hershey Kiss candies to encourage teenagers to use drugs wisely and to commit themselves to help friends with drug problems.

This activity was created for use in a worship experience following a presentation by a drug rehabilitation counselor. Plan a similar presentation and worship service. Ask a counselor to present the idea that we live in a drug-filled world. All of us make choices whether it be with drugs such as marijuana or drugs such as caffeine. Ask the counselor to give creative suggestions on how we can make wise decisions concerning drug use. After the presentation, move into the sanctuary for a worship service. End the worship service with the use of Hershey Kisses.

Place Hershey Kisses on the altar of your sanctuary (one for each person). Gather the kids and tell them that these candies can be considered drugs because they contain caffeine. The candies remind us that the choice of whether or not to use drugs is present in our everyday lives. We have the power to use drugs foolishly or wisely.

Invite the young people to kneel at the altar and take a piece of candy. Say to the students, "What you do with the candy is your choice. Just as what you do with drugs is your choice. You may choose to unwrap the candy as a symbol to open yourselves to care for your friends. Keep the strip as a reminder of this commitment. We should help each other when it comes to making choices about drug use. You can eat the candy, just as many people choose to eat chocolate or drink coffee. Although caffeine can be considered a type of drug, it is not as harmful as other drugs such as marijuana or cocaine. Life requires wise choices in all areas."

Allow time for the kids to remain at the altar to pray for a friend or family member with drug problems. Have the group members form a circle and place their arms on each other's shoulders. Close with a prayer asking God for guidance in making wise decisions in our lives. Offer thanks for the support of family and friends.

—Kathi B. Finnell

Variations

1. Invite four or five kids who would be willing to speak about drug rehabilitation experiences to come to the youth group meeting and be a part of a panel. Facilitate a discussion between the guests and the youth group members. Ask the youth group members to write their questions on 3×5 cards, then a discussion leader can ask the questions to the panel.

2. Sponsor another panel discussion with four or five people who have counseled those with drug problems; for example, a minister, a school counselor, a psychologist, etc. Facilitate a discussion between the guests and the group members.

Your Ideas and Variations

_____
_____
_____
_____
_____
_____
_____
_____
_____
_____

Symbols of Confession
TOPIC: LENT/CONFESSION

Use these ideas to discover a deeper meaning of the act of

132

confession. These ideas work well during Lent, but can be used any time during the prayer of confession.

For each of the six weeks of Lent, give the kids a symbol to hold during the prayer of confession. Leave plenty of time to discuss the symbols.

The first week of Lent, give each person a knot-shaped pretzel. Tell the kids how this food originated in the Middle Ages when monks wanted to teach about prayer. The tradition is that the shape of the pretzel represents the arms of someone who is praying. During the words of forgiveness, let the kids eat the pretzels.

The second week, give each person a piece of rock candy. Talk about the stumbling blocks in our lives and remind the kids of the stone that was rolled away on the first Easter morning. During the words of forgiveness, the group members can eat the candy. If you can't find rock candy, give each person a small stone. During the words of forgiveness have them place the stones at the foot of the cross.

The third week, give each person a chocolate, foil-wrapped piece of "coin" candy. Talk about how many of our sins are related to money—from shoplifting to coveting something we can't afford. During the words of forgiveness, eat the candy.

The fourth week, give each person a nail to hold during the prayer of confession. As the kids hear the words of forgiveness, let them pound their nails into a wooden cross.

The fifth week, give each person a candy cross to hold. Make the candy crosses by outlining the cross with basic sugar cookie dough and filling it with smashed hard candies such as Life Savers. The candies will melt and run together in the oven. Talk about how the ugly instrument of death becomes beautiful for Christians. During the words of forgiveness, the members can eat the cookies.

The sixth week, give each person a palm frond or confetti. They can toss them in the air when they hear the words of forgiveness. Celebrate that Christ died for our sins; he lives so that we may live with him.
                                        —Mardie H.C. MacDonald

Variations

1. Give each person a seed and say that without God's forgiveness and love we remain small, closed in and useless. During the words of forgiveness, give each person a flower. Say that God's forgiveness soaks through our tough exteriors and makes us blossom with new life, fresh happiness and love.

2. Give everybody a helium-filled balloon and a marker. Ask

each person to write on the balloon a sin that he or she wishes to confess; for example, "I lied." Have the kids take their balloons outside. As you read the words of forgiveness, have the young people let go of their balloons (**More ... Try This One,** Group Books).

Your Ideas and Variations

_____
_____
_____
_____
_____
_____
_____
_____
_____
_____
_____
_____

53

Worthwhile Treasures
TOPIC: VALUES

When we strongly desire to own something, it actually owns a part of us. This lesson allows youth group members to decide how badly they want certain items and what they would do to acquire them.

Gather one piece of candy for each person. Tape labels to

each piece of candy such as God's love, God's blessings, God's grace, etc. Place the candies on a silver tray. On newsprint, write the following menu. List the items without prices.

Menu

Item	Price
Own a sports car	
Earn a college education	
Be a famous star	
Write a best seller	

When the young people enter the room, give them time to study the menu. Let them choose one item they want. Mention that no prices are listed, but that you are going to set the prices now. Add these prices to the newsprint:

Own a sports car .... Steal It
Earn a college education .... Cheat
Be a famous star ..... Lead an immoral life
Write a best seller .... Copy another's work

Ask if the kids still want these things, knowing the price they would have to pay. What if they were absolutely assured that they would not get caught stealing or cheating? Would they still desire the item? Why or why not?

Read and discuss Colossians 3:1-17. Ask the students to use their own words to explain this verse, "Set your mind on things that are above, not on things that are on earth" (Colossians 3:2). Ask the kids, "What are other alternatives—positive ways to get the items on the menu?" For example, they could earn the money to buy a sports car. They could work part time or study hard enough to earn a scholarship to get a college education. They could suffer through years of training and preparation to become a famous star. Or spend years perfecting their writing skills before they write a best seller. Discuss whether or not the students want these things now. Why or why not?

Take the class members outside for a walk around the church. Have them look at the grass, trees, flowers and birds. Talk about how God gives these living things all they need to survive.

Go back in the classroom; pick up a silver tray. Ask if the young people have heard the expression: "It was handed to him on a silver platter." Say that it means a person didn't have to work very hard for the things he or she has. Explain that seldom does anyone get anything worthwhile this way.

Tell the youth group members, "God takes care of the flowers and the birds, but he gave us more and, therefore, he expects more. Let's say you really want that sports car. There are two ways to get it. If you choose to steal it, you are putting that car and your desire before what you

know is right; what you know God expects of you. If you choose to work and earn the money for the car, you are considering spiritual values first. You will get the car—nothing wrong with that—and your soul will remain intact. There is nothing wrong in wanting the good things in life as long as you don't sacrifice your relationship with God in order to get them."

Let the participants talk about the things they want, what they have to do to get them, and the price they will have to pay.

Pass around the silver tray and ask everyone to take a piece of candy. Explain that they are free gifts and they are sweet. As you pass the tray around, read the labels and talk about the gifts. Say, "These gifts are yours for the taking. All you have to do is accept them. They are handed to you on a silver platter. Free gifts from God. However, there are four things to keep in mind regarding God's gifts: You have to know that they are available to you—I offered them; a teacher, pastor, parent could tell you about them. You have to accept them—this is faith. You must take care of them—nurture through worship, prayer. Tell others about them—evangelism."

Close by reading the following verses: "And do not seek what you are to eat and what you are to drink, nor be of anxious mind. For all the nations of the world seek these things; and your Father knows that you need them. Instead, seek his kingdom, and these things shall be yours as well" (Luke 12:29-31).

—E. Jane Mall

Variations

1. Design a menu with qualities such as kindness, enthusiasm, love, positive attitude, etc. Ask the young people how they can acquire these qualities. What price do they have to pay?

2. Give the kids each five candies labeled "enthusiasm," five candies labeled "joy" and five candies labeled "positive attitude." Have the young people give the candies to other members and say why they possess that quality; for example, "Here's a piece of candy labeled 'enthusiasm.' You enthusiastically participate in all songs and activities. I wish I had half of your energy."

Your Ideas and Variations

_____
_____
_____
_____
_____
_____
_____
_____
_____

CANS

54

Crush the Can
TOPIC: FUND RAISING

One way for your youth group to make extra money is by recycling aluminum cans. Have members of your church save cans for your youth group, or have the kids pick up cans that have been thrown along roadsides. However, storing cans between trips to the recycling center can become a problem. Try this fun way to solve that problem.

Take several boxes filled with cans and dump them out onto

your church parking lot. Divide the youth group into four equal teams and assign team captains. Team members kick the cans to their team captain, who crushes the cans with his or her foot, picks the can up and puts it in the team box. After all the cans are crushed and put into boxes, declare the winning team with the most cans, "The Crushers."

—Gary Wheeler

Variations

1. Collect and recycle newspapers.

2. Plan a garage sale to raise funds for your youth group. Collect coupons as well as "stuff" to sell. As an incentive for attendance, advertise that the youth group will be giving away coupons at the garage sale.

Your Ideas and Variations

_____
_____
_____
_____
_____
_____
_____
_____
_____
_____
_____
_____
_____
_____
_____

55

Glimpses of God
TOPIC: CHRISTMAS/GOD

During Advent, it is a German custom for moms and dads to decorate their living room with a Christmas tree and presents. They close and lock the living room door until the family celebration on Christmas Eve. As you can imagine, German children spend most of the month of December peeking through the keyhole, trying to glimpse what awaits them on Christmas Eve. What a neat parallel of the Advent season and our lives in Christ. Our lives are filled with brief moments of understanding and glimpses of Christ's love.

Give the young people each a piece of cardboard and scissors. Ask them to cut out a keyhole shape, then peek through it. Discuss what they discovered when they looked at their surroundings through the hole.

Ask a volunteer to read 1 Corinthians 13:11-12. Say, "During Advent we catch many glimpses of the coming of Christ. In most churches, the Sunday lessons are prophesies which help us

get a glimpse of what life with Christ is like, and who our Savior really is.''

Ask your group to complete these sentences:

● Some things that I do to get ready for Christmas are . . .

● A time when I felt really close to God was . . .

● A time when I could "see" God working in my life was . . .

● Christ keeps coming to me when . . .

Say, "We tend to be so narrow, in our thoughts and in our vision. We think that what we see through the keyhole is the whole story. We don't trust that God can do far more for us than

what we are able to see right now.''

Give each young person a narrow strip of paper and a pencil. Ask the kids to write down a time when they made God a narrow God—a time when they made decisions without knowing the whole story; without praying about the decision. Gather in pairs and share the confessions.

Close by saying, "Hope is another important Advent word. We remember God's promise that life with Christ will bring us so much more than what we can see right now. Rather than believing the secular phrase, 'what you see is what you get,' we should know that with Jesus, it's 'what you get is so much more than what you see.' ''

—Nancy Going

Variations

1. Make keyholes out of posterboard, paper or paper plates.

2. Ask the youth group members who have their own set of keys to give "glimpses" of their lives by describing each key.

3. Serve Christmas cookies for refreshments; or serve a German dessert such as apple strudel.

Your Ideas and Variations

_____

_____

_____

_____

56

Home for Billions
TOPIC: HUNGER

Just in reading about the billions of poor people in the world and their living conditions, we somehow miss the impact of their situation. To help our youth group experience poverty, we had them create a model of a shantytown. Here's how your group can build a shantytown.

Gather a large cardboard base (cut out the side of a cardboard carton, possibly 2 feet by 3 feet, and lay it flat on a table); very small boxes to serve as bases for shanties; brown tissue paper for covering the boxes and delineating acreage for cultivation; chenille wire to create people and animals; twigs; glue; tape; card stock and markers for making a sign to advertise the shantytown; material scraps for clothes and bags.

When your group meets, show everyone the materials and say that they are going to make a shantytown to depict how billions of poor people in the world live. Let them use their creativity and imaginations. Have them consider these facts as they "build."

To live like the billions of poor people in the world, we would have to:

● Take away all our furniture except a kitchen table and one chair.

● Take away all our clothing except one old suit or dress per family member.

● Empty the kitchen cupboards except for a small amount of flour, sugar, salt and rice.

● Dismantle the bathroom, shut off the water and electricity to the house.

● Take away the house and move into the toolshed.

● Remove all the other houses and set up a shantytown.

● Cancel all magazine and newspaper subscriptions—but that's no loss because we can't read.

● Leave one small radio for the whole shantytown.

● Move all clinics, hospitals and doctors out of the area and replace them with a midwife.

● Throw away our bankbooks, stock certificates, pension plans, and insurance policies and leave each family $5 cash to hoard.

● Give each head of the family three tenant acres to cultivate; he can raise $300 in cash crops, 1/3 of which goes to the landlord and 1/10 to the local money changer.

● Take off 25 to 30 years from our life expectancy.

(This information is from **Reaching Out**, Heifer Project, page A14, where it is attributed to "Recycle Hunger." It is similar to the description of economist Robert Heilbroner's itemization found in **Rich Christians in an Age of Hunger** by Ron Sider; InterVarsity Press, page 31.)

Ask someone to make a poster with the above facts. When the "builders" complete the shantytown, display the town and poster in a prominent place for everyone to see. This display adds extra impact on a Sunday service that focuses on world hunger.

Ask your denominational office for the areas that could use help, or contact an interdenominational organization such as Bread for the World, 802 Rhode Island Ave. N.E., Washington, D.C. 20018, (202) 269-0200. For a small fee, you can join Bread for the World and receive a quarterly newsletter that points you to areas where you can become directly and immediately involved. The newsletter lists ideas such as writing letters to congressmen and congresswomen, and focuses your attention on bills that are before Con-

gress. Help all congregation members become more aware of world hunger and the need to help.

—Brethren House Ministries

Variations

1. Create a life-size shantytown out of similar materials. Use refrigerator-size cardboard boxes for the homes.

2. Raise money for a hunger project by planning a 12-hour fast. Have the youth group members collect pledges for every hour they go without food. During the 12-hour fast, "set up shop" in the life-size shantytown. Call your local newspaper or radio station for additional publicity—request donations from the entire community!

Your Ideas and Variations

_____
_____
_____
_____
_____
_____
_____
_____
_____
_____
_____
_____
_____
_____
_____
_____

CATALOGS °

57

The Eye of a Needle
TOPIC: VALUES/POSSESSIONS

Use catalogs to help your kids understand Jesus' statement about earthly possessions, "It is easier for a camel to go through the eye of a needle than for a rich man to enter the kingdom of God" (Matthew 19:24).

You'll need paper, pencils, catalogs, scissors and glue. In the meeting room, set up tables and chairs.

When the youth group members enter, give them paper and pencils and ask them to sit down. Have them list six things they wish they could have—tell them not to worry about the cost or how difficult it would be to get the items.

Next, distribute the catalogs, glue and scissors. Have everyone look through the catalogs and select several items they would like to have. Tell kids to cut out the items and glue them on the paper to form a collage.

Read and discuss Luke 12:13-21. Ask what "covet" means. What does it mean to "lay up treasures" for yourself? Have the kids look at their collage and answer these questions:

● What did you select?

● How expensive were the items?

● How many did you select?

● Are the items for play? pleasure? daily living? home? necessities?

● Would you want to be known by what you selected?

● Do the selections reflect your inward (spiritual) nature?

● Can material goods reflect the real you?

● Is there more to life than possessing lots of things?

Read and discuss Matthew 19:16-24. Ask how this passage relates to the activity. If the kids owned all of the items on their collages, would they have difficulty getting into heaven? Compare this to a camel going through the eye of a needle. Is that possible?

Ask the participants to turn over their papers and list six things they now wish they could have. Compare this list to the items on the collages. Post the collages on a bulletin board and label it, "The eye of a needle." Have the bulletin board serve as a reminder to strive for spiritual possessions not earthly ones.

—Wesley Taylor

Variations

1. Ask the young people to bring their "most treasured" possession from home. If this isn't possible, have them take a

picture of the item or draw it.

2. Carpool to a department store; give each person a pencil and a piece of paper. Allow 20 minutes for the kids to roam the aisles and write a shopping list of "most desired" items.

Your Ideas and Variations

_____

_____

_____

_____

_____

_____

_____

_____

_____

CHAIRS

The Encouragement Chair
*TOPIC: GROUP BUILDING/
AFFIRMATION*

Every youth group needs an Encouragement Chair. All kids need to hear words of encouragement from their peers and from adults.

An Encouragement Chair is easy to come up with. It can be as simple as a folding chair painted a special color, or as

elaborate as a recliner. Make the chair special by decorating it. The brighter and more distinctive the chair, the better. Keep the chair unique by storing it until it is used. Put rollers on the legs to make it easy to move in and out of storage.

At an appointed time during each youth group meeting, ask one individual to sit on the chair in the center of the group. Have the other group members share brief, sincere, encouraging statements about that person. This should be a serious time, but it shouldn't dominate the entire meeting.

Many young people feel uncomfortable giving or receiving compliments. Youth group leaders may have to set the pace by volunteering to go first. But after the Encouragement Chair is used a few times, group members will become familiar with, and will look forward to the activity.

Make sure all group members eventually have a turn, but do no more than one member per meeting. This helps maintain the special feeling connected with the chair.

—Doug Newhouse

Variations

1. Affirm guest speakers by having them sit in the Encouragement Chair after their presentations.

2. Affirm kids who are cele-

brating birthdays. Have them sit in the Encouragement Chair.

3. Rather than using a chair, have the kids form a circle and choose one person to stand in the middle. Proceed with the affirmation!

4. Light a candle and have one person hold it. Let everyone else affirm the "candle-holder." Pass the candle to the next person, let everyone affirm him or her, and so on. Let everyone have a chance to feel the warm glow of affirmation!

Your Ideas and Variations

_____
_____
_____
_____
_____
_____
_____
_____
_____

143

CHILDREN'S BOOKS

59

Sharing Children's Books
TOPIC: OUTREACH

This is a service project idea for your youth group. Plan to visit a children's hospital, children's home, day care center or Christian center in your area. In advance, meet with the appropriate person at the location to plan your eventual visit with the youth group.

Tell your youth group members about the upcoming visit to a children's hospital. Ask them to select one of their favorite books from childhood.

Explain to the youth group members that during their visit to the children's hospital, they each will be grouped with one or more children. They will read and discuss the book together. At the conclusion of the story-sharing time, they will donate the books to the organization so that other children can read them in the future.

If the group members don't have any children's books, ask for book donations to be made to the youth group from other church members. Allow time for the young people to select a book and become familiar with it in advance of the visit. Once the teenagers have chosen their books, ask them to bring the books to a youth group meeting. Answer the following questions about each book:

● How are values presented? (Good and bad, right and wrong, etc.)

● Who are the heroes in the story? (Men, women, children, animals, blacks, whites, etc.) What does the book teach us about heroes?

● What is the symbolism in the story? (Signs of hope, love, evil, etc.)

Make the book reading project a regular experience for your youth group. If the children's home has a great need for additional books, the youth group can join a children's book club and present new books monthly to the organization.

This project promotes reading as well as fellowship, care and concern for those who are less fortunate.

—Arlo R. Reichter

Variations

1. Give each person several sheets of paper and colored markers. Have the youth group members write and illustrate children's books. Share these creations with the children's home.

2. On butcher paper, draw the sequence of events for a Bible story. Have the youth group members tell the story as they unroll the paper. Hang it on a wall for the children to read and enjoy.

Your Ideas and Variations

_____
_____
_____
_____
_____
_____
_____
_____
_____
_____
_____
_____
_____
_____
_____
_____
_____

60

To Become as Children
TOPIC: FAITH/CHRISTIAN LIVING

There are many fascinating children's stories that relate to the Christian life. For example, **The Cat in the Hat** relates to our natural tendency toward sin, but grace abounds. **The Velveteen Rabbit** relates to the issue of being yourself—being real.

Plan a retreat around the theme "To Become as Children." Divide into groups of four and give each group a different children's book. Tell them to find analogies of the Christian life and relate them to how Christ wants us to become as children.

One group at our retreat was given the story **The Pied Piper**. The group said that everyone follows the tune of someone. The group asked everyone these questions, "As a Christian, whose tune are we following? the world's? our friends'? Jesus'?"

The children's books helped us have a fantastic discussion.

—Bob Hicks

Variations

1. Divide into small groups and let the kids rewrite the

children's books according to a Christian theme. For example, "Once upon a time there was a beautiful, Christian girl named Cinderella. She loved God and thanked him for all the things he had blessed her with. Throughout her life, she dealt with cruelty, jealousy and unjustness with love, help and concern . . ."

2. Prepare skits to the rewritten stories. Assign characters and roles, and develop props. Title the plays, "Lessons We Learn From Childhood."

Your Ideas and Variations

_____
_____
_____
_____
_____
_____
_____
_____
_____
_____

CLAY

All Things Were Created
TOPIC: BIBLE STUDY/CREATIVITY

The first two chapters of Genesis present a theology of God the Creator and a view of humanity as created "in the image of God." In the first creation story, God gives mankind dominion over the earth and all that lives and grows upon it. In the second creation story, the Creator invites Adam (mankind) to name the creatures that he has given Adam as companions. The man is to cooperate with the Creator. He is to create too. Our creativity is derived from God, as witnessed in a great cathedral, a moving poem, a fine meal, or the conception, birth and raising of a child.

Too many people believe that because they are not artists, they are not creative. This is to deny that they are created in the image of God, that in baptism they have received the creative gift of the Holy Spirit. In this session the participants are encouraged to explore the concept of creation as it applies to themselves. They will begin to see creativity in more than simple artistic terms.

Set up several work tables and place boxes of modeling clay on them. Provide a Bible for each group member. Put up on the walls, or on easels, pictures of nature and of people making things or playing. If you have a reproduction of Michelangelo's painting of God creating Adam, put it up as well. You will also need a record player and the

Fred Waring recording of "The Creation" from his album **God's Trombones**.

As the group gathers, give each person a lump of clay. Have the kids close their eyes and listen to the music. Have them imagine the swirling ener gy and colors of the creation events. Tell them to "listen" with their fingers as well—feel the texture of the clay and shape it into whatever form that the music and words inspire them to create.

At the end of the story divide into groups of two or three. In the small groups, ask the kids to share their clay impression of the story. After each has done this, ask each small group to combine each individual's clay creation. Refashion them to sym- bolize an important aspect of the creation story. After about 15 minutes, the entire group can share the ideas and experiences they had as smaller groups.

Read the first two chapters of Genesis aloud, or have several group members do so. Discuss these questions:

How many creation stories are contained here? Were you aware that there are two? Com- pare them. Which seems to be most suitable for a worship set- ting (because it uses repetition and an orderly progression)? Which seems like it might have been told around a campfire?

What do you think is the meaning of "created in the im- age of God"? What is the chief attribute or activity of God that is revealed in Genesis? In what ways do you feel or express a creative urge?

Do you feel you're creative? Why or why not? Have you been told you're not, or have you been put down when you've tried something? How can we enlarge our understanding of creativity so as to do justice to the teaching of Genesis?—that we are all created in the image of God. For instance, how can the following activities be exam- ples of creativity?

- Cooking a meal
- Setting a table
- Building a sand castle
- Cleaning your room
- Teaching a class
- Being a friend
- Writing a letter
- Writing a report
- Doing homework
- Doing housework
- Work (job)
- Raising children

In which of the stories is the equality of the sexes under- stood? Why is equality neces- sary for us to fully realize the doctrine of "created in the im- age of God"?

How did you feel working/ playing with the clay as you listened to the story? If you weren't comfortable doing this, what other form of expression would you prefer? Writing, music, dance, storytelling, painting or drawing?

How can your group and/or the church help people to create? How can looking at the ordinary from a different angle or viewpoint be creative? How can we be more creative in our group's meetings, worship, newsletter, or retreats?

—Ed McNulty

Variations

1. "Create" with tempera paints or finger paints instead of clay.

2. Write a creation history of your church—use Genesis 1 as a guideline. For example, "In the beginning, God chose several families to begin a new church in town. The building was without lights and electricity; and darkness was upon the interior . . ."

Your Ideas and Variations

_____
_____
_____
_____
_____
_____
_____
_____
_____
_____

62

A Healing
TOPIC: BIBLE STUDY

Create a slide show on John 5:1-15, the story of the healing at the pool of Bethzatha. Create the people and costumes out of clay. Design them to look "authentic," or more modern.

You will need an assortment of colored clay, some blue dye, a casserole dish, and any props you feel are necessary. You also will need a camera, color slide film and a projector.

Begin by deciding on the action you want to have for each Bible verse. For instance, John 5:1 depicts Jesus going up to Jerusalem for a feast of the Jews. For the first slide, create your clay Jesus walking along a road.

For the second slide, read the second verse and create your pool of water (by placing blue dye and water in the casserole dish). Fashion five colonnades. Continue through this story, passage by passage, creating each scene.

When we made a slide show for this story, we made a clay man without legs and sat him by the pool. We then added legs to him to coincide with verse 9 where it says, "And at once the man was healed . . ." During the slide show, it appears the man's legs pop on! It's always a hit with the kids.

—Mitchell M. Olson

Variations

1. Present the slide show to the children's Sunday school, the adult Sunday school, at potlucks or other special events. This clay-production slide show is a powerful and fun way to communicate Bible stories to kids of all ages!

2. Produce this same type of slide show with other Bible stories such as: John 6:1-15; 16-24; Luke 2:8-20; 5:17-26.

Your Ideas and Variations

_____
_____
_____
_____
_____
_____
_____
_____
_____
_____
_____

63

Molded Like Him
TOPIC: GOD'S LOVE

Here's an object lesson to help young people see that God

is the potter; we are the clay. Because of this we have a special relationship with him.

You'll need a handful of clay for each person and a lump of dry, hard, old clay.

Gather the young people in a circle. Pass around two samples of clay—one that's soft and pliable and one that's hard and crusty. Say, "We have a kinship with clay since we are made from it. Jesus used clay to heal. So often we resist God's will because of our pride, willfulness and fears. We are hardheaded and hardhearted, like cement (all mixed up and permanently set). We don't trust God. We won't let go of our egos. We need to be ourselves and to define our individuality; yet, the Creator wants us to surrender to his guidance—to be flexible, to stretch and grow like soft clay. Through the living water of Christ we stay moist and pliable. We need to remember that God is the potter and we are the clay, not vice versa.

Give each young person a handful of clay. Have the kids mold a symbol of how they see themselves in relationship to God. For example, a young person can shape a round ball and say that he or she tries to roll easily in the direction God points. While the kids are shaping their clay, read aloud Job 10:9; Isaiah 45:9; 64:8; John 9:11.

Have the kids each explain their clay creations. When they're finished, place the clay symbols in the center of the circle. Say, "We each have a relationship with God; and we, as a group, have a relationship with God. God affects all of our lives. We should listen and trust God to mold us in his image and guide us through life." Close by praying the Lord's Prayer.

—Lynn Potter

Variations

1. Pass out a handful of clay to each of the young people and ask them to create a symbol of the church. Symbols could be anything from a cross, to a chain with many links. Discuss the symbols and reflect on their meanings. Divide into several small groups. Ask each group to choose a symbol and role play its meaning. For example, a group could choose to role play the meaning of a cross. One person could stand with his or her arms outstretched—symbolizing Christ on the cross. The others could connect to Christ and each other by hooking arms—symbolizing the church's unity through Christ. Read 1 Corinthians 12 and discuss how these verses describe the church.

2. Give each young person a handful of bread dough. Ask the kids to shape a symbol of the church from the dough. Allow time for the dough symbols to rise; then bake 'em and eat 'em!

Your Ideas and Variations

_____

_____
_____
_____
_____
_____
_____
_____
_____
_____
_____
_____
_____

CLOCKS

64

Time to Praise God
TOPIC: TIME/PRIORITIES/WORSHIP

Your youth group will capture people's attention with this unique, "timely" exhibit.

Have the kids arrange to borrow several clocks from church members. Place the exhibit in a safe, yet visible location within your church building or in the front of the sanctuary. This idea is particularly effective on the Sunday in April or October if the region you live in changes to daylight-saving time. It will serve as a clever reminder for people to change their clocks.

Ask your worship committee and pastor to develop the entire worship service around one of

these themes: "It's Always Time to Praise God," "In Every Minute of Life, I Seek to Follow God" or "Daily Activities That Compete With Our Time With God." Use posterboard and markers to make a sign displaying the theme; place the sign by the exhibit.

The youth group members can inscribe, "Take Time for God" on 3×5 cards and distribute them to the congregation to place near their clocks at home.
—Arlo R. Reichter

Variations
1. Buy small, bright-colored stickers at a discount store. The youth group members can write, "Take time to pray" on the stickers and distribute them to others to place on their clocks or wristwatches.

2. Give each of the teenagers a pencil and a 3×5 card. Have them write a "timely" spiritual

growth goal such as, "Each time my alarm rings, I'll pray." Or, "Every evening before I go to sleep, I'll read three chapters in the Bible." Have the kids place the cards by their alarm clocks as reminders.

Your Ideas and Variations

_____
_____
_____
_____
_____
_____
_____
_____
_____
_____
_____

CLOTHESPINS

65

Clothespin Opinion Poll
TOPIC: DISCUSSION STARTERS

Looking for a unique way to get your kids to share their opinions? Try Clothespin Opinion Poll at each of your youth group meetings.

Hang a clothesline across the meeting room. On one end place a sign that says, "strongly agree." On the other end place a sign that says, "strongly dis-

agree." Mark the center of the clothesline for reference. You also will need one colored clip clothespin for each person.

Each week at the close of your youth meeting, read a strong statement to the group. Ask your group members to think about, talk about, and research the statement during the week. At the beginning of the next meeting, have each member clip a clothespin on the line where it best reflects his or her opinion. Spend the first few minutes of the meeting discussing the results. The topic can be independent of the meeting's main lesson, or it may be used as a great introduction to a related subject. Here are some examples:

• Christians should never date non-Christians.

• There should be prayer in schools.

• The legal drinking age should be raised.

• Church membership is a necessary part of the Christian life.

• It is okay for Christians to drink alcohol.

Clothespin Opinion Poll is a creative way to get the kids to discuss important topics.

—Linda Ferree

Variations

1. Use masking tape to create a line from one end of your room to another. Use this as a continuum. Designate one end of the room for those who strongly agree with a statement; and designate the opposite end of the room for those who strongly disagree.

2. Read a statement, then have the kids give a thumbs-up signal if they agree; thumbs-down signal if they disagree; and shrug their shoulders if they don't know. Gather in the three groups and discuss the statement. Then read another statement and proceed with the same process.

Your Ideas and Variations

_____

_____

_____

_____

_____

_____

_____

_____

_____

_____

_____

_____

CLOTHING

66

Blue Jeans Forever
TOPIC: PUBLICITY

Most of us love blue jeans—after all, we go through a lot together. Whenever a pair of jeans is finally worn out, wash them one last time and then use them again in all kinds of ways.

Reuse the back pockets. Cut around the outline of the pocket, leaving it intact, and include the section of waistband above it. Then tack the pockets to the church bulletin board and use them to hold and display camp brochures and other special fliers. What could be more appropriate than to pull a camp-information flier out of an old jean pocket!

Here are some more ideas:

• Two, six-inch squares of jean material and a cup of dried

beans make a fine beanbag.

● Take a section of leg, turn it inside out and sew the bottom. Then add a hem and cording on the top edge and turn the leg right-side out. This makes a sturdy draw bag to store game pieces or equipment.

● Braid three strips of jean material together to make a rope to hang a banner.

● Tie single strips of jean material around arms or legs of young people to designate team members when playing games.

There's no end to the uses for faded denim, so don't throw those old jeans away!

—Walter John Boris

Variations

1. Use old jeans to make costumes and blindfolds. Cut up jean material and use the scraps for collages and quilts.

2. Draw a large jean pocket on an 8½x11 piece of paper. Make copies and give one to each group member. Tell the kids to write their name on the pocket, then describe the kind of person who would wear these jeans. For example: "Mary Jones Jeans. The kind of person who wears Mary Jones Jeans likes summer more than winter, has long talks with old friends and watches the sunrise alone."

Afterward, each person shares his or her description. The leader notes that all have

identified themselves in a positive way. Read Psalm 139 (especially verse 14) and thank God for the "wonder of you" (**Try This One . . . Strikes Again**, Group Books).

Your Ideas and Variations

_____

_____

_____

_____

_____

_____

_____

_____

_____

67

Sock Offerings
TOPIC: OUTREACH

During vacation Bible school, Sunday school and youth meetings, collect money to go toward the purchase of socks for needy children. Use these ideas.

● Instead of offering baskets, collect money in empty socks.

● Conduct meetings and services in bare feet.

● Ask the youth group members to collect money from congregation members before and after church services. Collect the money in socks.

Use your sock-happy imagina-

tion to promote generous giving.
—Mark Reed

Variations

1. Stretch a clothesline across the front of the meeting room. Each week, count the money collected and hang the number of socks the current total will purchase.

2. During the announcement time in church, use sock puppets to publicize this unique project. Find an old sock for the main part of the puppet, sew on buttons for eyes and yarn for hair. Name the puppet "Sock Cousteau" or "Henry Sock from H&R Sock."

Your Ideas and Variations

_____
_____
_____
_____
_____
_____
_____
_____
_____
_____

T-Shirt Fund Raiser
TOPIC: FUND RAISING

Here is a great project that can raise funds for the youth

group and promote a spirit of fellowship among the entire church.

Design an emblem for your church. This may include a denominational symbol (such as the flame and the cross of the United Methodist Church), and the church name; or simply a cross and the church name.

Rather than designing an emblem yourself, plan a contest. Ask all interested artists in the congregation to submit an idea by a certain date. Then you and a committee of youth group members choose an emblem from all of the entries. Write about the winning artist in the church bulletin or newsletter.

Once you have an emblem, visit a local shirt shop to find out the cost of T-shirts, having a silk-screen made, as well as the amount they would charge for printing.

It may be less expensive to

buy your own shirts and just pay for the silk-screening.

Advertise your project by making announcements in church and displaying the finished product. Take orders for T-shirts and sweat shirts. Add a small extra charge for those wishing to have their names put on the back.

Selling T-shirts with a special emblem will help raise funds for your group as well as help build community in your church.

—Jim Farrer

Variations

1. Design shirts for special groups in your church: athletic teams, Sunday school classes, vacation Bible school, youth group, women's group, choirs, etc.

2. Tie-dye T-shirts and sell them. Purchase white T-shirts and several colors of dye. Have the youth group members design the T-shirts by tying rubber bands around gathered fabric. Drop the T-shirts into the prepared dye; let them dry; then untie them and admire the unique designs.

Your Ideas and Variations

_____

_____

_____

_____

_____

_____

_____

_____

_____

_____

CORKS

69

Floating Corks and Faith Journeys
TOPIC: FAITH JOURNEYS

Plan a meeting or retreat around the theme, "The Faith Journey." Meet by a small, flowing stream. Give each participant a cork and a permanent-ink marker. Ask the kids to write their name on their cork. Have each person place his or her cork in the water and follow it approximately 50 yards downstream. Tell the participants that the only time they can touch the cork is if it becomes lodged between rocks or branches. Otherwise, they are just to observe its journey down the stream.

After all the corks have reached the destination point, have the group members discuss the trip—the ease or difficulty their cork encountered as it

floated downstream.

Read the parable of the sower (Matthew 13:18-23). Divide into small groups and give each group a piece of paper and a pencil. Have them write a "parable of the cork"—illustrating how the journey the cork took downstream is similar to our journey through life and faith. For example: "Hear then the parable of the cork. As the cork floats down the stream it encounters many rocks. The rocks are like the difficulties we face in life . . ."

After everyone is finished, share the parables. Have the group members take their corks home as a reminder of what they learned.

—Arlo R. Reichter

Variations

1. Gather several packages of flower seeds, biodegradable egg cartons and a roll of biodegradable tape. Cut apart the egg cartons and give two "egg sections" to each young person. Have the kids fill one egg section with some seeds, place the other section on top (to form an egg shape), then secure the halves with tape. This creates a "seed bomb." Go to an empty lot and bomb it with the seeds. After several weeks, go back to the lot and see how many of the seeds have sprouted. Compare this activity to the seeds in the parable of the sower (Matthew 13:18-23).

—Kerrie Weitzel

Your Ideas and Variations

_____

_____

_____

_____

_____

COSTUMES

70

Fact-Finding Fiction
TOPIC: SPIRITUAL GROWTH/
DISCUSSION STARTERS

If you ask young people to reveal a personal problem that hinders spiritual growth, you will probably get a silent response. It's difficult for most people to be open in public. By creating fictitious situations, you can provide a non-threatening environment for discussing problems.

Gather several articles that could be used as costumes and props: scarves, coats, hats, canes, Bibles, magazines, glasses, etc.

Divide the youth group members into small groups and ask each small group to create a fictitious character by answering these questions:

● What is his or her name? age? appearance? job? hobby? family background?

● What does he or she want more than anything else in the world?

● What does he or she fear most?

● What makes people like or dislike him or her?

● Is the character a Christian? If not, what hinders him or her from becoming a Christian? If the character is a Christian, give his or her background in the church.

● What is a problem that hinders his or her spiritual growth?

Ask each small group to choose one person to portray the fictitious character. Dress him or her in an appropriate costume. An example of a fictitious person is "Sue Smith," a 25-year-old Christian. She thinks every issue has a right or wrong answer—there are no gray areas. An area that hinders her from spiritual growth is the expectation that all Christians should be perfect. Whenever members of her congregation fight or make mistakes, she wonders how they can call themselves Christians. The group could dress Sue Smith conservatively: button up shirt to the chin, pull back hair tightly with a rubber band, etc.

Allow time for all of the small groups to present their characters. Ask the other group members to offer ideas on how to overcome the problems that hinder spiritual growth.

A youth group member could tell Sue Smith that we all are sinners. As Christians we struggle with sin and ask God for forgiveness. Christians need to love and forgive one another just as Christ loves and forgives us.

Very often some personal concerns or attributes will be projected to the fictional character. Sometimes the kids will mirror the situation of a close friend. Whatever the case, the problems portrayed in the stories make good topics for discussion as group members offer possible solutions.

—Esther M. Bailey

Variations

1. Use puppets to portray the fictitious characters.

2. Present the dramas or puppet plays to junior high and senior high Sunday school classes. Title the presentation, "Roadblocks to Spiritual Growth."

Have a discussion time on how to break through those roadblocks.

Your Ideas and Variations

_____
_____
_____
_____
_____
_____
_____
_____
_____
_____
_____

71

The Living Picture
TOPIC: DRAMA/WORSHIP/BIBLE STUDY

The Living Picture is a dramatic way to present the "high points" of a scripture passage. The main events of the story are presented as a series of "still-life" pictures.

Members of our high school fellowship presented the parable of the good Samaritan as a Living Picture during the Sunday morning worship service. It was a good way for the young people to participate in worship and it added interest to the scripture reading that day. Because no speaking parts were involved, a brief practice before worship was all that was necessary for a polished presentation.

Here's how you can present a Living Picture of the parable of the good Samaritan. Choose youth group members to portray the following characters. Gather the corresponding costumes and accessories.

Characters	Costume/Accessories
Narrator	None
Man (traveling from Jerusalem to Jericho)	Backpack, cane
Robbers (2)	Bandanna
Jewish priest	Bible
Levite (a lay assistant to the priest)	Briefcase
Innkeeper	Apron, towel
Samaritan (a hated enemy of the Jews)	Two coins

Instruct actors that the parable will be presented through "still-life" acting. Youth group members will portray scenes of the parable by freezing in their posed positions for three to five seconds while that portion of scripture is read. Then an off-stage leader will snap his or her fingers (or give another signal) and the characters will quickly take their places for the next scene. Here are ideas for several still-life scenes to this parable:

●**Scene 1:** The man, center-stage, lays on the floor as two robbers appear to beat him. Freeze. Read Luke 10:29-30. An off-stage person snaps fingers and actors move to next position.

●**Scene 2:** The man on the floor reaches out as the priest holds a Bible and looks at him. Freeze. Read Luke 10:31. An off-stage person snaps fingers and actors take next position.

●**Scene 3:** Man continues to reach out as the Levite with the briefcase looks at him. Freeze. Read Luke 10:32. An off-stage person snaps fingers and the actors take next position.

●**Scene 4:** The good Samaritan pretends he is tending to the man's wounds and begins to take him to the innkeeper. Freeze. Read Luke 10:33-34. An off-stage person snaps fingers and the actors take next position.

●**Scene 5:** The good Samaritan takes out two coins and gives to the innkeeper. Freeze. Read Luke 10:35. An off-stage person snaps fingers and the actors move to next position.

●**Ending:** All characters stand in a line in front of the audience for three to five seconds. Read verses 36-37. Exit.

The Living Picture also could be used with Bible study groups and as part of the activities during a fellowship meeting. Young people will vividly remember important points of scripture portrayed through this type of acting.

—Walter John Boris

Variations

1. Create a Living Picture to Mark 12:1-11. Ask youth group members to play the roles of the vineyard owner, the servants, the son, and the tenants.

2. Create a Living Picture on the main events of Jesus' life: visited the temple (Luke 2:41-50); baptized (Matthew 3:13-17); tempted by Satan (Matthew 4:1-11); called his disciples (Matthew 4:18-22); transfigured (Matthew 17:1-8); entered Jerusalem (Matthew 21:1-11); the Lord's Supper (Matthew 26:26-29); betrayed and arrested (Matthew 26:47-57); crucified (Matthew 27:31-56); Resurrection (Matthew 28:9-20).

Your Ideas and Variations

_____

_____

_____

_____

_____

_____

_____

_____

_____

_____

72

What's My Cult?

TOPIC: DISCUSSION STARTERS

Want an interesting attention-getter when you lead a meeting on cults? Use costumes and dress the part!

I found several old costumes in the prop room of our church. I found a "sari" type of outfit that made me look like a Hare Krishna. I also found a white shirt, thin black tie and black shoes that made me resemble a Mormon missionary.

During the lesson, I changed costumes, and changed the tone of my voice as I discussed each cult.

It was funny trying to get in and out of costumes during the presentation—the kids saw me transform in front of their very eyes!

—Tom Franks

Variations

1. Divide the youth group members into pairs. Give the pairs one week to research a cult (they decide which one) and think of a representative costume. At the next meeting, have one person in each pair wear the costume, as the other person presents information on the cult.

2. Ask a person who specializes in religious movements in America to present a series on cults. Contact local universities, city offices or police departments for suggestions of speakers. Ask the speaker to define the term "cult" and answer questions such as how do they lure new members? How can

kids respond to cult members? How do kids react if a friend or family member gets involved with a cult?

Your Ideas and Variations

_____
_____
_____
_____
_____
_____
_____
_____
_____
_____
_____

COTTON

73

Whiter Than White
TOPIC: GOD'S LOVE

Did you know cotton balls can be used for more than removing nail polish? Here are some ways they can be used to help young people learn about God's cleansing power.

Simulate a snowstorm by throwing cotton balls up in the air or blowing them from an electric fan. Have a miniature snowball fight. Share the frustrations of winter (shoveling snow, driving on ice, having to

wear so many clothes). Also talk about the joys of winter (brightness, brisk air, time to enjoy warm fires). Say, "Snow is the peanut butter of nature—it's crunchy, kids love it, and it clings to the roof of your house! Isaiah used snow to illustrate the cleansing power of God's forgiveness. 'Come now, let us reason together, says the Lord: though your sins are like scarlet, they shall be as white as snow!' (Isaiah 1:18). You think your favorite detergent has cleansing power—that's nothing compared to the power of God's mercy. Snow can give junkyards and garbage cans a cloak of beauty. That's what Christ does for us in covering us with his garment of white. And his grace is not seasonal, but eternal!"

Ask each of the youth group members to take a handful of

cotton balls and place them in their coat pockets. Every time they reach in their pockets this week, they'll be reminded of God's power to cleanse us from sin and make us whiter than white.

—Lynn Potter

Variations

1. Serve sno-cones or cotton candy for refreshments.

2. Advertise the meeting with the following poster—make the bubbles with cotton balls.

Wash Your Sins Whiter Than White!

GOD'S FORGIVENESS

A POWERFUL DETERGENT

Come to the youth group meeting on March 20 at 7 p.m. Learn more about this sparkling idea!

Your Ideas and Variations

_____
_____
_____
_____
_____
_____
_____
_____
_____
_____
_____

74

Wind and Clouds
TOPIC: GAMES

Enthusiasm is essential for effective group dynamics. When your youth group members are enthusiastic, they are much more open to learning. The most obvious indication of enthusiasm is participation.

To help develop group participation use this simple, competitive game called Wind and Clouds. The game requires both individual and team effort. Very little skill is needed; desire is more important than ability.

Divide your group into teams of four. Have each team form a line and each team member space themselves approximately 3 feet apart. If your group is small, the team can compete against the clock. Give each participant a straw. Make the person on the far right of each line the starting player for his or her team; make the person on the far left the finishing player for his or her team. Just before the game starts, dump a bag of cotton balls on the floor to the right of the starting player for each team; and place a bucket 3 feet to the left of the finishing player. When you give the signal to start, the first player must

163

pick up a cotton ball by sucking in air through the straw and blow the cotton ball to the player on his or her left. The same procedure is done by each player until the last player has all of the cotton balls. The last player then blows the cotton balls into the bucket. Once each player has finished blowing the cotton balls to the player on his or her left, the players may congregate around the bucket to help the last player. But, the last player must make the initial attempt before others can assist. The team that has all of its cotton balls in the bucket first wins. Let all of the teams finish.

Wind and Clouds is a great game that "puffs up" the group members' participation and enthusiasm!

—Steve Roberts

Variations

1. Fill a bowl with cotton balls and place it next to an empty bowl. Blindfold a young person and give him or her a spoon. Allow 30 seconds for the person to spoon the cotton balls into the empty bowl. This is a hilarious game! It's impossible to tell how many cotton balls are on the spoon, because they're so light. Let everyone have a turn.

2. Play pingpong—only use a cotton ball as the ball.

3. Play Keep Away with a cotton ball. Divide the young people into two teams. One team tosses the cotton ball from person to person trying to keep it away from the other team's members.

Your Ideas and Variations

_____
_____
_____
_____
_____
_____
_____
_____
_____
_____
_____
_____
_____

CRAYONS

75

Crayon Creations
TOPIC: CHRISTIAN SYMBOLS

Don't throw away those old, broken crayons. Use them for this colorful art project.

Before a youth group meeting, separate the crayons by color. Use a knife to make shavings out of them. You also will need scissors, wax paper, newspapers, newsprint, markers and an iron. Place several newspapers on the

table to protect it.

Start the meeting by discussing Christian symbols. On the newsprint, have the kids draw as many Christian symbols as they can think of (cross, fish, chalice, etc.). Ask why they think these symbols are used by Christians and why they are important. Ask everyone to choose a symbol that has special meaning for him or her.

Give each of the members two 7-inch-by-7-inch sheets of wax paper. Say to the group members, "Place one piece of wax paper wax-side-up on the table. Then arrange the crayon shavings on the wax paper in the form of your chosen symbol. Be sure you leave a 1-inch border. The final step is to place the other sheet of wax paper wax-side-down on top and seal it with a warm iron. The crayons will melt and create a stained glass symbol."

When the art projects are finished, decorate a window in the youth room or church. Let everybody enjoy the colorful creations!

—Karen Darling

Variations

1. Add other items to the Crayon Creations such as construction paper symbols, leaves and fabric scraps.

2. Glue a 1-inch border around the creations. Use materials such as aluminum foil, construction paper or gold braid. Make a hanger by attaching a piece of yarn to the top of each stained glass symbol.

Your Ideas and Variations

_____
_____
_____
_____
_____
_____
_____
_____
_____
_____

CUPCAKES

76

Outward Appearances
TOPIC: PREJUDICE

In our fast-paced, media-saturated world, we sometimes are fooled by sweet talk and fancy frosting. This fun activity highlights this point. Use this activity to top off a lesson on friendship, or as a study on, "What is real?"

You will need napkins and enough cupcakes for everyone in the group. Carefully cut off the tops of four cupcakes, hollow them slightly and fill them with cotton puffs. Place the tops back on the cupcakes. Take two of these cupcakes and two of those not hollowed and decorate lavishly with frosting, nuts, coconut, cherries, etc. Arrange all the cupcakes on a platter. Pass the platter to the group members, but tell them not to eat the cupcakes until after discussing these questions:

- Do these cupcakes look good enough to eat? Why or why not?
- Which will be better, the plain ones or the fancy ones?
- Do you know what's inside them?
- How can we compare these cupcakes to friends?
- Does a person's (or cupcake's) outside appearance have anything to do with what is on the inside?
- Can a fancy person (or cupcake) be good on the inside? Explain.
- Can a plain person (or cupcake) be bad on the inside? Explain.
- How can we find out what's inside a person?
- Should we know what a person is like before we become friends? Why or why not?

After the discussion, let everyone eat the cupcakes. Compare the cotton-filled cupcakes to people. Tell the kids, "Know your cupcake before you eat it. In other words, know your friends. Don't be fooled by sweet talk and fancy frosting."

—Janet R. Balmforth

Variations

1. Have the youth group members present this lesson to the elementary Sunday school children.

2. Buy a cake-size piece of foam at an art supply store. Lavishly decorate it with frosting, candies and candles. Ask everyone to describe the cake and why he or she wants to eat a piece of it. Let someone try to cut it. After the surprise has died down, bring out a real cake to eat as you discuss "sweet talk and fancy frosting."

Your Ideas and Variations

_____
_____
_____
_____
_____
_____
_____
_____
_____
_____

CUPS

77

Coffee Cup Messages
TOPIC: WORSHIP

Does your church have a coffee hour before or after worship or church school? Do they use Styrofoam cups? If they do, your group can plan a surprise for the coffee hour participants.

Have your youth group members use colored markers to write messages on the Styrofoam cups. The messages can be in harmony with the worship theme for that day or fun phrases such as, "Jesus loves you" or "You're special." You also could publicize future events of the church: "Baptism next Sunday," "Communion Wednesday evening," "Youth fund-raising event," "Church anniversary reminder," "Invite a friend to worship," etc. The message possibilities are endless. Take special care not to soil the insides or rims of the cups since these will be used for drinking.

Use this same idea to share a message for a youth group meeting or retreat. Give it a try, be creative!

—Arlo R. Reichter

Variations

1. Build community during refreshments with a variation of this idea. On each cup write a question similar to the following: What is your favorite television show and why? What is your happiest memory of grade school? Who is your favorite Bible character and why? Pour a beverage into the cups and dis-

tribute them to the youth group members. Ask them to find a person and answer each other's cup-questions. Once they've answered the two questions, have them move on to another person—keep mingling!

2. Write questions on the cups according to a meeting's topic or a retreat's theme. Discuss the questions as you enjoy refreshments.

Your Ideas and Variations

_____
_____
_____
_____
_____
_____
_____
_____
_____
_____
_____
_____
_____
_____
_____
_____

78

Judge Not
TOPIC: PREJUDICE

Demonstrate why racism is wrong with a simple visual display.

On a small platform or table, place three paper cups filled with water. Use food coloring to color one red, one yellow and one blue. Except for the color of the water, the cups should be identical.

Gather the youth group members around the cups. Tell the group you think the red cup is best and you would choose it above the others every time because it's the winning cup. Tell the kids the blue and yellow cups just aren't good enough.

Then ask the following questions: "What makes this red cup better than the other two? What makes it a winner? Is it a different size? Is it sturdier than the other two cups? Is it easier to drink from the red cup?"

Explain that choosing a cup just because it's a certain color, or ignoring the other cups for the same reason, is as bad as choosing or rejecting a friend just because he or she is of a different race. Explain how, even though the cups are different colors, they're all the same. Just as we, as a multitude of

races, are all God's children.
We should treat each other with
love and respect, and be treated
the same in return, no matter
what race we are.
—Mary Joyce Porcelli

Variations

1. Don't simply stress racism;
stress judging by male vs. fe-
male, old vs. young, rich vs.
poor, Christian vs. non-Christian.

2. One youth worker, Tom
Franks, used some unique
"stuff" to present a lesson on
judging by outward appearances. Here's his explanation:
"Every church has a junk closet,
better known as the audio-visual
room. In our AV room, I discovered 100 urine specimen cups
which someone had donated. I
still have no idea what they
were doing in the closet. To illustrate a lesson on judging, I
filled the cups with ginger ale
and offered a cup to each student as he or she entered the
room. Needless to say that upon
examining the cup, most of the
students wondered what was going on. I made the point: You
can't judge people by their outward appearance!"

Your Ideas and Variations

_____
_____
_____
_____

79

Seeds and Soil
TOPIC: FAITH

Use this Bible study to make
the parable of the sower meaningful to the young people.

Begin by giving each group
member a cup and a plastic
spoon. Give the kids five minutes
to go outside and fill their cup
with dirt that describes them in
some way. Examples: Kids who
see themselves as insecure
might spoon mud into their cup;
those who see themselves as
tough could mix dirt and rocks
in their cup. Regroup and share
the soil types.

Ask a volunteer to read Mark
4:1-9. Ask the young people to
explain why Jesus would tell this
parable. What did he mean?
Then read the explanation for
the parable in Mark 4:10-12.

Divide into four smaller
groups. Give each group paper,
pencil and one of the following
discussion guides which you
have written on separate 3×5
cards. Give the groups 20 min-

utes to answer the questions and follow the directions on their card.

Group #1:
The Path (Mark 4:4)
What kind of soil is this? Draw a picture of the kind of person who's representative of this path. What would he or she look like? What would he or she do? Describe his or her lifestyle.

Group #2:
The Rocky Ground
(Mark 4:5-6)
What kind of soil is this? Do you know anyone like this? Draw a picture of a person who is like this kind of soil. What would he or she look like? What would he or she do? Describe his or her lifestyle.

Group #3:
The Thorny Ground
(Mark 4:7)
What kind of soil is this? Draw a picture of a person who represents this kind of soil. Do you ever feel "choked" by activities in your life? Do the activities overwhelm your faith? take away your energy/ability to be filled with the Spirit? What are some of the things that are choking your life right now? Do you want to change those things? Explain.

Group #4:
The Ground That Brings
Forth Grain (Mark 4:8)
What kind of soil is this? Describe the kind of life this soil represents. Each of you name four "grains" (or "fruits") that people bear who represent this soil. How can you begin to make your own life more fruitful? Do you want to do this? Why or why not?

Regroup and discuss the four types of soil. Ask, "What kind of soil do you identify with right now in your life? How does God enable us to be like the soil that bears fruit?"

Gather in a circle and have the young people tell how the person on their right bears the fruit of God's love. For example, "You always bring your friends to our youth group events. You really show Christ's love by your enthusiasm."

—Bill Zieche

Variations

1. Ask each small group to prepare and present a skit that describes their soil-type. For example, Group #1 could present a person whose life has been like a well-worn path. "People walk all over me; they take me for granted . . ." Group #2 could present a person whose life has

been filled with difficulties. "One rock after another has been thrown into my life. I can't deal with all the problems. How do you expect me to think about Christianity when I have all of these troubles?" And so on.

2. Give each youth group member a small plant or flower as a symbol of God working in their lives.

Your Ideas and Variations

_____
_____
_____
_____
_____
_____
_____
_____

DICE

Bunko
TOPIC: CROWDBREAKERS

Just about any age group can have an evening of fun with just a few dies—so start robbing your board games.

Bunko is a game played at card tables, with four people seated at each table. There are partners in this game, but they change a lot, so it's a good mixer. You should have at least four tables, one of them designated as the head table. Place three dies at each table.

One person at the head table rolls a die, and the number of that die is the number everyone is rolling for. For example, a person at the head table rolls a six (or any number except one) and yells it out. Then the game begins. After "six" is called out, everyone takes a turn at rolling the dice. You and the person sitting across from you are partners, but you keep your scores separate. One point is given for each time you or your partner roll the right number. If anyone rolls all sixes he or she yells "Bunko" and that round of the game is over. If you or your partner gets Bunko, you each get 25 points. Everyone tallies up the number of points they earned in that round. For exam-

ple, you and your partner rolled 10 "sixes." Each partner gets 10 points for that round. Also, if you roll three "ones" at any time in the round, you and your partner each lose the points you've earned in the round.

After someone has yelled Bunko, the partners with the highest score at each table move up to the next table, but must split up. Those with the lowest score stay at the same table, but split up. The goal is to get to the head table and stay there. If you lose at the head table, the two of you go to the last table and split up. You may continue playing until a specified score is reached, or until people tire of the game.

Award prizes for the highest and lowest scores.

—Julie Sevig

Variations

1. Carry the "dice" theme into devotions by talking about the cloak the soldiers gambled for while Jesus was on the cross. Discuss how Jesus, and the soldiers, might have felt.

2. Talk about how we gamble with our lives—using drugs, abusing alcohol or smoking cigarettes. Do we gamble away our relationships with poor friendship skills? Do we gamble away our relationships with parents and relatives when we do that which we know is harmful?

Your Ideas and Variations

_____
_____
_____
_____
_____
_____
_____
_____
_____
_____

DOLLS

81

Youth Group Bond
TOPIC: GROUP BUILDING

Paper dolls can be used to create a visual image of the bond between members in your youth group. Here's how you can do it.

You will need matches, tape, markers and a candle. Out of various colors of construction paper, cut a paper doll, about 6 inches tall, for each member of your group. Cut through the section where the hands and hips meet. See top of next page.

When the group members arrive, gather in a circle around a lighted candle. Give each member a doll and marker. Ask each young person to write his or her name on the doll's face.

Read aloud Colossians 3:12-14. Note especially verse 14 which speaks of the binding that can occur among the people of God. Say, "Our group will now have the opportunity to see how we are bound together." Ask one person to think of a word that reminds him or her of the youth group; write that word on his or her doll's body; say the word aloud; and place the doll on the floor in front of him or her.

Ask the next young person to think of a word that begins with the last letter of the word chosen by the first person. For example, if the first word is "respect," the second word could be "togetherness."

After writing the word on his or her doll, this second person says the word aloud and connects the two paper dolls by slipping one of the doll's arms through the other doll's arm. This process continues around the circle until a line of dolls is created.

Conclude this activity by standing together with arms linked. Offer a prayer thanking God for the bonds that unite your group. Tape the dolls to-gether and display them on the wall of your meeting room!

—Kathi B. Finnell

Variations

1. Give the youth group members some crayons or colored markers. Have them each decorate the dolls to resemble themselves: hair, eyes, favorite sport or activity. For example, if a person plays high school football, he could draw a jersey and a football on the paper doll. Connect the dolls, and hang them on a wall with a sign that says, "Our group."

2. Give the young people each a pencil and have them write on their paper doll their favorite hobbies. Share the hobbies and see how many group members enjoy similar activities.

Your Ideas and Variations

_____
_____
_____
_____
_____
_____
_____
_____
_____

DOORBELLS

82

Ring 'n' Run
TOPIC: OUTREACH

Celebrate special holidays or special people with this fun idea. Help others experience God's love in a surprising way.

Ask your group to purchase or make simple gifts. You may want to solicit gifts from church members as well. Ideas are: flowers, stationery, gift certificates for free car washes, etc. Ask group members to include an encouraging note with each gift such as, "Have a great day" or "You're fantastic." Target special groups such as visitors, senior citizens, elders, deacons, etc., or randomly select homes in your community.

Once you've purchased the gifts and written the notes you're ready to "Ring 'n' Run." Load up the church van and take off for designated stops. Set your gift at the door, ring the doorbell then run like crazy! It's not important that the recipients see who placed the gift at their door. They will have a pretty good idea when they see the church van pull away. In this manner God will receive the glory, not the group or one person. Your group will receive the joy of giving and those visited will experience God's love in a special way. Make Ring 'n' Run an annual event!

—Tommy Baker

Variations

1. Instead of purchasing inexpensive gifts, use your imagination and "artistic talent" to create cards. Decorate construction paper with glitter, glue, yarn, fabric scraps, aluminum foil— anything you can find! Deliver each card, ring the bell, and run away!

2. Make banners out of butcher paper. Paint a colorful message such as, "Have a beautiful day, you wonderful person!" After the paint dries, roll up the paper and tie a bright ribbon around it.

Your Ideas and Variations

_____

_____

_____
_____
_____
_____
_____
_____
_____
_____
_____
_____

DOUGHNUTS

83

The Gourmet Doughnut
TOPIC: GAMES

Here is a game that not only gets young people excited; it also makes them laugh.

Stretch a thin rope through the holes of glazed doughnuts. (One doughnut for each group member.) Attach the rope to two poles. Lay a clean sheet under the string of doughnuts.

When the group members arrive, divide them into teams. Have the kids remove their shoes. At the word "go," one person from each team runs to the rope and chooses one doughnut to eat without the use of his or her hands. If the doughnut falls off the rope and onto the

floor, he or she still must eat it—no hands allowed. Then he or she runs back and tags the next player. The game is finished when one team of kids have eaten all of their doughnuts.

—Bob Hicks

Variations

1. For a messier time, use chocolate-covered doughnuts!

2. Vary the food—try salty pretzels or spicy raisin-cinnamon bagels.

Your Ideas and Variations

_____
_____
_____
_____
_____
_____
_____
_____
_____
_____

EGGS

84

Family and Faith
TOPIC: FAMILY

MOTHER!

"Who is my mother?" What a question! In Matthew 12:46-50, Jesus is preparing the people to receive a precious gem of truth. Jesus is not talking about being self-righteous and performing good works. He is reminding the people that faith is what counts and that the spiritual ties between the believer and Christ can be closer than family ties. The youth group members can learn of these ties during this meeting.

You will need one raw egg for each student and one for yourself. Bring egg salad and crackers.

When the students enter the room, give each one an egg. Ask them, "In what ways is an egg like a family?" (Do not give any answers. You will be surprised and thrilled with the students' creative analogies.) "Accidentally" drop your raw egg on the floor. Ask, "What things can change a family—shatter it?"

Spread egg salad on crackers and pass one to each student.

Explain that we can change the consistency of an egg to make it better. For example, we can make omelets, French toast or add them to cake batter, etc. Ask how a family can be changed to make it better.

Read and discuss Matthew 12:46-50. Say, "The egg is a beautiful and wondrous creation. We cannot duplicate it. But we can benefit from it in many ways. However, so many things can happen to it—it's so fragile! Our faith must be stronger. Unbreakable. Rooted in Jesus Christ."

—E. Jane Mall

Variations

1. As you are discussing the scripture passage, have the students put their eggs into a pan of boiling water. The eggs will be hard-boiled by the end of the class time. Ask them to take their hard-boiled eggs home, eat them and think about the wondrous gifts God gives us—espe-

cially the wonderful gift of family.

2. Plan a breakfast Bible study for the youth group members and their families. Organize a team of young people to help cook and serve sausage, toast and scrambled eggs. After the breakfast discuss the lesson as a large group. The families will get food for thought as well as food for their bellies!

Your Ideas and Variations

_____
_____
_____
_____
_____
_____
_____
_____
_____
_____
_____
_____
_____
_____

85

Stretching the Truth
TOPIC: INTEGRITY/HONESTY

In this object lesson, the youth group members will learn not to stretch the truth because it doesn't do a bit of good.

You will need a 2-foot piece of 3-inch white elastic. With a ball point pen, crayon or marker, write the word "truth" on the elastic. Don't use fingernail polish, it will crack, and truth shouldn't be cracked. You also will need a marker and a 6-inch piece of elastic for each person.

When the group members arrive, ask for two volunteers and have them each take hold of one

end of the elastic. Have them stretch the truth by pulling, twisting, winding, tossing and stomping on it. Now, hold it up in its original shape. The group will see that truth, no matter how people may try to distort it, will always be truth.

Ask volunteers to read each of these verses: Proverbs 8:7; John 3:21; 8:32; Galatians 4:16. Ask the young people what each of these verses say about truth. Then discuss these questions with the youth group members:

● Why does truth, no matter how distorted, remain the same?

● How can truth be stretched?

● Why do some people seek to change and destroy the truth?

● How can we twist and change our lives by not living by the truth?

● Are the scriptures old-fashioned because some people don't live the truths taught there? Explain.

Give each person a piece of elastic and a marker. Have the youth group members write the word "truth" on the elastic. Ask them to keep the pieces of elastic as reminders of the lesson. Challenge them not to stretch the truth—keep it straight every day.

—Janet R. Balmforth

Variations

1. At the end of the meeting, give each person a Hershey Kiss and say, "It's the truth! God loves you."

2. Eat Popsicles for refreshments. Clean the sticks, then form crosses by attaching two together with yarn. Use permanent-ink markers to write on the crosses, "It's true; Jesus lives."

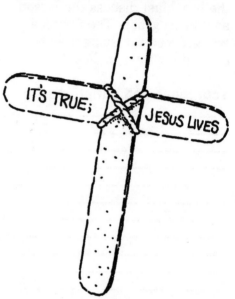

Your Ideas and Variations

_____
_____
_____
_____
_____
_____
_____
_____
_____
_____
_____
_____
_____
_____

FABRIC

Build-a-Quilt
TOPIC: RETREATS/GROUP BUILDING

For one of the last activities at a retreat, preserve your memories by building a quilt. Give each person a 10-inch square of muslin and some fabric crayons (available in craft shops). On the fabric square, ask each person to add his or her name and the date. Then ask each person to write a poem, prayer, words to a favorite song, or draw a picture that best describes his or her favorite experience of the retreat.

When every square is completed, place them on the floor so that all can see what the quilt will look like when it is finished.

Ask a seamstress to sew the squares together. Once the quilt is finished:

● Hang it in your church for a couple of weeks.

● Allow each person to take

the quilt home for two weeks.

● Hang it permanently in your meeting place or in the central office.

● Take some pictures of the quilt and distribute them to your group members.

● Give thanks for the individual young people who make up your youth group.

—Mary Kay Fitzpatrick

Variations

1. Make a quilt for other special occasions. For a church anniversary you could give every family a fabric square and have them draw a favorite memory of their church experience, or write a word that describes how they feel about the church. Have a seamstress sew together the squares to create a giant quilt or wall hanging.

2. Instead of a quilt, make a memory tablecloth. Buy one large piece of fabric and let all of the youth group members draw or write on it. Sew a hem around the edges and use it for special youth group meals or to cover the refreshment table at each youth group meeting.

Your Ideas and Variations

_____

_____

_____

_____

_____

_____

Fabric Scraps
TOPIC: WORSHIP

Want to perk up or personalize a special worship service in your church? Fabric scraps add a unique and special touch of brightness.

In advance, discuss the feelings that colorful windows, fabrics and clothing give us: They lift us up; they present a festive mood; they make us notice something we hadn't noticed in the past; they represent "youth"; the different colors represent the variety of gifts of the Spirit, etc. Everyone should understand the purpose for using the colorful fabric scraps.

For this experience, select several seamstresses and ask them to help with this project. The basic idea is to make one or more of the following in a colorful, patchwork design: a stole for your pastor, stoles for the choir, a cloth for the altar, a wall hanging for the front of the church, a wall hanging for the pulpit. Ask the sewing helpers to design patterns for the projects. Ask the youth group members to bring bright-colored fabric scraps to be used in this project. The young people also can ask others in the church to donate fabric scraps. Schedule special work times and gather equipment for the cutting, sewing and fitting.

Once the garments and hangings are complete, have the youth group members present them to the church as a sign of joy and celebration. Dedicate the items for use on special occasions.

These bright-colored, patchwork garments and wall hangings definitely will brighten up your church building and worship services—a special touch to show God's uplifting love for his children.

—Arlo R. Reichter

Variations

1. Plan a youth Sunday and use the garments as special symbols for this special day. Center the service around God's colorful promise of forgiveness as seen in rainbows, or God's promise of eternal life with him.

2. Ask the pastor to develop a service around Ephesians 4 regarding the varieties of gifts God gives. The various bright-colored patches can symbolize

the many gifts.

3. The pastor could wear his or her colorful stole and give a sermon on Joseph and his multicolored coat!

Your Ideas and Variations

_____
_____
_____
_____
_____
_____
_____
_____
_____
_____
_____
_____
_____
_____

FENCES

88

Climbing Over Fences
TOPIC: HONESTY/OUTREACH

Bridges bring people together; fences separate. In this activity, the kids will experience separation and seek to understand the things that come between us.

Bring a roll of plastic garden-bed fence, or make a fence from string, crepe paper and rope. You also will need newsprint,

markers and tape. Before your youth group arrives, set up the meeting room with many fenced areas. Make it impossible to get from one side of the room to the other without going around the fences. Place chairs inside the fenced areas. As the youth group members arrive, encourage them to seat themselves in one of the areas.

Discuss things that isolate us from each other: lying, money, greed, moral issues, different ethnic backgrounds, languages, etc. As the kids list situations that separate, have them use the newsprint and markers to make signs. Hang the signs on different sections of the fence throughout the room.

Discover ways we can cross over the fences that separate

us. Consider each item the kids have listed on the signs and then write on the opposite side of the paper things that can help us to build bridges to each other: love, help, thoughtfulness, understanding, etc.

After each isolating factor has been "overcome," have the group rearrange the fence to make a large circle where everyone can sit together. Celebrate the unity and the discovery that can come when we build bridges to each other.

Follow up the experience with a discussion using these questions:

● What barriers keep people from coming to the youth group? to church?

● How can we abolish cliques?

● How can we reach the unchurched in our community?

Using fences illustrates the need to remove barriers and to build bridges to the inactive and unchurched. The kids learn to refocus their attention on others.

—Arlo R. Reichter

Variations

1. Have your youth group lead this activity during a church service. Use the fence to divide the sanctuary into parts; follow the same discussion.

2. Have the kids place their arms around each other and

close their eyes. Say, "Sometimes we separate ourselves and can't enjoy the love God intends. Everyone who has been a part of a group and has ever let that group down, drop your arms from your neighbors." After a brief period of silence say, "Sometimes we say things that are harmful to other people. Anyone who has ever said something that was harmful to another, fold your arms." After a period of silence say, "Often we exclude others from our group. If anyone has ever made someone feel left out, step away from the group." After a brief silence say, "It is important to listen to others. If you have ever listened to another, take one step back together." Allow a time for silence then say, "If you have ever made someone feel welcome, open your eyes." Allow for silence then say, "If you have ever forgiven someone, then place your arms around the people beside you." End with a group squeeze (**The Giving Book**, by Paul M. Thompson and Joani Schultz, John Knox Press.)

Your Ideas and Variations

_____
_____
_____
_____
_____
_____

_____
_____
_____
_____
_____
_____

FILM CANISTERS

89

Guess the Stuff Inside
TOPIC: GAMES

Set up this guessing game for early arrivals to a meeting, activity or retreat to play.

Fill opaque film canisters with granulated or powdered substances such as flour, sugar, salt, sand, rice, coffee, cereal, aquarium gravel, soap flakes. Number each canister with masking tape and a pen. Distribute paper and pencils and ask the youth group members to record guesses. Individuals try to identify the contents by shaking the canisters.

Award a prize for the person with the most correct guesses—a film canister filled with coins or a coupon for a free ice cream cone.

—Linda Ferree

Variations
1. Divide the teenagers into

small groups. Give each group a film canister and ask the members to search for an item to fill it with such as pins, sand, pebbles, paper clips, tacks, etc. Gather after several minutes and let each group try to guess what the other groups' canisters contain.

2. Thoroughly wash the film canisters and fill them with beverages such as lemonade, soft drinks, water, grape juice, etc. Blindfold the kids and let them take turns guessing the beverages.

Your Ideas and Variations

_____

_____

_____

_____

_____

_____

_____

_____

_____

_____

_____

_____

90

Many Uses for Film Canisters
TOPIC: OFFERINGS/RETREATS

People who use 35mm film are likely to have a collection of empty film canisters. Ask church members to donate their collection to the youth group. Put those canisters to use with the following suggestions:

● Plan a youth retreat around a key scripture or phrase. At the retreat have the participants write the scripture or theme on a small piece of paper and place it in a canister. This canister is theirs to take home as a memento of the retreat. Have the kids fill additional canisters to give to friends who were unable to attend.

● During a youth retreat, ask the young people to set some personal goals. Have them write the goals on a slip of paper, place it in a canister and take it home. Another option is to have the leader keep the canisters for one month. At that time, the kids can open their canisters and see how many of their goals they have reached. This is a fun way to introduce the young people to the valuable concept of setting goals.

● As part of a youth program or service, have the kids prepare messages in canisters and give them to church members. The messages could be reminders of the theme of the service, or thoughts such as, "Remember that God loves you."

● As a part of a retreat or worship service, have the kids write "offerings" on slips of paper and place them in the canisters. Offerings could include: "more patience at home," "less swearing," "better cooperation with brothers and sisters," etc.

● Use the canisters to collect a special offering for peace, hunger or a church project. Have a contest to see who can collect the most money. The canisters are small enough to be placed in offering baskets. Build a symbol with the canisters to show the amount of offerings received. This is most effective if the offering is collected over a period of several weeks. As the offering grows, glue the canisters together in a shape such as a cross, animal, building, etc.

—Arlo R. Reichter

Variations

1. Label each canister with a name of each youth group member. Fill the canisters with "love-notes" such as, "I love you because you always take time to listen to others." Give the canisters to the young people as an affirmation activity at the end of a meeting or retreat.

2. Give a canister, piece of masking tape, small slips of paper and a pen to each group member. Have them write their name on the piece of tape and place it on their canister. Then ask all group members to write affirmation notes to the others and place the notes in the corresponding canisters. Have them take the canisters home and read the notes for an uplifting time of affirmation and good feelings.

Your Ideas and Variations

_____
_____
_____
_____
_____
_____
_____
_____
_____
_____
_____
_____
_____

FILMSTRIPS

91

A Refreshing Renovation
TOPIC: MEDIA/CREATIVITY

Many filmstrips have important things to say, but they don't make an impression on us because they are outdated or because we don't know the people featured in them.

Using the following technique, you can revive an outdated filmstrip while sharing a creative experience with your youth group. You won't change the script or soundtrack but you'll recast the visuals, making your group members the stars of the show.

You'll need an old filmstrip, 35mm camera and equipment, a few rolls of 35mm slide film, a slide projector and screen, a tape recorder for playing the original soundtrack. Gather the necessary costumes and props.

Review filmstrips your church has on file and pick a few that look interesting. Bible stories are great.

Schedule a time and place to present your finished product, perhaps to the Sunday school members or to the entire congregation. This gives your group even more reason to do the project, and a timetable for completing it.

Show the original filmstrip and explain the idea to your youth group. Tell them they have a chance to create a new filmstrip from the old filmstrip, using themselves as the stars.

Once the group agrees to do the project, write down and make copies of the script, watch the original again, and take notes about each scene.

Divide into small groups and assign each group a portion of the show. Ask the young people to personalize each scene with their own ideas about their parts, costumes or props.

Plan a time when everyone can get together to remake the filmstrip. Use a 35mm camera to shoot each scene, keeping careful notes about what you've shot.

Ask for helpers to assemble the film by placing the slides in proper sequence in a slide tray. View the filmstrip as a group and make any changes members consider appropriate.

Present the finished product as scheduled; try to have your "actors" present to receive the accolades they so richly deserve.

Take them out to celebrate after the presentation. They have earned it!

—Walter Mees

Variations

1. Use this same idea to renovate old slide shows or films.

2. Use this same idea with a videocassette recorder. A significant difference between slides and videotape is that motion can be recorded on the latter. This means in planning each scene, you'll have to consider motion.

The other major difference between videotape and slides is that you'll need to set the visual part of the presentation to go with the audio. The easiest way to accomplish this is by simultaneously recording the narration, dialogue and background music live, while you tape the scenes.

Lighting can really spell the difference between a so-so production and an excellent one. At least two lights are needed angling in from each side. Experiment to see what works best, but the ultimate goal is to eliminate any shadows.

Most church videotape efforts will probably be done in ½-inch VHS format, using one camera. This format is very difficult to edit; therefore, it is easiest to shoot in proper sequence, using only the pause button and the time it allows the kids to set up the next scene. This same pause button, used on a machine connected to another source machine, is your best ally in later editing if changes are needed.

Your Ideas and Variations

FLASHLIGHTS

92

Flashlight Lessons
TOPIC: GOSSIP/HOLY SPIRIT

A flashlight without batteries is like a non-Christian. Although both were created with a purpose in mind, without a power source, they are incapable of functioning at full capacity.

Have the kids brainstorm ways a flashlight without batteries might be used. Possible answers are: a weapon, an object to play catch with, a container to store things, etc. A flashlight without batteries could have

many uses, but none as good as what it was designed for.

Put batteries in it—fill it with power (the Holy Spirit). Now what can it do? All the things it did before, *plus* light up the way.

Is it possible for a flashlight to contain batteries, yet still not light up? Sure! The power which is there must be used; the connection must be made.

Use a flashlight to illustrate another point: Our mouths can get us into trouble!

Disassemble a flashlight and display the pieces on a table at the front of the room. Keep one small piece in your pocket—something that will prevent the flashlight from working properly.

Invite several young people to assemble the flashlight. They can easily put it back together, but it won't work.

Reveal the little piece you hid in your pocket. Ask them, "How can one little piece be so important?" Discuss the following questions that focus on the mouth—one little part of our body that can cause a lot of trouble.

● How often does your mouth get you in trouble?

● How could the trouble have been avoided?

Ask one of the kids to read James 3:1-12. Have the youth group members make a list of the images used to describe the tongue. What are these verses saying?

Present topics such as white lies, gossip, swearing, anger, etc. Ask the kids to brainstorm what can be done to confront each of these situations. For example, "Don't pass on any gossip you hear; don't start any gossip either." "Don't say things in a burst of anger that you'll be sorry for later."

Distribute paper and envelopes to the participants. Have them each write a goal to "clean up their act." For example, "I will count to 10 each time I'm angry." Or, "I will not spread any gossip I hear."

Ask the kids to put the paper in the envelope and seal it. On the envelope, have them write a date six months from now. Have the youth group members take the envelope home, open it in six months and see how they're doing in "controlling their tongues."

—James D. Walton

Variations

1. Use other battery-powered machines such as tape recorders, pencil sharpeners and radios.

2. Discuss more about gossip by dividing the young people into three groups. Give each group a 3×5 card with one of the following case studies and questions:

Case Study 1: A friend catches you in the hallway between classes. She says: "Did you hear about Sandy and John? Last Saturday, they told their parents they were going to a friend's house to watch television. They didn't get home until 4 a.m. They said they fell asleep during a boring show. Sure!"

● What would you say to your friend?

● How would Sandy or John feel if they knew they were being talked about?

● Why do you think the friend is passing along this story?

● How could you stop this talk from going further?

Case Study 2: A rumor is floating around school that one of your friends is pregnant. You know this isn't true.

● What would you do or say if you heard this?

● If the story isn't true, why would somebody make it up?

● How could you stop it from going further?

Case Study 3: You overhear two friends talking about you. They're saying you failed a math test they thought was really easy. The truth is, you *did* fail the test.

● If something is "the truth," is it okay for people to talk about it? Explain.

● How would you feel if you overheard someone talking about you?

● What would you do?

Your Ideas and Variations

_____
_____
_____
_____
_____
_____
_____
_____
_____
_____

93

Flashlight Pictures
TOPIC: CREATIVITY/
CHRISTIAN SYMBOLS

How about putting on a light show with flashlights? Think of the possible shapes 20 to 30 flashlights could make: a cross, fish, communion chalice, loaf of bread, stick person. The flashlights also could be used to spell short words such as love, peace, joy, hope, etc.

The flashlight holders will need to rehearse their positions so that each form will be projected correctly.

Light up a special evening service with these fun flashlight formations!

—Arlo R. Reichter

Variations

1. Decide upon a theme for a service such as "The Law." Use flashlights to form the Ten Commandments tablets:

2. Sing a song such as "This Little Light of Mine" and shine the flashlights on the walls and ceilings.

3. Read a scripture such as

1 Corinthians 13:1-13. Form the word "love" or a heart with the flashlights.

Your Ideas and Variations

_____
_____
_____
_____
_____
_____
_____
_____
_____
_____

94

Light the Way
TOPIC: OUTREACH/EVANGELISM

Jesus wants us to let our lights shine so that all will know the glory of God. This object lesson uses flashlights to illuminate that concept!

The best place to utilize this concept is in a darkened hallway during a youth group meeting or on a camp trail at night during a retreat. Keeping the subject of the activity in mind, at an effectual moment, turn the light on. As the group walks along, ask someone to shine the flashlight so as to light the way for others. Then ask the person holding the flashlight to hold it close to his or her chest. Try to keep walking along the path or hallway. Stop for a few moments and discuss these questions:

● What is the difference between shining the light on the path ahead or shining it downward in front of your feet?

● When a person lights the path for others, does he or she also light it for himself or herself? Explain.

● Could a person light the path for others and not himself or herself? Explain.

● When we light the way for others, how do we develop physically? mentally? emotionally? spiritually?

Ask the person to turn the flashlight back on the path and light the way again. As you walk back to the meeting place or camp area, discuss how the youth group members can light the way for others the next week. Encourage everyone to bring a friend to the next youth group meeting.

—Janet R. Balmforth

Variations

1. Develop a Bible study around the theme of "light." Use these verses: Genesis 1:3; Psalms 27:1; 119:105; Isaiah

42:6; John 9:5; Acts 13:47.

2. Give the group members each a candle to take home and light each time they have a daily devotion. Remind them to let their lights shine for everyone to see.

Your Ideas and Variations

_____
_____
_____
_____
_____
_____
_____
_____
_____
_____
_____
_____

95

Liquid Picture
TOPIC: DRAMA/BIBLE STUDY

Liquid Picture helps young people focus on the major parts of a Bible story. The technique is similar to a modified choral reading.

Several key phrases are chosen from a parable. The first short phrase is spoken (with appropriate motions) three times at full volume. Then the same phrase is whispered three times (with appropriate motions) until

it's time for the speakers to change to a new line. As the story is told, the phrases add on, layer by layer, full volume and whispers.

Members of our high school fellowship presented the parable of the wise and foolish maidens (Matthew 25:1-13) as a Liquid Picture during the Sunday morning worship service. The young people arrived about 45 minutes before the presentation to rehearse lines and movements. By the time the congregation members started arriving, everything was ready to go. You can present a Liquid Picture too. Here's how:

Choose 10 girls (five to represent the wise maidens; five to represent the foolish maidens). Choose one guy to play the bridegroom. Give one flashlight to each maiden to represent the lamps. Ask the wise maidens to stand stage left and the foolish maidens to stand stage right. Follow these instructions:

● All maidens hold hand above eyes and search the horizon. They repeat at full volume three times, "We are waiting for the bridegroom."

● The wise maidens continue the phrase, "We are waiting for the bridegroom," in a stage whisper for three times. While the wise maidens are whispering, the foolish maidens hold out their arms, palms up, and shake their heads from side to side as they say their new line three times at full volume, "We are foolish."

● The three foolish maidens continue the phrase, "We are foolish," in a stage whisper for three times as the wise maidens change to their new line. The wise maidens point to their heads, nod them up and down, and repeat three times at full volume, "We are wise."

● The foolish maidens and four wise maidens continue these same lines in a stage whisper while the fifth wise maiden points to the horizon and adds the next line three times at full volume, "Here comes the bridegroom."

● The foolish maidens repeat three times in a stage whisper, "Here comes the bridegroom," as the wise maidens point their lighted flashlights to the ceiling and say at full volume, "Our lamps are lighted."

● The wise maidens continue their line three times in a stage whisper as the foolish maidens shake their unlighted flashlights upside down to check for oil and say three times at full volume, "Our lamps are out."

● The foolish maidens continue their lines three times in a stage whisper as the wise maidens use their thumbs to give an "out" signal. The wise maidens say three times at full volume,

"Go and buy some more."

● All maidens continue their lines in stage whispers as the bridegroom enters and stands between the two groups. He places his hand on his chest and says three times at full volume, "I have come."

● The foolish maidens wave and say three times at full volume, "We are back."

● The foolish maidens continue in a stage whisper as the wise maidens and the bridegroom hold up their hands to make a door and say three times at full volume, "The door is locked."

● All young people drop their hands to their sides and stand in silence for five seconds, then exit.

Liquid Picture is a valuable opportunity for young people to participate in worship and it helps make the scripture reading "come alive." Have fun when you try it with your youth group!

—Walter John Boris

Variations

1. Present the Liquid Picture to Sunday school classes, other churches or nursing homes.

2. Record the Liquid Picture and give away the tapes. Better yet, sell them to raise funds for your youth group.

3. Instead of flashlights, use candles or lamps and oil.

Your Ideas and Variations

_____
_____
_____
_____
_____
_____
_____
_____
_____
_____
_____

FLOUR

96

Ring in the Flour
TOPIC: GAMES

Taking chances is what this game is all about.

Take a 6- or 8-ounce paper cup and pack it with flour. Turn it over on the table and gently lift the cup off the packed flour. Place an inexpensive ring (such as those found in gum machines) gently on top of the packed flour.

Ask everyone to line up and take a turn carving away flour with a butter knife without letting the ring fall. The one who takes too big of a chance and makes the ring fall must dig it out without using his or her hands. The use of his or her

teeth is all that is acceptable.

Be ready for flour-covered faces and a great time!

—Bob Hicks

Variations

1. Give everybody a toothpick and divide into equal-numbered teams. Ask everyone to put the toothpick in his or her mouth. Place a ring on the toothpick of the first person in each line. On the word "go" the teams must pass the ring from toothpick to toothpick—no hands allowed.

Your Ideas and Variations

_____
_____
_____
_____
_____
_____
_____
_____
_____
_____

FOOD

97

Fat Tuesday Celebration
TOPIC: CELEBRATIONS/LENT

Make arrangements so that your youth group can host a Fat Tuesday Celebration the evening before Ash Wednesday. The point is to simulate a Mardigras festival or carnival held regularly on Shrove Tuesday (or Fat Tuesday). It is an evening of good food, rich dessert, fun and games.

Plan the celebration for the youth group, or have the youth group sponsor it for your church. The easiest way is to plan a potluck, with the youth group members providing the beverage, setup and cleanup. Ask people to bring dishes from a variety of nations and cultures. You also will need 3×5 cards, envelopes and pencils.

Plan several fun, energetic games such as Dragon Dodgeball (**Try This One . . . Strikes Again**, Group Books). For this game, you separate the participants into teams of four people. Then choose one team to be the first dragon; have the kids line up and put their hands on the waist of the person in front of them. Instruct the other teams to join together and form a large circle around the dragon. Give a ball to the players in the circle; they need to throw the ball at the last person of the dragon and hit him or her below the waist. When hit, he or she joins the circle and the players try to hit the (new) last person of the dragon. This continues until only one person of the dragon is left and he or she, too, is hit. Then the next team of four forms a new dragon that must dodge the ball. Be sure to time the life span of each dragon; the team whose dragon survives the longest is the winner.

When the meal and games end, invite everyone to the sanctuary for a few minutes. There, begin with a prayer for the Lenten season. Say, "Tomorrow is Ash Wednesday. It marks a period of 40 weekdays until Easter. Lent is a time to balance both fun in life and solemn dedication to God. Lent is a time for us to repent of our sins." Distribute the pencils, blank cards and envelopes. Ask the participants to write down a word or phrase that dedicates themselves for the Lenten period. Examples of dedications are: "I will give up red meat for Lent." Or, "Every day I will do a kind act for someone else." Or, "I will have a 30-minute devotion each morning.''

Once the dedications are written, ask the participants to seal their cards in the envelopes, come forward, deposit them on the altar, then quietly depart. Explain that you'll keep their private dedications until Easter, then destroy them—unopened.

At the youth meeting after the Fat Tuesday Celebration, talk about the dedications. Emphasize Jesus' final dedication—his death on the cross. Discuss how we balance in life both food and fun, and solemn, sacred dedications to God and to one another.

—Russ Jolly

Variations

1. Add to the festivity of the Fat Tuesday Celebration—have everyone wear costumes. Award candy and balloons for most colorful costume, most creative costume, and most-sure-to-attract-attention costume. Give each of the participants a kazoo and have them parade around the area. During the solemn part of the evening, have the people remove one part of their costume as a symbol of their dedication for Lent.

2. Host a community Fat Tuesday Celebration at the high school. Use the pool, gymnasium, weight room and cafeteria for all of the fun. For the second part of the evening create a solemn atmosphere in the audito-

rium. Drape a black cloth over a cross and place the cross on the stage. Surround the cross with several lighted candles; dim the lights in the auditorium.

Your Ideas and Variations

_____

_____

_____

_____

_____

_____

_____

_____

_____

_____

98

A Fruitful Dinner
TOPIC: GROUP BUILDING/FELLOWSHIP

Gather everyone for a unique, fun experience with food. Ask each youth group member to bring one can of soup (no creamed soups), one piece of fruit and some bread. (Don't explain why they need each item.)

You'll need kitchen facilities, a large pan to mix the soup, plates, bowls, glasses, silverware and napkins. On a large table, place a large bowl, soup ladle, sharp knives and a cutting board. Place a chair for each person around the table.

As the youth group members

enter the room, ask them to put the fruit and bread on the table and bring their soup to the kitchen. Gather around the stove, open the cans and prepare the soup. Ask the young people to think of ways the youth group is like the soup. For example, "Just like there are many different soups added to one pot, we're many different people who make up our youth group."

While the soup is heating, sit at the table. Ask the kids to examine their piece of fruit for a few minutes. Ask how they resemble the fruit. Then ask how they are different. Distribute the knives and ask the youth group members to cut up their fruit in silence and put the pieces into a large bowl. Read 1 Corinthians 12:12-26, substituting the words "fruit salad" for "body" and specific fruits for the parts of the body.

Ask for helpers to set the table, then bring out the hot soup As everyone eats the soup, fruit salad and bread, ask the members to compare their faith to the bread. For example, "My faith is like this bread because it fills me up when I'm spiritually hungry."

After everyone is finished eating, close with a prayer. Ask each participant to add a word or sentence giving thanks for the person on his or her right.
—Therese Caouette

Variations

1. Take the leftover fruit, soup and bread to shut-ins, nursing homes or other members of the church—share the fruitful dinner!

2. Out of the different pieces of fruit, make "people" salad. Use a pear half for the body, peach half for the head, slices of apples or oranges for the arms and legs, etc. This activity really illustrates that a body is made up of many parts.

Your Ideas and Variations

_____
_____
_____
_____
_____
_____
_____
_____
_____
_____

99

Home Cookin' Craze
TOPIC: PROGRESSIVE EVENTS/
FELLOWSHIP

Looking for a fun way for your group to take advantage of those sensational cooks in your church? If so, plan this activity.

Contact 12 cooks and ask them if they would prepare their "specialty" dish and open their home to your youth group in order to play Home Cookin' Craze. Inform your cooks of the date and time your game will begin. They also will need to know how many servings to prepare; one serving for each team.

When your group arrives at church divide them into teams of four or five and give each team a Home Cookin' Craze game sheet. You will need 12 items on your game sheet. Here is a sample game sheet:

Home Cookin' Craze

_____ A bowl of Mrs. Dunavann's homemade ice cream.

_____ A cup of Mrs. Jones' homemade custard.

_____ A piece of Mrs. Baker's "famous" lasagna.

_____ A piece of Mrs. Hayden's cake.

_____ A slice of Mrs. Campbell's banana nut bread.

Give the teams a map of the game route, which should include names, addresses and phone numbers of the cooks. Allow team members a few minutes to chart their courses. Use adult drivers. Remind all participants to wear seat belts.

Allow each team 90 minutes

to complete the course. Release each carload at one-minute intervals to take away the "Indy 500" effect. Assign the teams each a different house for their first stop, so they don't begin at the same place.

The entire team must go into each house, but only one person can eat at each location. No one can leave until the bowl or plate is clean. Whoever eats that item signs his or her name by it on the game sheet. That person can't eat again until everyone else on the team has eaten an item as well.

The first team to complete the route and return to the starting point before the 90-minute limit, is the winner.

For prizes, give away gum or after-dinner breath mints. Have all of the participants write thank-you notes to the talented chefs who shared their mouthwatering creations.

—Tommy Baker

Variations

1. Ask cooks in your congregation to donate a few of their favorite recipes. Compile the recipes into a church cookbook, then sell them to raise funds for your youth group.

2. Plan Home Cookin' Craze according to various themes: favorite Mexican food, best beverage, delightful desserts, scrumptious salads, etc.

Your Ideas and Variations

_____

_____

_____

_____

_____

_____

_____

_____

_____

_____

100

Spiritual Picnic
TOPIC: SPIRITUAL GROWTH/
BIBLE STUDY

We spend a lot of time preparing and eating food. This study will make the young people aware of the importance of feeding our bodies spiritual food every day, as well as physical food.

● Make the following invitations and distribute them to the youth group members. Have them give extras to their friends.

> You are invited to a
> Spiritual Picnic!
>
> Date:
> Place:
>
> FREE! EVERYONE INVITED!
> BRING YOUR FRIENDS!

● Assign six young people to make six 3×5 cards with the following information:

1. Read Psalm 119:103
Item of food: honey—symbolizes God's promises

2. Read 1 Corinthians 10:4
Item of food: rock candy—symbolizes Christ

3. Read John 6:35, 58
Item of food: bread—symbolizes Christ's life

4. Read 1 Peter 2:2-3
Item of food: milk—symbolizes basics of Christianity

5. Read Revelation 2:7
Item of food: pretzels—symbolizes eternal life

6. Read Revelation 2:17
Item of food: dry cereal—symbolizes the spiritual sustenance God gives

● Have the six volunteers who made the cards read the cards during the picnic as they distribute the appropriate food item.

● Before the picnic, gather enough food, serving containers, paper plates, cups and silverware for everyone.

● Set a table with the food and place settings for all of the youth group members and their guests.

Gather the kids around the table and discuss physical food. Read John 6:27-29 and discuss spiritual food and why it is important. Explain that Jesus always gave thanks before meals (Matthew 14:19; Acts 27:35) and ask someone to offer a prayer.

Have the first volunteer pick up the container of honey, serve a small portion to himself or herself, pass it on, then read the corresponding 3×5 card. Discuss how quickly physical food perishes. Think about what the honey symbolizes and how God's promises are eternal. Pause briefly between each verse to meditate upon it. Continue this process for all six food items.

Conclude by saying together, "Life is more than food. Don't be anxious about anything. Trust God for everything."

—Gloria Menke

Variations

1. Ask the young people to evaluate their daily spiritual diet each time they eat or prepare food.

2. For the picnic, have the kids make deviled eggs. Give them each a hard-boiled egg and ask them to peel off the shells. As the young people do this, discuss how Christ "peels away" our sinful nature with his forgiveness. Cut the eggs in half and put the yolks in a bowl. Add spices and mayonnaise and discuss how we spice up our Christian lives with prayer, Bible study, worship and fellowship. Drop the mixture in the egg halves and arrange them on a platter. Celebrate how Christ makes us new through his life

and love.

—Sue Fries

Your Ideas and Variations

_____
_____
_____
_____
_____
_____
_____
_____
_____
_____
_____
_____
_____
_____

101

Winter Cookout
TOPIC: FELLOWSHIP/WINTER

A cookout in winter may sound crazy, but it's a lot of fun! Where we live, it is cold and snowy during the winter. We have other activities in the snow, why not a cookout? After all, the charcoals don't care.

Ask the youth group members to dress warmly. Have the guys bring buns and beverages; girls bring chips and dessert. Ask everyone to bring meat to grill.

Cook the hamburgers and hot dogs on an outdoor grill. Play volleyball, Frisbee and have a

tug of war. If there is snow, try snow sculpting! See who can build a snowman that looks the most like the youth group sponsor.

Be sure that there is some place where the kids can get warm when they need to. But go ahead and enjoy the winter weather!

—Jeffrey A. Collins

Variations

1. Meet by a frozen lake. Have the kids bring beach towels and ice skates. After they skate for a while, they can relax on their beach towel and dream of the summertime: warm weather, swim suits, beach towels and swimming.

2. Add to the frozen fun by making homemade ice cream.

Who says homemade ice cream only can be enjoyed during the summer?

Your Ideas and Variations

_____
_____
_____
_____
_____
_____
_____
_____
_____
_____
_____
_____
_____
_____
_____
_____
_____
_____
_____

FRUIT

102

Fruit of the Spirit
TOPIC: SPIRITUAL GROWTH

A luscious bowl of grapes, bananas, pears, apples, oranges and strawberries can facilitate a discussion on the fruit of the Spirit.

Gather the youth group members in a circle around the bowl of fruit. Ask a volunteer to read Galatians 5:22-23. Ask the young people to meditate on a spiritual fruit they feel manifested right now in their lives. They don't have to be limited to the biblical list, they also can think of fruit such as enthusiasm, loyalty, fun, sincerity, etc. When each person decides on a spiritual fruit, ask

him or her to pick a fruit from the bowl that illustrates that quality. When all have made their selection, ask them to share their spiritual fruit and how it is symbolized by the actual fruit. For example, "I picked grapes because the clusters symbolize how my fruit of love draws me together with all of you."

After all have shared, celebrate the gifts God has given by having a love feast. Eat the fruit and serve grape juice or orange juice. A truly "fruitful" experience!

—Lynn Potter

Variations

1. Make fruit salad by cutting up pieces of fruit and mixing them in a large bowl. Discuss our uniqueness as individuals—and the totally delicious combination we make as a group.

Give each person a small bowl of fruit salad and a spoon. Dab a spoonful of whip cream to each person's portion and say, "Jesus' love and forgiveness add a sweet flavor to our lives." Enjoy the salad!

2. A messy, but fun crowdbreaker is The Orange Peel Relay. Divide the young people into two teams; place an orange in the mouth of the first person in each team. The object of the relay is to peel the orange by using teeth only—no hands. The

first person bites off a piece of the peel as he or she passes the orange to the second person, and so on, until the orange is totally peeled. Then, the members can use their hands to divide and eat the orange. First team finished eating their orange wins!

Your Ideas and Variations

_____
_____
_____
_____
_____
_____
_____
_____
_____
_____
_____

103

Preparing for Communion
TOPIC: COMMUNION/WORSHIP

Conduct this meaningful experience in a study, retreat setting, or in a worship service before the celebration of communion.

You'll need bread, juice, seedless grapes and a bowl. Ask the group members to sit in rows as they would in a worship service or classroom.

Pass the bowl of grapes down the rows and ask the participants to each take one grape. Admonish them, "Please don't bruise the grapes. Gently hold them until you receive further instructions."

Ask a volunteer to read John 15:1-8, 16-17. Ask the group members to look at their grape and think about the relationships between the vinedresser, vine, branch and fruit. Focus on the fruit and the fact that scripture does not assign it a specific meaning. Ask what the fruit might symbolize. What does it mean "to bear fruit"? The discussion should lead to words such as nurture, nourishment, renewal, sustenance, growth and love. Designate the word "love" as that which embraces all of the others. For this study, let the grape represent love.

Instruct each person to carefully take the grape and pop it into the mouth of his or her neighbor to the right. If that person claims not to like grapes, then say, "This isn't a grape, it's a small morsel of love." If a person did not heed your earlier advice, then a grape might have been dropped or squashed. It will not be fit to feed anyone and, if offered, probably would be refused. Make the point that love is tender and should not be abused.

A problem will arise when the

person at one end of each row will not receive a morsel of love, while the person at the opposite end will have no one to feed. At that point, the participants must make a decision. Will they be gluttons and feed themselves more grapes, or will they make the effort to feed the person on the end who didn't get fed? Challenge the kids to make a decision and to carry it out. Discuss these questions:

● Realistically, how do we as Americans. share our wealth and resources with the rest of the world?

● Gluttony is said to be one of the seven deadly sins. What happens to the glutton? How does gluttony relate to hunger?

● What does the word "abide" really mean? Jesus says, "Abide in me, and I in you. As the branch cannot bear fruit by itself, unless it abides in the vine, neither can you, unless you abide in me. I am the vine, you are the branches. He who abides in me, and I in him, he it is that bears much fruit, for apart from me you can do nothing" (John 15:4-5).

● After this discussion about vines, branches and fruit, Jesus says, "This is my commandment, that you love one another as I have loved you" (John 15:12). Can you imagine that the whole grape symbolizes the love of God in Christ? What does the cele-

bration of Holy Communion mean to you?

After the discussion, sing a song such as "His Banner Over Me Is Love" (**Songs,** by Yohann Anderson, Songs and Creations, Inc.). Be sure to sing the verse, "He is the vine and we are the branches" and celebrate the fact that we share God's love with others.

Close with communion. As you eat the bread, give thanks to God for sending his Son to the world. As you drink the juice, give thanks that Jesus died for our sins. Eat the rest of the grapes and ask God to help us show love to others and spread his Word.

—Russ Jolly

Variations

1. Enjoy refreshments such as grape bubble gum, grape Popsicles, grape fruit bars, or sandwiches made with peanut butter and grape jelly!

2. Give each participant a small bunch of grapes with a 3×5 card attached to the stem. On the card write, "Morsels of God's 'grape' love." Each time the kids eat a grape, have them offer a prayer thanking God for his boundless bunches of love.

Your Ideas and Variations

_____
_____
_____

104

The 12 Days of Christmas
TOPIC: CHRISTMAS/FELLOWSHIP

This is a fun twist to the familiar Christmas tune, "The 12 Days of Christmas."

Ahead of time, prepare the following items, which will be handed out to 12 volunteers. Wrap and number each item.

1. A can of pears, with a note attached that reads, "It's not a partridge. It's not a pear tree. It *is* something from a pear tree."

2. Two bird-shaped scented soaps (found at bath stores).

3. An empty egg shell with a note attached, "From a French hen."

4. A note that reads, "For a prize, imitate the sound of any calling bird, such as a whippoorwill, quail, crow, etc." (The prize is a pack of gum.)

5. Five small gold rings. Find these at a craft store or use gold curtain rings.

6. Any item with a geese motif such as a piece of stationery or a napkin.

7. A note that reads, "Demonstrate a swimming stroke on land."

8. An emery board with a note that reads, "Cows do not like to be milked by maidens with rough hands or nails."

9. A note that reads, "Select a partner and demonstrate any dance step." (After the two do this, give each a packet of bath oil for soaking their weary feet.)

10. A note that reads, "Leap for joy when you receive this gift." Attach a small gift such as a granola bar.

11. A toy harmonica or flute with a note that reads, "Pipe your favorite Christmas carol on this."

12. An item with a drum on it. Perhaps a tea towel with "The Little Drummer Boy" pictured or a small, toy-drum tree ornament.

When you're ready to begin, choose 12 volunteers to stand up in front while the rest of the group sings "The 12 Days of Christmas." After each line, the group members stop and the volunteers must open the appropriate item. When the song is finished, volunteers get to keep what they opened and the rest of the group receives packs of gum for being the chorus. Give a pack of gum to the volunteers who received gag gifts.

This activity promotes giving and receiving in a unique way. Enjoy spreading Christmas cheer!

—Karen Musitano

Variations

1. Rewrite the song according to a school theme. For example: "On the first day of high school my teacher said to me, 'Do all your homework on time.' On the second day of high school my teacher said to me, 'Don't come to school late . . .' " etc.

2. Have the young people use their creativity and rewrite the song to other themes such as Easter, summer vacation, guidelines for getting along with family members, etc.

Your Ideas and Variations

_____
_____
_____
_____
_____
_____
_____
_____
_____
_____
_____
_____
_____
_____
_____
_____
_____
_____
_____
_____

GAMES

105

Detrivializing a Popular Game
TOPIC: BIBLE STUDY

Trivia games are a lot of fun. The problem is, the facts are so "trivial." Use this game idea to create a great learning experience for Christian young people.

Borrow a Trivial Pursuit game board. Obtain 50 index cards in six different colors—so you'll have a total of 300 cards. (We found the brown color hard to match, so we substituted white for brown.) Gather enough pens or pencils for the whole group and ask everyone to bring a Bible.

Divide the youth group into six teams, and assign them to six different sections of the Bible (for example, Genesis, Exodus, Psalms, Prophets, Gospels, Revelation). Give each team a set of 50 index cards. On one side of the cards, instruct them to write as many questions about their section as they can in 30 minutes. On the other side of the cards, have them write the answers and scripture references. For example:

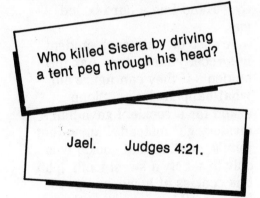

Who killed Sisera by driving a tent peg through his head?

Jael.   Judges 4:21.

Gather the group and place the cards in six piles, by color. Have each team choose a game piece and determine who goes first, etc. Follow the rules of Trivial Pursuit, adapting the following special rules: Landing on your own color gives you an extra roll; After consultation, a group's agreed-upon answer must be prefaced by the announcement, "Our answer is . . ."

While this variation of Trivial Pursuit is great fun, it also is educational. Since most information will be learned during the question-writing phase, this game is preferable to purchasing prepared Bible questions from another source.

—Walter Mees

Variations

1. Read the answers on each of the cards and see if the participants can guess the questions!

2. Host a biblical trivia bowl. Divide the youth group into two teams. The teams compete with each other to answer the questions on the game cards. Flip a coin to see which team goes first. Ask that team a question. If they answer correctly, they receive a point; if they answer incorrectly, the other team tries to answer the question. After the trivia bowl, serve refreshments such as bowls of ice cream, bowls of grapes, or bowls of Jell-O!

Your Ideas and Variations

_____
_____
_____
_____
_____
_____
_____
_____
_____

GIFTS

106

The Wisdom of God
TOPIC: PRAYER

Even though we sin, God still calls us his children. He promises to answer our prayers. All we have to do is ask and know that he will answer. In answer to our prayers, he gives us love gifts—just as a loving parent gives to his or her children.

You'll need a pencil and a piece of paper for each person. Then wrap several mystery gifts: a nickel in a small box with a question mark on the outside, or a stone in a paper sack. On a table, place the mystery gifts, a plate of cookies, a bag of candy, an orange and a hard-boiled egg.

As the young people enter the room, give them a pencil and piece of paper. Ask each student to write his or her name on the paper. Let the students walk around the table, decide which item they want, put their name next to the item and return to their seats.

Read Matthew 7:7-11. Talk about God's wisdom and his love for us. We can and should go to

God on a daily basis and ask him not only for guidance, but for the things we want. Talk about parents and how they show their love for their children.

Go to the table and read the names aloud one by one.

"John asked for a cookie." Hand John a mystery box with the nickel inside.

"Mary asked for a mystery gift." Hand Mary an orange.

"Ben asked for a piece of candy." Hand Ben a hard-boiled egg.

And so on until each student has received one item. Ask the students if they can figure out what happened. Say, "John asked for a cookie. I gave him a mystery gift instead. I knew that John's wanting that cookie was only to satisfy a sweet tooth. John has cookies at home, so I gave him something far better than what he asked for. I know that John will be unselfish and wise in spending that nickel.

"I gave Mary an orange. She can either eat it or make orange juice with it. Mary asked for a mystery gift but I knew something that Mary didn't. The mystery gift that Mary chose was a stone.

"I gave Ben a hard-boiled egg because Ben is going to be very hungry before lunch time. That egg will keep him going. Ben asked for a piece of candy but that would not have satisfied his appetite as well. (And so on.)

"Your prayers are always answered, although they are not always answered in exactly the way you're hoping. You have to learn to look for the blessings. Look to God as your loving Father. He doesn't want to withhold anything from you. Remember that God knows more than you do and he knows what's best for you. He will not give you anything that will be harmful to you. It's not wrong to ask your heavenly Father for what you want. However, every prayer should end with these words: 'Not my will, Lord, but yours.' That way you'll be able to accept God's answers to your prayers. And you're not just saying 'Gimme, gimme' like a greedy child. You're acknowledging the truth that God will give you only good things. There is a saying: 'Be careful what you ask for. You may get it.' What kinds of things could you ask for, that if you got them it would be disastrous?"

Allow several minutes for discussion. Then close with a prayer thanking God for being a wise and loving Father. Thank him for knowing the things that are best for us.

—E. Jane Mall

Variations

1. Gather everyone in a circle.

Have each person tell of a time he or she prayed for something and didn't get it. What happened? Did God answer the prayer in another way? Explain.

2. Ask everyone to keep a prayer journal for three months. Each day, have the kids record their prayer requests. Have them mark the date the prayer was answered and the way it was answered. For example, "April 3: I prayed that my brother would drive safely to college." "April 4: My brother's trip went smoothly. He arrived safe and sound."

After a few months, discuss the journals. Talk about all of the answered prayers. Are there some unanswered prayers? How long should we wait for God to answer? How do the journals help us be aware of God's action in our lives?

Jesus says all of our prayers will be answered. Read and discuss these verses: Matthew 7:7;

21:22; John 14:13; 16:24; James 4:2.

Remind the kids to balance their prayers with praise and thanksgiving for a gracious, loving Father.

Your Ideas and Variations

_____
_____
_____
_____
_____
_____
_____
_____
_____
_____
_____
_____
_____

GLOVES

107

God Fills Our Lives
TOPIC: INCARNATION

Help kids visualize how God fills our lives with his love. Gather several types of gloves such as those used for formal outings, skiing, working or cleaning. Place a wad of paper in the wrist of one glove. Display them on a table in front of the room.

Invite the youth group members to gather around the table and look at the gloves. Discuss the types of gloves, where and how they could be used. Say, "Right now these gloves are not doing their job, because they are empty. There is no life in them. Just like our lives when we don't allow God to fill us."

Ask a volunteer to read John 3:3. Say, "Each of us was created and born into this world. Jesus talks about a second birth—to be born from above. This happens when we let God fill our empty lives with his love and promises."

Ask another volunteer to read Galatians 2:20. Explain, "We are crucified with Christ. That means that he lives in us. Sometimes because of our human nature, fear and sin get in the way of God using us fully. We want God to use us, but only on our terms. It is like sticking one finger in this glove and expecting to get full use out of it. (Demonstrate.)

"Sin blocks the way for God to get into our lives. (Demonstrate by attempting to put your hand into the glove with the wad of paper in it.)

"To have a full, meaningful life, let God fill you. Ask for forgiveness and trust him for all of your needs. (Demonstrate by taking out the paper and putting your hand into the glove. Shake someone's hand or pat someone on the back.) Let God live, in you and through you."

Distribute a pencil and piece of paper to each of the group members. Have each one trace his or her hand on the paper. Point out that there are different types of people just as there are different types of gloves. But God wants to fill all of us.

Ask the kids to write in their hand outline one way that they will let God fill them and use them this next week. For example, "I will pray every night this week and ask God to give me patience with my little brother." Or, "I will offer to help the youth pastor plan the upcoming talent show."

Have the youth group members take home their hand outlines as a reminder to let God use them every day of their lives.

—Mary E. Albert

Variations

1. Make puppets out of the fingers of the old gloves. Decorate them with yarn and fabric; use a marker to make faces on the finger tips. Create "finger plays" to illustrate how God fills our lives.

2. Give each group member a handful of clay. Have the kids roll the clay flat, then make a print of their hand. Using a pencil or other sharp object, have them carve into the clay, "Jesus molds my life."

Your Ideas and Variations

_____
_____
_____
_____
_____
_____
_____
_____
_____
_____
_____
_____
_____
_____
_____
_____
_____
_____

108

God's Protecting Armor
TOPIC: CHRISTIAN LIVING

Our walk through life is warfare. The Christian must be equipped to win the battle. Help the young people learn that God has provided armor for us: truth, righteousness, the peace of God.

On a table, place as many of the following items as possible (or pictures of the items): potholders, gloves, calorie counter, dropcloth, suntan oil, umbrella, ski mask, ChapStick, rain boots. Ask the students to look over the items on the table. Then hold up each item and ask:

● From what is this used to protect us?

● What are the things that we need to be protected from?

● What do you encounter in your daily life that you need protection from?

● How do you protect yourself? Do you fight? carry a gun?

Ask a volunteer to read Ephesians 6:11-20. Discuss how we are to arm ourselves with truth. We can do that through Bible study. We are to put on the breastplate of righteousness. We can do that through prayer—asking the Holy Spirit to help us. We are to use the shield of faith. We can do that by knowing what we believe— what our faith has done for us. We are to wear a helmet of salvation. We can do this by knowing that we are saved. Ask the kids to think of other ways we can protect ourselves with the "armor of salvation."

Ask each student for a quick yes-or-no answer to the question, "Are you saved?" All should answer with a resounding yes! However, some may say: "I hope so" or "Well, I'm trying."

Assure them, "If you are a Christian and you accept Jesus Christ as your Savior, you are saved. You do not have to hope for salvation, you have it. You can't earn it, you already have it.

"Before you use a potholder, you make sure it is thick enough to withstand heat. Before you use an umbrella, you make sure it will open and that there are no holes in it. We can also test our faith. We can put on the armor of God . . . go through all the avenues that are open to us. Does this mean that evil or tragedy or sadness will never touch us? Of course not. Just because we have an umbrella, doesn't mean it will never rain. But it won't rain on us. We won't get wet. Because of our faith, we can withstand anything."

—E. Jane Mall

Variations

1. Ask the young people to each choose an item from the table. Have them adapt each item as a part of their "armor of righteousness." For example, a person could choose the rain boots and say, "I put on these boots to protect myself from the muddy puddles of sin, remembering that Jesus died to save me from my sins." Or, "I put on these gloves and work hard to make the glory of the Lord known to all." Have fun with the adaptations!

2. Ask for a volunteer. Have the kids dress him or her in a full set of armor using the items on the table. For example, the volunteer could spread suntan oil on his or her arms; wear the ski mask, gloves and rain boots; hold the umbrella in one hand; and hold the potholder in the other hand. Adapt Ephesians 6:11-20 to describe this new set of armor.

Your Ideas and Variations

_____
_____
_____
_____
_____
_____
_____
_____
_____
_____
_____

GOLF CLUBS

109

Night Owl Golf
TOPIC: GAMES

Most teenagers like to play miniature golf. Here's a way to play it with an interesting little twist.

Arrange with the manager of a miniature golf course to let your youth group come after hours to play a golf game in the dark. Ask the youth group members to meet at the church. Carpool to the golf course and let everybody select clubs and balls. Divide into groups of four and give each foursome a flashlight. Instruct them as follows:

"We are going to golf in the

dark. A person from each foursome shines the flashlight directly on the hole. Do not light the entire green; you may as well play with the lights on. There will be no stroke limits for the course. In other words, don't pick up the ball after five or six strokes. Scores of 10, 12 or higher won't be unusual. As in any golf match, lowest score wins!"

At the end of the activity, give prizes for lowest score, highest score and craziest technique. Prizes can include a candle and match, a pair of sunglasses or a light bulb!

—Thomas F. Bronson

Variations

1. After Night Owl Golf, gather the group members for a star-gazing study. Discuss God's heavenly creations; or discuss the shepherds' wonder and amazement when they saw the Bethlehem star; or discuss God's fulfilled promise to Abraham, "I will multiply your descendants as the stars of heaven" (Genesis 22:17).

2. Play miniature golf during the day—blindfolded!

Your Ideas and Variations

_____

_____

_____

_____

_____

_____

_____

_____

_____

_____

_____

_____

GRASS SKIRTS

110

Hip Charade
TOPIC: GAMES/PARTY IDEAS

Plan a Hawaiian luau with your youth group. Organize a pig roast and have everyone bring fruit such as oranges, bananas, coconuts and pineapples. Open the luau with activities like this one. It doesn't require much preparation or many materials. All you need are several grass skirts, 3×5 cards and pencils. Buy the grass skirts at a costume shop or novelty store.

Divide into teams of five. Give each team 10 3×5 cards and a pencil. Ask them to write 10 different Hawaiian-type words (one per card). For example, volcano, coconut, islands, etc.

Collect the cards, shuffle them and place them in a pile at the front of the room. Ask for one volunteer per team to come to the front and put on a grass skirt. Select one of the cards and show the word to the "dancers" only. The dancers will now stand in front of their teams and spell out the word, one letter at a time, simply by using their hips. For example, the dancers could form the letter "Z" by moving their hips to the right, diagonally back to the left, then to the right again. When the teams guess the correct letter, the dancers nod. If the teams guess incorrectly, the dancers shake their heads. No other signs or signals are permitted. The first team to correctly guess the word wins that round. The person who guesses correctly gets to dance.

Play several rounds of Hip Charade. The winning team members can don the grass skirts and serve dinner to the hungry group members.

—Tim Smith

Variations

1. Make a grass skirt by attaching 4-foot strips of green, crepe paper streamers to a 4-foot-by-4-inch strip of fabric. Place the skirt around the waist of a "dancer" and secure the ends with a safety pin.

2. Make a grass skirt by stapling strips of newspaper to a 4-foot-by-4-inch piece of fabric. Spray on green paint for that "authentic grass look"!

Your Ideas and Variations

_____

_____

_____

_____

_____

_____

_____

_____

_____

_____

_____

_____

GREETING CARDS

111

Giant Greeting Cards
TOPIC: OUTREACH/CHRISTMAS

Greeting cards serve as ways to express our feelings to one another on significant days such as birthdays, anniversaries and holidays. This project will enable the youth group to express their feelings to the community. The goal is to create the largest greeting card your community has ever seen.

After the kids decide which holiday they want to focus on, discuss possible location sites. A shopping mall would be an ideal spot for your giant card. The youth group should get permission to display the card from the location's manager.

Have a committee of young people create the basic design and assemble the necessary supplies. Be certain each youth group member participates in the actual making of the card and have them each sign the card when it's finished.

Think big! Make a 4-foot-by-8-foot card out of two pieces of plywood hinged together. Cover the plywood with a collage of old greeting cards. On white posterboard, write a colorful greeting and include the name of your church. The kids might also like to add an appropriate scripture. Glue this on top of the collage.

The giant card is a bold, creative, sparkling witness to the community. Store the giant card and use it each year.

—Arlo R. Reichter

Variations

1. Leave a majority of open space on the oversized card. Invite people in the community to tape up their greeting cards to others—a cheery way to extend holiday greetings.

2. Create a colossal Christmas card for your church.

3. Deliver a giant, bright card to an ill member of your group. The sight of the colorful creation will lead him or her to the road of recovery.

Your Ideas and Variations

_____
_____
_____
_____
_____
_____
_____
_____
_____
_____
_____
_____

"Behold, I Bring You Good Tidings of Great Joy! . . ."

NOW YOU CAN SEND YOUR GOOD TIDINGS to a brother or sister in Christ, neighbors, friends, or relatives who live nearby by sending them a Singing Christmas Card!

Your part:
- Provide the card
- Give a donation of $5 or more
- Fill out registration form

Our part:
- Hand deliver the card
- Sing a Christmas carol

Proceeds:
- Will go toward the purchase of a wheelchair for the local nursing home.

112

Singing Christmas Cards
TOPIC: CHRISTMAS/FUND RAISING

This is a great way for your kids to make money as well as have a lot of fun at Christmas time. Singing Christmas cards are very much like singing telegrams.

Have the people of your church buy a Christmas card and sign it. The youth group then delivers the card and sings a Christmas carol. The giver is asked to give a donation of $5 or more. Following are examples of a flier and the registration form that we gave to our congregation members:

Singing Christmas Card Registration Form

Giver's name_____
Donation _____ Date _____
Name of recipient _____
Address _____
_____ Phone _____
Best time to deliver_____

Please return this form along with your check by December 10 to the church office.
Singing Christmas Cards will be delivered on December 13, between 7 and 9 p.m. Exceptions will be made on an approval/availability basis.

The money you earn can go toward the youth group program, missions, world hunger or needy people in your congregation. The kids have a good time and are able to support a worthy cause. It gives Christmas caroling a whole new twist!

—Jeffrey A. Collins

Variations

1. As a group, design a large, colorful Christmas card from two sides of a refrigerator box. Cut and fold the box to create a card-like effect. Use bright tempera paints or wrapping paper to add pictures and words on the front. On the inside, cut holes for people's heads. The kids stand behind the card, stick their heads through the holes and sing the Christmas carols (**Try This One . . . Strikes Again**, Group Books).

Your Ideas and Variations

_____
_____
_____
_____
_____
_____
_____
_____
_____
_____
_____
_____
_____
_____

HATS

113

Christian Boasting
TOPIC: SELF-IMAGE

We all want to accomplish something in life, even if it's simply finding happiness. This study will help the young people seek self-esteem and a sense of accomplishment in God, rather than in self or the world. It offers positive encouragement of the self, especially for those with a confused, overblown or crippled self-image.

Gather *lots* of hats, at least as many hats as you have group members. Hats should represent vocations such as a carpenter, policeman, fireman, construction worker, nurse, businessman, football player, baseball player, farmer, cowboy, artist, graduate, soldier, etc. Toy hats work fine and are more amusing. You also will need pencils and paper.

Ask everyone to select a hat, put it on and take a seat. Then ask each person to briefly tell why he or she chose the particular hat.

Say, "Every person needs something he or she can do well,

something he or she can contribute to society. Everybody wants to feel needed by others."

Ask the kids to imagine they are actually the characters represented by their hats. Then ask what things their character might boast about. Where would he or she find his or her security? For example, an artist might find security in recognition. The artist could boast of his or her first private art exhibit.

Ask a volunteer to read Jeremiah 9:23-24. Explain that this passage is a part of Jeremiah's declaration of the punishment to come to the people of Judah for their sin. Jeremiah says the Lord offers an alternative to his people, calling them to trust him rather than their own strength or skill or position in society. He shook the foundations of Judah's security with this proclamation, but did not leave Judah without hope. He told them real security could be found only in their God.

Divide into three small groups. Assign each group one of the false boasts of Jeremiah 9:23: wisdom, might (or strength), riches. Each group must come up with modern-day examples of their boast. Explain that "wisdom" can refer to a skill, quickness or knowledge. "Might" can refer to power, authority or athletics. "Riches" can include any area of abundance or over-indul-

gence. A modern-day example of "riches" could be, "My name is Max Millions. I am a self-made millionaire. I began with my own business in carpentry and made a fortune by the time I was 24."

Ask the groups to report their examples. Select some examples from each group and discuss the security of those individuals. The ultimate test of one's security is death. How does their boast hold up against the enemy death? If a person is secure because he made a fortune while he was young, can that person take that fortune with him when he dies?

Compare these boasts to Jeremiah 9:24. Does it stand the test of death? How can we find security in knowing God? How can we be secure in understanding his kindness, justice and righteousness?

Ask each young person to pinpoint a particular boast or center of security in his or her life. For example, first-string quarterback, car-owner, popular, honor student. Allow a time of reflection. Then, ask everyone to abandon his or her hat in a pile in the center of the room. Tell group members this symbolizes the casting away of their greatest earthly boast. They can be almost anything in life they choose, but they can find security in only one place.

Encourage the kids to commit

themselves to God. Say, "In God you will find your greatest boast, never in your own accomplishments, but in the accomplishments of God within you."

Brainstorm ways to understand and know the Lord (prayer, Bible study, fellowship). Ask each young person to select one idea to implement in his or her life; then close with a prayer of commitment.

—Mark Reed

Variations

1. Give the youth group members cardboard, yarn, newspapers, construction paper, magazines, scissors, crayons and glue. Instruct them each to make a hat that describes one of their goals in life. For example, a person could make a mortarboard out of cardboard and a tassle out of yarn and say, "A goal of mine is to graduate from college."

2. Go to a fast-food restaurant and gather a cardboard crown for each youth group member. If you can't find the crowns at a restaurant, make them out of yellow posterboard. Cut out the crown, curl it into a hat shape, then staple the sides. Crown each youth group member and say, "God has crowned you with many blessings. You are his child."

Your Ideas and Variations

_____
_____
_____
_____
_____
_____
_____
_____
_____
_____
_____

114

The Mad Hatter
TOPIC: GAMES

Plan a crazy party for your group around the theme of "hats." Require that everyone wear a hat to get in. Encourage the youth group members to come up with their own hat creations. Offer prizes for the biggest, smallest, cutest, and the most original. You'll be amazed at what you'll find on their heads when they arrive.

Secure two or three large cardboard boxes and cut round holes in the top, big enough to stick your head completely through. Have a couple of sponsors and the youth minister put their heads through the openings. Place party hats on their heads. This is where the fun begins! From a distance of 10 feet, everyone gets three chances to knock the party hats off with 3-inch Nerf balls. The results are hilarious!

Keep score as follows:

- 1,000 points if the hat is knocked off in one throw
- 500 points in two throws
- 250 points in three throws

Whoever has the most points after three rounds, is the winner.

For refreshments, serve sundaes in plastic baseball hats, which can be purchased from any novelty store.

—Tommy Baker

Variations

1. Ask the kids to bring hats representative of the vocations of their parents or other relatives. Discuss the importance of each vocation in our society.

—Arlo R. Reichter

2. Display the hats in the church. Near the display, place a poster that reads, "This church ministers daily through the people who wear these hats."

—Arlo R. Reichter

Your Ideas and Variations

115

Ready for Action!
TOPIC: GAMES

Ready for Action! is a game where there are no losers—only winners and lots of fun.

Before your group meets, write down a list of activities for the kids to do (see the following suggestions). Cut up the list, separating the activities, and place the pieces in a hat.

Seat the kids in a circle, pass around the hat and have each member draw one activity. Ask each person to read the activity out loud, then act it out in the middle of the group. Within a few minutes the group will be roaring with laughter.

20 Suggested Activities
- Hug somebody in the room.
- Act like a puppet on a string.
- Tell a joke.
- Pretend you're taking a bath or shower in the middle of the room.
- Select somebody else to sing a Christmas carol with you.
- Recite a nursery rhyme.
- Imitate a comic strip character until somebody guesses the character's identity.
- Behave like a duck for 45 seconds.
- Say something nice about three different people in the room.
- Shake hands with two other people in the room.
- Pantomime a 2-year-old child taking a bone away from a German Shepherd dog.
- Walk from one end of the room to the other with a dime between your knees.
- Act like an egg being cracked and fried.
- Do an impression of a well-known celebrity; identify the person first.
- Confer with another person and make up a short poem about the group leader.
- Select a few people to aid you in presenting a scene from a popular Bible story such as Jonah and the whale.
- Draw a picture of yourself and give it to somebody else in the room.
- Find something in your pocket or purse to give as a gift to the person on your left—even if it's a penny.
- Challenge another person in the room to a bubble gum contest: Who can blow the biggest bubble?
- Retell the story of **Goldilocks and the Three Bears**, using the names of four other people in the room as the bears and Goldilocks.

—Sherry Westergard

Variations

1. Make the questions correspond to a meeting's topic or a retreat's theme.

2. Look through a cookbook for a recipe for fortune cookies. Place one of these questions in each cookie. Be prepared for a fun refreshment time!

Your Ideas and Variations

_____
_____
_____
_____
_____
_____
_____
_____
_____
_____
_____
_____

HEADSTONES

116

R.I.P.
TOPIC: DEATH/ETERNAL LIFE

For a good discussion about the value of life, talk about death.

Decorate your meeting room to look like a funeral parlor. Dim the lights, set chairs in rows and light candles. Ask the leaders to dress in black and adopt the somber, serious manner of a funeral director.

Gather pens, bright-colored markers, magazines, somber music and a record player. On newsprint, write the discussion questions. Post them in a prominent place. Make copies of the following headstone drawing—use different headings such as R.I.P. (Rest in Peace), Here Lies, In Memory Of, etc.

Have the music playing as youth group members enter the room. Ask them to sit in silence. Give them each a headstone drawing, pen and magazine to write on.

Have each person think about his or her death for a few minutes. Ask the members to write a personal epitaph. Explain that an epitaph is a brief statement usually inscribed on a tombstone. Allow 15 to 20 minutes.

Divide into groups of eight to 10 people. Have each person share his or her epitaph. Ask the groups to discuss these questions:

● Are you living in a way that you want to be remembered? Explain.

● What changes would you like to make?

● By whom do you want to be remembered? For what?

● Who has died the way you expect to die?

● Share some examples of what another person's death has meant to you.

● Describe your funeral. Who would you like to have attend your funeral? Who would you like to have deliver the eulogy?

● What are some fears you have about death and dying?

Close with a prayer service on the theme of life, death and resurrection. Ask volunteers to read these scripture passages: Micah 6:8; John 3:11-21; Romans 8:18-25.

Give the group members each a bright-colored marker. Have them write in bold letters across their headstone drawings: "JESUS DIED FOR ME. I HAVE ETERNAL LIFE!"

—Mary Kay Fitzpatrick

Variations

1. Rather than decorating your meeting room as a funeral parlor, arrange for your youth group to visit a funeral parlor in your community. Ask the director to tell the kids about the steps for planning a funeral.

2. Before the meeting, take your group to a nearby cemetery. Ask the kids to walk silently around the area and think about death. The walk through the cemetery will cause everyone to think about the finality of our life on earth; the meeting will help the kids think about our everlasting life in heaven.

Your Ideas and Variations

_____
_____
_____
_____
_____
_____
_____
_____
_____
_____
_____
_____
_____
_____

HYMNALS

117

Hymn-Sing
TOPIC: SINGING

Make a joyful noise to the Lord by hosting a Hymn-Sing with your church.

Have your youth group members look in your church's hymnals and research the dates when some of the hymns were written, the composers, and the countries where the hymns originated. Have them look for as many details as they can. Ask the kids to write a brief history on each of the hymns.

Plan a Hymn-Sing and invite the congregation to come exercise their vocal cords. Have the kids each introduce a hymn by reading the history. Then encourage everyone to sing to the Lord their familiar, favorite songs!

—Mardie H.C. MacDonald

Variations

1. Have your youth group choose one hymn per month, research its history and practice singing it. One Sunday per month have the kids introduce the hymn and sing it to the con-gregation.

2. Sponsor a Hymn-Sing using new, popular songs. Find these tunes in a book such as **Songs**, by Yohann Anderson, Songs and Creations Inc., San Anselmo, CA 94960. Really make a joyful noise by accompanying the songs with guitars, tambourines, drums and rhythm sticks.

Your Ideas and Variations

_____

_____

_____

_____

_____

_____

_____

_____

_____

_____

_____

_____

INDEX CARDS

118

Accepting Advice
TOPIC: AUTHORITY/ADVICE

This meeting focuses on authority and advice. It will help the kids decide who they should listen to; and help them learn that Jesus is the true authority.

Have on hand enough 3×5 cards for each member of the youth group. On half of the cards write situations such as:

● You have just received your first driver's license.

● You are to leave tomorrow for college.

● You are getting married tomorrow.

● You start a new job tomorrow.

● You get your first pair of glasses tomorrow.

● Your parents are divorcing tomorrow.

On the other half of the cards write:

● I do not have a driver's license, but this is my advice to you:

● I have never been to college, but this is my advice to you:

● I have never been married,

but this is my advice to you:

● And so on for each situation.

Divide the class into two groups and hand out the cards. The group with the first batch of cards will stay in the meeting room. They can discuss how they will cope with the situation on their cards.

The group with the second batch of cards will go into another room with you. Tell them to write on their cards the advice they would give. For example, observe speed limits; write home often, etc. You will need to help them with this part of the exercise. Give pieces of advice that they might not know about or think of on their own.

Have the two groups meet together again and match cards. Pair off so that the "advisors" can give their advice. After 10 to 15 minutes ask:

● How did you feel taking advice from someone who didn't know any more about the subject (at least firsthand) than you did?

● Could you accept the advice? Why or why not?

● Would you follow the advice given?

● If the person had experienced these things would you have found it easier to accept the advice?

Then tell the members, "I am the leader. I know about all of these things and have experienced most of them. I helped the advisors with the advice they gave you. In other words, I gave them the authority to advise you. In what other areas do we have to accept advice—and truth—even though the person teaching may not have experienced what they are teaching?" Answers could include the pastor who tells us about heaven and has never been there. Parents who tell us about the dangers of drugs, sinful life and have never used drugs or lived bad, sinful lives. Ask for more examples.

Conclude by saying, "These people have the authority to teach and advise us and we should listen to them. If you don't listen, or follow their advice, who will suffer? Who will be hurt? They can't force you to listen or heed their advice. All they can do is give it. Listen to them and grow."

—E. Jane Mall

Variations

1. Write each of the following case studies on separate 3×5 cards. Divide the young people into small groups and assign each a case study. Have the members decide what to do in each situation. Discuss the case studies as a large group.

● You are at a clothing store and you see your close friend put a scarf into her purse without paying for it. What do you do?

● Your friend tells you that he sometimes gets so depressed that he wants to kill himself. What do you do? What do you say?

2. Distribute a piece of paper and a pencil to each of the youth group members. Ask them to think of a problem they are having right now. Then have them write a letter to God asking for advice about handling the problem. For example:

Dear God,
My best friend has been drinking a lot lately. It's more than "just for fun". She drinks even when we aren't at a party. What should I do?
Love,
Kim

Gather the papers, then randomly redistribute them. Have the kids read the letter, think of how God would advise the person, then write an answer. Discuss the letters in small groups.

Your Ideas and Variations

_____

_____

_____

119

Build a House of Support
TOPIC: GROUP BUILDING

Support among youth group members is crucial for effective youth ministry. Use the following items to help illustrate this important concept: matches, pencils, index cards, a candle and a camera. On an index card, write the word "Christ."

Gather your group in a circle around a lighted candle and read aloud Ephesians 2:19-22. Note especially verse 22 which speaks of how people can be built into a dwelling place for God in the Spirit. Then place the card in the center of the circle with the word "Christ" written on it. As verse 20 explains, Christ is the cornerstone of the church.

Give each person an index card and pencil. Ask them to write on the card what they will do to support the youth group. What will they do to make the group a "strong building?" For example, "I will come to youth group every week." After all have written, you go first. Read aloud your card, fold it in half and stand it on top of the "Christ" card in the center of the circle. This card becomes the first support for the house that will be built. Continue around the circle with each person reading aloud his or her card and then adding it to the house structure. Build the house in levels by folding some cards in half and standing them on the ends. These form supports for other cards laid flat across the folded cards. Take a picture of the house when completed and display it in your meeting room.

Conclude this activity by standing in a tight circle. Have the group members turn to the right and put their hands on the waist of the person in front of them. On the count of three, everybody sits down on the knees of the person behind him or her. Pray in this position, thanking God for the group and the support you give each other.

—Kathi B. Finnell

Variations

1. Ask the teenagers to invite their families to a youth group meeting. Use this activity to close the session. Have each

family member write on a 3×5 card how he or she will support the family. For example, "I will help plan a family night once a week. This evening will be for fun, laughter and time together—as a family." Have the members discuss the cards, then build a house with them—a house that is filled with concern, caring and support.

2. Use this idea to help the kids commit to a goal after any session. For example, if the topic is helping your neighbors, a group member could write a goal such as, "I will sit with the new person at school during lunch, every day next week." Or if the topic is using your talents, a person could write a goal such as, "Since I write well, I will write to my grandmother this week. It's been a long time since she's heard from me!"

Have the group members write their commitments on the cards, then build the support structure. Say that the youth group is a place for support as the kids reach out to others.

Your Ideas and Variations

_____
_____
_____
_____
_____
_____
_____

120

Mother's Day Booklet
TOPIC: MOTHER'S DAY/FAMILY

Help your youth group give special gifts on Mother's Day. Three weeks prior to Mother's Day, have one of your young people announce during Sunday worship that the youth group will be compiling "quotes by mothers" or "special things that mothers do." These will be typed up and printed in a small booklet to be handed out on Mother's Day.

Distribute 3×5 cards to the congregation members. Ask them to write on their card something special about their mother (limit it to two or three sentences). Have them give the cards to a designated member of the youth group, or put the cards in the collection plate. Unless they wish to, members need not sign their names.

Ask several of the young people to design an appropriate cover for the booklet. Ask others to type the quotes, copy and compile the booklet. Include in the booklet, scripture passages about mothers such as Mark 7:10, a poem about mothers, a song about mothers, and a prayer for all mothers. At the end of the church service on Mother's

Day, have two youth group members distribute the booklets

This is a touching way to show mothers in your congregation how special they really are.
—Karen Musitano

Variations

1. Do this same project for Father's Day.

2. Plan a Mother's Day potluck and fashion show. Ask everybody to bring food and a table setting. Request that the women wear an outfit that their mother would have worn when she was a teenager. Enjoy the food and fashion show of "styles through the ages."

Your Ideas and Variations

_____
_____
_____
_____
_____
_____
_____
_____
_____

121

The Oops Method
TOPIC: BIBLE STUDY

This method teaches scripture concepts to your class members that they probably think they al-

ready know. The object is for the kids to make the necessary corrections to seemingly correct verses.

Find 10 familiar verses of scripture such as the examples included here. On separate 3×5 cards, write a couple of the verses correctly. Write the rest incorrectly, maybe omitting or changing one word or perhaps an entire phrase. Following is an example of a scripture assignment for Matthew 5:38-48:

● **Verse 38:** "You have heard that it was said, 'An eye for an eye, and a tooth for a tooth.' "

● **Verse 39:** "And I say to you, that is exactly right. Don't let people walk on you."

● **Verse 40:** "And if any one would sue you at the law, provide for yourself adequate counsel so that you will not be taken for granted."

● **Verse 41:** "And if any one forces you to go one mile, impress upon him the unfairness of his demand."

● **Verse 42:** "Be careful who you give money to and make sure that you don't lend money to any one without good credit."

● **Verse 43:** "You have heard that it was said, 'You shall love your neighbor and hate your in-laws.' "

● **Verse 44:** "But I say unto you, 'Bless those of your own nationality, except for those who curse you, have nothing to do with those who hate you, pray that you never come in contact with those who despitefully use and persecute you.' "

● **Verse 45:** "So that you may be sons of your Father who is in heaven; for he makes his sun rise on the good, and sends rain on the just."

● **Verse 46:** "For if you love those who do not love you, what sense does that make? We should certainly be more kind to those who love us."

● **Verse 47:** "And if you salute only your brethren, what more are you doing than others? Do not even the publicans do this?"

● **Verse 48:** "You, therefore, must be as perfect as you possibly can be, ever trying to follow the example of your Father who is in heaven who himself is perfect."

If you use the King James Version, do so in your "incorrections" also. They will sound more correct and be more difficult to spot.

Gather in "listening research teams." Have the kids combine their knowledge to try to come up with the best correction possible.

After 15 to 20 minutes, allow the team members to open their Bibles to check for the correct verses. The kids will find that they do not know the scriptures as well as they thought. They will remember The Oops Method for a long time!

—Gary G. Jenkins

Variations

1. Let the group members choose their favorite scripture and create subtle boo-boos for the others to try and catch.

2. Design an "Oops Method Game Booklet." Combine all of the scriptures the kids "fixed" and have them design a cover. For a fun fund raiser, sell the booklets.

3. One week, in the church bulletin, print a passage filled with subtle boo-boos. Encourage congregation members to make the corrections (without consulting their Bibles), then phone the church office with the number of errors they caught. Give the one with the most caught errors "The Theological Proofreader Award." In the next bulletin write a brief paragraph about the sharp, detail-oriented congregation member!

Your Ideas and Variations

_____
_____
_____
_____
_____
_____
_____
_____
_____
_____

122

Talking With Jesus
TOPIC: BIBLE STUDY

The purpose of this session is to give the group members a chance to personalize scripture. Before the session begins, write this question on a chalkboard: Wouldn't it be wonderful to talk with Jesus today? Gather 3×5 cards, pencils and Bibles.

Announce to the youth group members that they are going to talk with Jesus. Begin with prayer and ask God to help each person discover something of value from the session.

Ask the students how they think it is possible to talk with Jesus today. When someone suggests prayer, agree with him or her and then say that Jesus taught the disciples to address the Father directly in prayer. Help the students discover how they can talk to Jesus by asking these questions:

● Can the Bible help us talk to Jesus? Explain.

● Which books of the Bible are more likely to bring us into a dialogue with Jesus?

● Which books tell what Jesus did and said while he was here on earth?

Explain to the teenagers that they can personalize the Gospels by substituting their names for the names of people to whom Jesus was speaking. Pass out Bibles, pencils and 3×5 cards. Assign each teenager one of these verses:

● "He said to them, 'Why are you afraid? Have you no faith?' And they were filled with awe, and said to one another, 'Who then is this, that even wind and sea obey him?' " (Mark 4:40-41).

● "The Pharisees came and began to argue with him, seeking from him a sign from heaven, to test him. And he sighed deeply in his spirit, and said, 'Why does this generation seek a sign? Truly, I say to you, no sign shall be given to this generation' " (Mark 8:11-12).

● "And they came to Capernaum; and when he was in the house he asked them, 'What were you discussing on the way?' But they were silent; for on the way they had discussed with one another who was the greatest" (Mark 9:33-34).

● "Now it happened that as he was praying alone the disciples were with him; and he asked them, 'Who do the people say that I am?' And they answered, 'John the Baptist; but others say, Elijah; and others, that one of the old prophets has risen.' And he said to them, 'But who do you say that I am?' And Peter answered, 'The Christ of God' " (Luke 9:18-20).

● "Jesus said to the twelve, 'Do you also wish to go away?' Simon Peter answered him, 'Lord, to whom shall we go? You have the words of eternal life; and we have believed and have come to know, that you are the Holy One of God' " (John 6:67-69).

Say to the students, "Sometimes Jesus asks a question that you can answer in your own words from your own experiences. On one side of the 3×5 card personalize Jesus' question. On the other side of the card answer him."

For example, one girl personalized Jesus' question in John 6:67-69 like this: "Then Jesus said to Pam, 'Will you also go away?' " Pam answered the question with, "No, I will not leave because when I was in need at the lowest times of my life, you were always there to help me."

Encourage the kids to put their questions into the framework of their own personal experiences. For example, in Luke 9:18-20 Jesus could ask, "What do the kids in your school say about me?" Mark 8:11-12 could be adapted for questions about current events.

Look through a red-letter Bible edition for other verses to turn into a personal dialogue with Jesus.

Putting personal names to Jesus' teachings increases the impact of the advice. It is an adventure that the kids will talk about for a long time.

—Esther M. Bailey

Variations

1. Personalize a Proverb by rewording it to fit a current situation. For example, Proverbs 4:13 could be reworded, "Value education, try your best; education adds interest and quality to your life."

2. Personalize a Psalm. For example, Psalm 100:1 could be reworded, "Worship should be joyful. Be happy and enthusiastic as you sing, shout and play instruments for God."

Your Ideas and Variations

_____

_____

_____

_____

_____

_____

_____

_____

_____

123

Working Together
TOPIC: GROUP BUILDING

Galatians 6:1-10 talks about love for our brothers and sisters. Especially love and concern for a brother or sister in trouble. The verses also talk about meekness—being aware that we too can easily slip into sinful ways. We may need a brother or sister to help us.

Acts 15:10 discusses the law of Moses and the burden it placed upon the people. The law of Christ is not a burden. Beware of feeling superior. Test yourself and be grateful but do not become boastful.

We do not stand alone. We need our brothers and sisters and they need us. We help each other; we give to each other. We should not let a brother or sister go hungry, or homeless. This is how we work together with Christ.

On 17 3×5 cards, write each of these ingredients or directions (one ingredient or direction per card):

½ cup butter
1 egg
½ teaspoon salt
1 cup chocolate chips
½ cup brown sugar
½ teaspoon vanilla
½ teaspoon soda
½ cup white sugar
1 cup flour
½ cup nuts
cream butter
beat in egg and vanilla
stir in flour, salt, soda
stir in nuts
stir in chocolate chips

drop from spoon on cookie sheet
bake 10 minutes

On 10 more 3×5 cards, write these ingredients:

4 gallons milk
1 quart molasses
½ cup chili powder
8 cups salt
5 pounds butter
10 pounds flour
1 box oatmeal
5 cups black pepper
2 dozen eggs
6 tablespoons sage

Mix all of the cards together; divide them into two groups. You also will need a plate of chocolate chip cookies.

When the students come into the room, gather them in a circle. Briefly read and discuss Galatians 6:1-10.

Divide the class into two groups; give each group a set of cards. Tell them to put the cards together and decide what recipe they have. The group who figures it out first will win a prize. Stress the prize so that each group feels they are competing against the other group.

After 10 to 15 minutes, go to each group separately and ask what they have. Of course, neither group has anything. Tell them you can't see why they haven't figured it out since there is a genuine recipe there. Give them a few more minutes.

Then ask the two groups to get together, sit in a circle and see what happens. Now they very quickly should be able to discard the unnecessary items and put together the recipe for chocolate chip cookies.

Refer to the scripture and say, "When you were divided, you could not put the correct recipe together. Once you pooled what you had you were in great shape. How does this principle work in life? in the church?"

Allow time for them to give examples. Then ask, "Are there times when we know a little but not quite enough—and someone else knows a little but not quite enough—and if we get together, it will work out?"

Allow time for them to give examples, then say, "If we have a spirit of helpfulness—of wanting to work together—we won't waste time trying to do everything ourselves. You were not told that you couldn't work together. Each group was working for that prize and you didn't even know what the prize was. Let me tell you what it was: one penny. Not a great prize. Now you have a better prize. Because you worked together you have a plate of cookies to enjoy. (Pass around the cookies.) When we compete with our fellow believers instead of wanting to help and cooperate, we end up with less than nothing: no recipe, maybe one penny. When we work together our reward is there. And we are doing the will of God, which carries its own reward."

—E. Jane Mall

Variations

1. Another game that stresses teamwork is Climbing the Walls. Divide the young people into two groups. Give each group some tape or chalk (depending on the type of wall you use). Give the group members eight minutes to see how high a mark they can make on the wall. Tell them that they only can use the wall, and others in the group, for support. Instruct the youth about the importance of using "spotters" to soften the landing if someone takes a tumble. For safety's sake, the groups should not be allowed to get higher than three people in height. Afterward, discuss these questions:

● What part did you play in this exercise?

● What did you learn from this exercise?

● What surprised you during this exercise?

● How did your group work together to accomplish the task?

2. Another game that stresses teamwork is Electric Fence.

Tie a string 5 feet off the ground between two objects that are at least 10 feet apart.

Tell the students that their goal is to get the whole group over the string without touching it. It is illegal to use the objects the string is tied to for support. Have the group members visualize an "electric field" extending from the string to the ground. If they touch the string or cross beneath it they become "electrocuted." The "shocked" individual must try again.

To prevent twisted ankles, use spotters, especially for the first few people over the fence. Don't allow the group or individuals to make uncontrolled leaps over the fence. They must be caught.

To make the exercise more difficult, don't allow the participants to talk. Afterward, discuss these questions:

● What do you see as the purpose of this exercise?

● What were some examples of teamwork you observed during this activity?

Your Ideas and Variations

_____

_____

_____

_____

_____

_____

_____

_____

_____

_____

_____

_____

INNER TUBES

124

Tube Hockey
TOPIC: WINTER/GAMES

This is a winter game that combines the sports of soccer and ice hockey. You will need to find, or purchase, an inner tube from a Mack truck tire.

We went to a baseball field after a deep snow and plowed off a huge rectangle for our Tube Hockey field. There was ice underneath the snow, which made it even more slippery. We built 4-foot snow walls all around the field for the boundaries. At each end of the field, we cut out two holes for the goals. Then we divided into two teams.

The fun began as we tried to get the tube into each other's goal by kicking it—no hands allowed. If a foot got caught in the middle of the tube, we had a tossup; we threw the tube into the air and started the game again.

The next year it didn't snow, but that didn't stop us from playing Tube Hockey. We turned a sprinkler on the field and left it to freeze overnight. It made a great Tube Hockey playing field!
—Bob Hicks

Variations

1. Use the icey field for other sports such as soccer, football or kickball. Be sure to bundle up and stay warm.

2. Plan a winter carnival at night. Play games on the field, roast hot dogs on portable grills, drink hot chocolate, and thank God for crisp, brisk winter weather.

Your Ideas and Variations

_____
_____
_____
_____
_____
_____
_____
_____
_____
_____
_____

JARS

125

Glass-Jar Collections
TOPIC: FUND RAISING

Use jars as "visible offering baskets" around your church. Before using the jars, have the youth group decide on a project and get approval from the church board. Publicize the offering project through church newsletters, posters, bulletin boards and fliers.

Place the jars at high-traffic church areas. Use posterboard to make signs describing the project. The jars could be labeled "pennies only," "nickels only," "dimes only," etc. Place a jar in the youth room and Sunday school area—young people will be certain to contribute

loose change. If you have a soft-drink machine in your church, place a jar near it to collect change received after a purchase.

The jars are a crystal-clear means in which to collect money for a youth camp, for world hunger or for a community project.

—Arlo R. Reichter

Variations

1. Fill jars with candy kisses, jellybeans or other candies; decorate the lids with fabric and ribbon. Sell the gifts as a fundraising project.

Your Ideas and Variations

_____
_____
_____
_____
_____
_____
_____
_____
_____

126

Saturation Test
TOPIC: VALUES/POSSESSIONS

How we spend our time reveals where our priorities lie. This object lesson helps kids examine their priorities and see where Christ fits into their lives.

You'll need one eyedropper and one Mason jar for every two people. You also will need red, blue, green and yellow food coloring.

Divide the youth group members into pairs; give each pair an eyedropper and a Mason jar. Ask them to fill three-fourths of the jar with water. Tell them the water represents a week of their time—roughly 112 waking hours.

Ask the pairs how many hours they spend in worship or in service to the Lord each week. Provide red food coloring and say that one drop equals one hour. Have them use the eyedroppers to place the corresponding amount of drops in the water. Discuss the pale result and how we should be more saturated with Christ.

Bring out the blue coloring; this represents the teenagers' various priorities. Have the pairs decide what the blue will represent for them: music, cars,

books, magazines, television, sports, anything to which they willingly devote a good portion of their time (school doesn't count unless the pair would go by choice). Ask them to place one blue drop into the glass for every hour spent on that priority. Let the young people comment on the result.

Continue the same process with yellow and green representing sin. Allow time for discussion. The young people will have plenty of humorous comments, but their observations provide a self-reflective lesson. Once the yellow and green are added, most of the water will be black or ugly gray, depending on the strength of the coloring used. Ask the kids where Christ is in all that mess. Can he be detected anywhere?

Say that how we spend our time reveals where we place our priorities. Priorities are changed, then, not by a mental rearrangement, but by action—a time rearrangement. The remedy for the murky water is not just more red, but less of everything else as well.

—Mark Reed

Variations

1. Help the kids prioritize their activities by having them complete the worksheet on the next page.

Priority Worksheet

List tasks and activities:	Check one:	TOP PRIORITY	SO-SO PRIORITY	NOT-IMPORTANT PRIORITY

(A copyrighted resource from **Youth Ministry Cargo**. Permission granted to copy this handout for local church use only.)

Your Ideas and Variations

_____
_____
_____
_____
_____
_____
_____
_____
_____
_____

JUGS

127

Floating Boats
TOPIC: CAMPING/GROUP BUILDING

We used plastic jugs at one of our junior high summer camps to build boats. Not toy boats—real boats.

In the spring we asked church members to bring in gallon-size, clean, empty, plastic jugs (with the caps)—we had a special room to store them. We didn't tell anyone what we were going to use them for. This sparked everyone's interest, especially the junior high kids'. By summer, we had collected 1,500 plastic jugs.

At camp, the kids had to earn their jugs by participating in a variety of contests. These contests included scripture memorization, games, cabin cleanup, etc. Different events earned the participants a different number of jugs. We waited until the middle of the week to tell the kids that we were going to build boats with the jugs. Waiting to tell them added incentive halfway through camp—they worked harder to earn more jugs.

On Friday, the plastic jugs were distributed and each cabin built a boat. They were allowed to tie logs, or other buoyant materials, to the jugs to construct their boats. Finally, we held a race down a portion of a river. Lifeguards in canoes and rowboats were present to rescue those kids whose boat sank. We removed all debris from the river and tossed it into a truck bound for the junkyard.

The campers responded enthusiastically. They can't wait to build boats again next summer!
—Tim Pontius

Variations

1. Award prizes for "best-looking boat," "most likely to float forever" or "most likely to sink in the sea." Prizes could be toy boats, nose plugs, earplugs or goggles.

2. Give each young person a plastic jug, then host a jamboree. Sing songs such as "Breathe on Me Breath of God," "They Call the Wind Maria" or "Children of the Wind." Blow into the jugs for an appropriate musical accompaniment!

Your Ideas and Variations

_____
_____
_____
_____
_____
_____

_____
_____
_____
_____
_____
_____
_____
_____

JUNK

128

Creating Something Out of Almost Nothing
TOPIC: VALUES/CREATIVITY

Here's a fun project that could result in some interesting works of art and, hopefully, lead young people to a new appreciation for things normally considered to be of little value. The project is inexpensive yet it can prove to be an invaluable experience in creativity and growth.

Invite the group members to go through their wastebaskets, garages, basements and attics, and bring the stuff they find to the next meeting. Gather up some choice stuff yourself—broken rulers or yardsticks, old clocks or watches, broken radios and other appliances, hangers, toys, etc. Also provide paste, picture wire, string, tacks, poster paints and brushes, ink markers, large pieces of corrugated cardboard (cut from boxes and cartons), magazines and newspapers.

Spread a large dropcloth or sheet of plastic on the floor for the group to put their junk on. Print in large letters on a blackboard words such as sin, death, Crucifixion, love, Resurrection, hope, and so on. Write one or more related scripture references beneath each word.

Tell the group that they're going to create an art project from the stuff on the floor, based on one of the themes printed on the board. They can work on a project individually or as a group. (Keep the groups to three or four members, otherwise some of the quieter young people won't have much input.) As they choose their theme, assign them a related scripture passage to look up and discuss. Once they

understand the passage and the theme, the group should discuss how to best express it. The art project can be a junk sculpture. collage or montage. If they choose one of the latter two forms, give them one or more pieces of heavy corrugated cardboard to use as a base. You will want to circulate among the youth to help get them started. (Getting started is usually difficult for kids who haven't done much creative artwork—once they get their idea and begin, they come up with some amazing ideas for the junk!) If you have artists in the church, use them as resources, but don't let them help the youth *too* much.

After about an hour, call the group together and ask each artist to discuss his or her project. It might be fun to first see if the group can tell what theme the artist worked from.

Single out several of the projects in which the creator had made clever use of an object. From that which was worthless the kids have fashioned something very precious.

State that too often we look at people as if they were throwaway, expendable junk. This was as true in Jesus' time as today. Ask, "Who were some of the people in Jesus' day who were regarded by the leaders of the faith as 'junk'?" If the group members can't think of anyone,

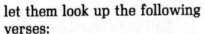

let them look up the following verses:

Matthew 9:10-13 and Luke 5:27-32; 19:1-10—Tax collectors

Matthew 12:22-32—The insane (possessed by demons)

Matthew 15:21-28—Gentile woman

Matthew 19:13-15—Children

Mark 1:40-45—Lepers

Mark 10:46-52—Blind beggar

Luke 7:36-50—Woman of the street

Luke 15—Sinners

John 4:1-42—Samaritan woman

John 8:1-11—Woman caught in adultery

Note that the Lord was able to see beyond people's sins to what they could become, as potential sons and daughters of God.

Ask the kids who could be considered junk today. Some possibilities:

- Welfare recipients
- Junkies
- Racial groups
- Elderly people
- Street people
- Unattractive people
- Homosexuals
- Communists

Ask: "How do we show that such people are 'junk'? By language? put downs? cruel humor? stereotypes? segregation? other? Are there those in your school and community who might be regarded as junk? What can we do to reach out to them?"

Close with the singing of "In Christ There Is No East or West" or "They'll Know We Are Christians by Our Love" and the reading of James 2:1-8. Say that faith, creativity and care can bring new life to what the world regards as junk.

—Ed McNulty

Variations

1. Go to a dump to collect the junk.

2. Display the projects in the church foyer.

3. Develop a Bible study around Revelation 21:5, "Behold, I make all things new." Other verses you can use are: Matthew 9:16; Mark 2:21-22; 2 Corinthians 5:17.

Your Ideas and Variations

_____
_____
_____
_____
_____
_____
_____
_____
_____
_____

KEY CHAINS

129

Driver's License Ceremony
*TOPIC: DRIVER'S LICENSES/
RESPONSIBILITY*

Getting a driver's license is one of the most significant accomplishments for teenagers today. Whenever someone in your group gets his or her license, use the following ceremony to observe this important event.

Purchase enough key chains to give one to each young person who is being honored. (We give key chains with our denomination's emblem.) Ask young people who are not being honored to volunteer to read the various leader parts and the parts labeled "All." Have an adult read the part labeled "Charge to the New Driver." The new drivers should read the parts labeled "People." Gather your group in a circle around a lighted candle and dim the lights.

Call to Celebration
Leader: "We are gathered to celebrate a crucial point of passage in the life of youth."
People: "That magical rectangular card! It symbolizes achievement! power! freedom!"
Leader: "Let us praise God for guiding this person to this moment of achievement in receiving his or her driver's license. A new freedom has been given—accompanied with powerful responsibility."
People: "Let us praise God for being with us to enjoy the freedom and to enable us to soberly assume this responsibility."

Hear God's Word
Leader: "Let us hear what guidance God's Word can give us concerning freedom and responsibility when we are behind the wheel of a car."

● "You shall not kill" (Exodus 20:13).

● "You shall love the Lord

your God with all your heart, and with all your soul, and with all your strength, and with all your mind; and your neighbor as yourself" (Luke 10:27).

● "And as you wish that men would do to you, do so to them" (Luke 6:31).

● "Live as free men, yet without using your freedom as a pretext for evil; but live as servants of God" (1 Peter 2:16).

● "Jesus said to the Jews who had believed in him, 'If you continue in my word, you are truly my disciples, and you will know the truth, and the truth will make you free' " (John 8:31-32).

● "So each of us shall give account of himself to God" (Romans 14:12).

● "He has showed you, O man, what is good; and what does the Lord require of you but to do justice, and to love kindness, and to walk humbly with your God?" (Micah 6:8).

Words of Confession and Proclamation

People: "We confess there are times we want freedom *without* responsibility. We care little for justice. We do *not* want to consider our responsibility to ourselves, to others, or to God.

"However, getting a driver's license is such a big event in our lives that we pause for a moment of reflection. God gives this moment for each of us to re-

new and restate our faith. Therefore, we can proclaim together these beliefs as Christians: Christians always choose life over death. Christians respect one another. Christians are free to live in love. Christians are responsible for others' lives and property. Our driving is an accountable act of faith.

"Yet the question remains: Will my Christian beliefs make a difference in how I drive?"

Moments of Prayer for the New Driver

Leader: "Would the person receiving his or her license to drive please sit in the middle of our circle? Those who wish may pray aloud for this person, asking for God's protection and guidance that he or she might drive with enjoyment and wisdom."

245

Charge to the New Driver
Adult Leader: "Only you will determine how you will use the power now within reach of your hands and feet. Accept this key ring as a reminder that you are loved and supported. May this love protect and guide you through any decisions or danger you may face while behind the wheel of a car."

Youth Group Affirmation
(All stand. All young people read aloud except the one who has just received the key ring.)
All: "Now that this person has reached the point in time between childhood insecurity and Social Security, he or she has acquired the right to drive legally. This means that he or she doesn't have to have parents drive on dates. Through the years, he or she has graduated from training wheels to a bicycle, and now to four wheels. This person has worked at least 15 long, hard years to receive this card. We now affirm the right of passage onto the nation's streets and highways. AMEN!"

Benediction
All: "The Lord bless you and keep you: The Lord make his face to shine upon you, and be gracious to you: The Lord lift up his countenance upon you, and give you peace" (Numbers 6:24-26).

—Kathi B. Finnell

Variations
1. Let your youth group members create ceremonies for other special occasions such as high school graduation, acceptance to a college, first job, etc.
2. Work with your pastor and create a special ceremony for baptism. Have the youth group members lead the ceremony and present a gift to the one being baptized: a banner or card, which the youth group has made.

Your Ideas and Variations
_____
_____
_____
_____
_____
_____
_____
_____
_____
_____

KITES

130

Flying High
TOPIC: SPRING/BIBLE STUDY

There is an old saying that

kites fly highest against the wind—and there is nothing like an old saying to inspire a fantastic youth program.

Ask each youth group member to purchase an inexpensive kite-making kit from a discount store. Have them decorate the kite to symbolize themselves. (Use markers to draw favorite activities, animals, food, etc.) Have the members bring the completed kites to a youth group meeting. Plan this program for a windy day, otherwise you'll have to be more creative at kite flying than you ever really wanted to be! (Go to an alternate plan in the event of no wind.)

Gather the kids and have them describe their kites. Continue with a Bible study on Romans 8 and the fact that God loves each of us very much. No obstacle can separate us from his wonderful love.

Talk about a difficult time in your life—when you had to fly your kite against the wind. Encourage the young people to share some difficult times they've experienced.

Go outside to fly your kites together. Discuss God's freeing love and how he lifts us through our difficult times and helps us grow stronger.

You also can use a kite theme in other ways. If you have a group of young people who enjoy art projects, let them design

their own kite posters from posterboard, marking pens, scissors, tape, yarn and construction paper. Use the kites to decorate the youth room. Above the kites, post a sign that says, "God lifts us up through difficult times."

Another idea is to ask each Sunday school class to design its own kite. Post these on a wall. Display the kite of the class with the largest attendance, above the others each week.

Use these kite ideas to help you create some of your own—let your imagination soar!
—Denise Turner

Variations

1. Draw the following kite on an 8½x11 piece of paper, then make copies for the youth group members:

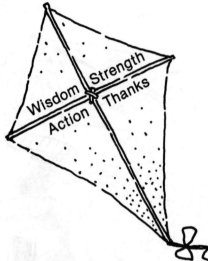

Lead your young people in this Bible study. Have them write their answers in the appropriate kite sections—discover the joy of being set free!

● **Wisdom.** Read Colossians 1:9; Proverbs 2:2-6; 9:10. Complete these two sentences: God's Spirit fills me with understanding when . . .

The key to wisdom and understanding is . . .

● **Action.** Read Colossians 1:10; James 2:18, 22, 26. Complete: Good deeds help me grow in the knowledge of the Lord by . . . List three times when your faith has come alive through your actions.

● **Strength.** Read Colossians 1:11; Ephesians 6:10-18. List three things you do to maintain a strong faith. Complete: One thing I'm not already doing that I can do to strengthen my faith is . . .

● **Thanks.** Read Colossians

1:12; Philippians 4:4-6. Complete this sentence five times: I'm thankful for . . .

Now look at your freedom-kite. Let the cross piece in the center remind you of the importance of having Jesus in the center of your life. Because of his death on the cross, you can be free!

Your Ideas and Variations

_____
_____
_____
_____
_____
_____
_____
_____
_____

LABELS

131

Personal Labels
TOPIC: AFFIRMATION/SELF-IMAGE

Why is it easier to share negative qualities about ourselves rather than positive qualities? Make it easier for your youth group members to share their positive qualities through this activity.

Gather a couple of the following items: cereal box, soup can, pop can, coffee can or other item with information on its label. You also will need tape, markers and two copies of the following handout for each person.

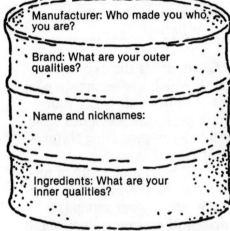

Manufacturer: Who made you who you are?

Brand: What are your outer qualities?

Name and nicknames:

Ingredients: What are your inner qualities?

(A copyrighted resource from **Youth Ministry Cargo**. Permission granted to copy this handout for local church use only.)

When the group members arrive, show them the boxes or cans and say, "These labels tell us all about the products: the name, ingredients and manufacturer. You are going to get the chance to design a label that describes you."

Distribute one copy of the handout and a marker to each person. Let the kids have a chance to describe themselves. An example is:

● Name and nicknames: Dan, "Hans," Flash.

● Manufacturer: good family, friend Kent, good church.

● Brand: blond hair, green eyes, athletic physique.

● Ingredients: energetic, consistent, caring, thoughtful.

After the participants complete the labels, share them as a large group. Then give everyone another copy of the handout. Ask the kids to write their name in the appropriate spot and tape the papers on the wall. Let the group members go around and fill out the labels with positive qualities they see in others.

Have the youth group members take both sheets home with them as a double dose of affirmation!

—Therese Caouette

NET WT. 85 LB.

Variations

1. Tape a blank piece of paper to each person's back; give each person a crayon or marker. Allow several minutes for the youth group members to write positive qualities on each person's paper such as, "You have a great smile." "You contribute so much to the group." "Your friendship brightens up my day." Let the kids take their paper home and reread it for uplifting affirmation.

2. Give each of the group members a piece of paper. Ask them to write their name on it and place it in a hat. Mix the papers and redistribute them. Have each student share something he or she appreciates about that person. Instruct each group member to keep his or her slip and pray for that person throughout the coming week (**Building Community in Youth Groups**, by Denny Rydberg, Group Books).

Your Ideas and Variations

_____
_____
_____
_____
_____
_____
_____
_____
_____
_____

LEAVES

132

Nature-Print Place Mats
TOPIC: NATURE

Creativity is the expression of ideas, which are an innate part of our individuality. Let your youth group members use their creativity in preparing Nature-Print Place Mats.

You'll need a quantity of unbleached muslin in accordance to the size of your group (1⅛ yards will make six place mats), jars of textile paint in various colors, 1-inch brushes, paper towels and old magazines.

Take the youth group members to a city park. Ask them to observe and appreciate the intricate patterns of nature. Ask them to try and identify the various trees and plants; and talk about their strengths or weaknesses, their beauty or delicacy. Ask a volunteer to read Luke 12:27-29. Allow time to "consider the lilies of the field." Ask:

● How do these verses make you feel?

● How would you describe the gifts of nature that you see?

● How would you describe yourselves?

● Why does Jesus say not to be anxious about what you are to eat or drink?

Tell the group that you are going to make nature place mats to serve as reminders of these verses. Ask the youth group members to gather several leaves. Give them each a magazine, paper towel, paint, brush and fabric.

Have the youth group members lay the fabric on top of a magazine, paint the face of a leaf, carefully lay it on the cloth, cover it with a paper towel and press firmly. Remove the leaf by lifting straight up. It will leave a beautiful pattern. When all of the place mats are finished, ask a seamstress to fringe, border or hem them. The place mats are impressive reminders of God's love for us.

—Margaret Kelchner

Variations

1. Use this same procedure to make tablecloths or dresser scarves. Pre-cut the material according to the project. These make great Christmas presents; or the youth group could sell them as a fund-raising project any time during the year.

Your Ideas and Variations

_____
_____
_____
_____
_____
_____
_____
_____
_____
_____
_____
_____
_____
_____

133

A Christmas Message
TOPIC: CHRISTMAS/GROUP BUILDING

Instead of just hanging a string of lights on the church's Christmas tree, use the lights to illustrate that Christ was born for us all, and that we are all a special part of the body of Christ.

Depending on the size of your group, take a string or two of lights (enough so that each young person can receive a light bulb). As you know, on most light sets, if one bulb is removed the circuit will be broken. All of the bulbs have to be in place for the lights to shine forth with their beauty!

One by one, have each young person place his or her light bulb in the string and share one special thing about himself or herself. This could be a feeling about the Christmas season, or a feeling about being a part of the youth group. When everyone's bulb is in place, the string will light up.

This experience helps your kids realize that they are all important in the body of Christ.

They will personalize the Christmas message: Christ was born as a gift to everyone.

—Steven J. Bolda

Variations

1. Decorate the tree with strings of popcorn and cranberries. Supply construction paper, glitter, glue, markers and magazines. Have the kids each make an ornament that describes themselves. For example, they could use glitter and glue to write their name and cut out magazine pictures such as jogging shoes, books, puppies and food. Make hangers for the ornaments out of pipe cleaners.

2. Follow up this lesson with an affirmation idea. Give each person 10 pieces of peppermint candy. Instruct the group members to mingle and give a piece of candy to 10 different individuals, telling them what they appreciate about them. Tell the students to continue until all of

their candy is gone. As a leader, plan ahead and make a point of affirming individuals who may get neglected. The larger your group, the more candy you give to the members to distribute (**Building Community in Youth Groups**, by Denny Rydberg, Group Books).

Your Ideas and Variations

_____
_____
_____
_____
_____
_____
_____
_____
_____

134
Fluorescent Light: What an Experience!
TOPIC: MEETING SETTINGS

Using long-tube fluorescent lights, you can create one of the most exciting worship or meeting areas that you have ever used! Almost every church has an abundance of these light bulbs. All you have to do is learn how to carry 50 at a time without breaking one. Here is how you set up this "electric" meeting area.

Find a hill or an area directly below some high-voltage power lines. Take as many of these bulbs as you can to the hill and prepare your group for a surprise. The electric current in the air causes the bulbs to light up.

Stick the bulbs in the ground to form a path leading to a circle. A piece of tape can be used to hold two bulbs together to form a cross. Place the cross in the center of the circle. As you might imagine, the results at night are breathtaking. Plan a service around this theme: "Jesus Is the Light of the World."

It is hard to believe that this idea really works. That is exactly how I felt until I tried it many years ago. The "enlightening experience" will not damage the bulbs; put them back in the box and they are as good as new!

—Steven J. Bolda

Variations

1. Get as many bulbs as you can and stick them in the ground to outline a large cross. Stand inside the cross.

2. Plan a service of light to celebrate Epiphany or Pentecost. Meet in the "fluorescent" worship area and give each person a candle or flashlight. Sing songs such as, "I Saw the Light"

and "Walkin' in the Light" (**Songs**, by Yohann Anderson, Songs and Creations, Inc.).

Your Ideas and Variations

_____
_____
_____
_____
_____
_____
_____
_____
_____
_____
_____
_____
_____

LURES

135

Making Lures
TOPIC: TEMPTATION

If you're teaching a lesson on temptation, here's a fun project that will help young people understand it.

Prepare several work areas. In each one place coat hangers, fishing line, magazines, store catalogs, modeling clay, construction paper, markers, scissors and tape.

Divide the youth group members into small groups; assign each group a work area. Tell the kids that they are to make lures for people—lures that will tempt people to sin or cause them to withdraw from Christian fellowship. Have them bend the coat hangers to resemble fishing hooks, and bait the hooks with all kinds of material temptations. They can use pictures of boats, parties, luxurious homes, or make a money symbol out of clay, etc. When everyone is finished, assemble in a large group and discuss the lures.

This no-fail activity will "hook" the kids' attention when talking about temptation!

—Gloria Menke

Variations

1. Attach a strong cord from one end of the meeting room to the other. Hang the fish hooks on the cord and make a poster that says, "Temptations That Lure Us Away From God."

2. Take your youth group members to a hill, tower, or tall building overlooking your city. Have them look all around the area as you read about Jesus' temptation in the wilderness (Matthew 4:1-11). Discuss the things the kids see that tempt them; for example, bars, new cars, a fast-paced lifestyle, etc. Discuss how God helps us overcome temptations (**Dennis Benson's Creative Bible Studies**, Group Books).

Your Ideas and Variations

_____
_____
_____
_____
_____
_____
_____
_____
_____
_____
_____
_____

MAGAZINES

136

Magazine Gifts
TOPIC: ELDERLY/OUTREACH

This project will help your youth group members reach out to the elderly.

Select a retirement home or convalescent hospital and meet with a staff member to facilitate your group visit. Work together to pair the young people with the elderly for optimal interaction. For example, an elderly person interested in music may best be paired with a young musician.

Prior to the visit, ask each youth group member to bring a current magazine to a youth group meeting. If their families don't subscribe to any magazines, collect a supply from church members.

Tell your youth group members about the upcoming visit to a retirement home. Ask them to look through the magazines and select an article which may be of interest to an elderly person. Have the kids read the article several times to become familiar with it. Explain that reading the entire article may not be appropriate for some of the elderly people. Ask the kids to be prepared to "tell" the story—possibly reading only the important portions of the article.

On a prearranged day, take your youth group to the retirement home. Have the young people share the articles with their new friends. Have the kids donate the magazines to the facility. After the visit, have the young people share their experiences and feelings.

Challenge the young people to accept an ongoing interaction project with the elderly. Have them give a magazine subscription to the facility and pay for it from their youth group fund. The values gained from this type of experience are endless, for the young and the elderly alike.
—Arlo R. Reichter

Variations

1. Subscribe to a newspaper and give it to a nursing home. Ask the youth group members to visit the residents, and read and discuss newspaper articles with them.

2. Give the residents other gifts such as stationery and stamps. Help them write letters to their friends and relatives.

Your Ideas and Variations

_____
_____
_____
_____
_____
_____
_____
_____
_____
_____
_____
_____
_____
_____
_____

137

Magazine Madness
TOPIC: BIBLE STUDY/GOD'S LOVE

It's amazing how young people enjoy looking through magazines—just for pleasure or for a serious purpose. This activity will provide a fresh perspective on biblical values and a challenge for further spiritual growth.

Have each member bring a Bible to the meeting. You also will need magazines, glue or tape, scissors and cardboard—enough for several small groups.

As you begin the study, have everybody turn to 1 John 2:15-17; read the verses in unison. Explain briefly that following Jesus means not following the world.

Divide into small groups of about four or five people. Supply each group with magazines, glue, scissors and cardboard. Ask the kids to thumb through the magazines and choose pictures that portray "the world." Give each group 20 minutes to create a collage of these pictures.

When everyone is finished, have one spokesperson from each group share how his or her group's collage illustrates the world. After each group has shared ask, "If I am not to love the world, what am I to do?"

Have the group read together verse 17, "And the world passes away, and the lust of it; but he who does the will of God abides for ever."

Form a large circle and have each person complete the sentence, "God's will is . . ." Go around the circle again and have each person say one thing he or she learned from the meeting. Close with a circle prayer and a massive squeeze!

—David Olshine

Variations

1. Make a mega-newspaper by taping together the edges of full sheets of newspaper. Tape both sides, including the outside edges so that it won't rip.

Spread out the mega-newspaper. Ask the kids to lift the paper and walk under it so that it creates a tent-like paper over them. Then ask certain people to step back. The few remaining people will be almost buried by newspaper. Ask the few people how it feels to hold up the giant newspaper. Of course, they'll complain that it is impossible without more help.

Invite everyone to return to the outside edge of the newspaper. Ask them to remove their shoes. Explain that the world needs to be sustained by the prayers of all. Invite the young people to walk carefully to a spot on the huge newspaper and sit down. Explain that the prayers for others need to be focused.

Ask the students to search the newspaper for stories of people who need their prayers. Share the prayers. Between each one, have the group recite, "For God so loved the world that he gave his only Son, that whoever believes in him should not perish but have eternal life" (John 3:16).

The mega-newspaper gets the kids to think about others. It is a meaningful prayer of intercession for the world in which we live (**Creative Worship in Youth Ministry**, by Dennis C. Benson, Group Books).

Your Ideas and Variations

_____

_____

_____

_____

_____

_____

_____

_____

_____

_____

_____

_____

_____

_____

138

Random Verses
TOPIC: BIBLE STUDY

This activity allows the young people to work together, use their creativity and memorize scripture.

Divide your young people into groups of two or three. Give each group magazines, one glue stick, scissors for each member, five sheets of paper, and five Bible verses. For example, write out Genesis 1:1-5. You can write different verses for each team or have each team work on the same five verses.

Give the kids 20 minutes to duplicate the verses by cutting out letters from the magazines and gluing them onto the paper until they have done all five verses or until time runs out. They may use symbols instead of letters (for example, the number 4 instead of the word "for"). Here's an example of part of a verse:

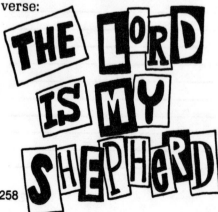

Follow the activity with a devotion using the verses. Random Verses is a time-consuming activity, but while the youth group members are looking for the letters, they also are memorizing the verses!

—John Miller

Variations

1. Send the Random Verses to inactive members as "We-miss-you" messages.

2. Meet in a carpeted area. Divide your young people into small groups and have them spell out the letters with their bodies. For example, to form an "E," one person could lay down and three others could lay perpendicular to his or her right. Have the other youth group members guess the verse by decoding the letters.

3. Create cards for special occasions by cutting out letters and pictures and gluing them onto colored construction paper.

Your Ideas and Variations

_____
_____
_____
_____
_____
_____
_____
_____
_____
_____
_____

MAGNIFYING GLASSES

139

Name Tag Magnifying Glass
TOPIC: NATURE

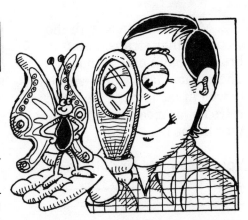

At a mountain retreat, on a nature walk, or on a hike through the woods, a magnifying glass will help the youth group members discover and study God's wonderful creations.

Gather paintbrushes; varnish; leather straps or shoelaces; glue; pocketknives; electric, wood-burning tools; small limbs of cedar, pine, or other suitable woods not more than 2 or 2½ inches in diameter. Cut the limbs at a slant to present a nice grain with bark trim. Cut more than one for each person so that they will have a variety to choose from. You also will need a 1-inch magnifying glass for each student. Purchase these from Edmund Scientific, 101 E. Gloucester Pike, Barington, NJ 08007, 1-800-222-0224.

Let each young person choose a piece of wood. Have them use the pocketknives to carve two holes: one hole just large enough for the strap to slip through; the other hole for the magnifying glass to snugly fit into.

Have the members take turns etching their names in the wood with the wood-burning tool. Varnish the wood, then insert the magnifying glass. Secure the glass with glue. The completed magnifying glasses should look like this:

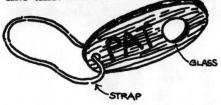

These magnifying glasses are a great way for youth group members to take a closer look at the intricate beauty of God's world.

—Margaret Kelchner

Variations

1. Earn money for the youth group by selling these magnifying glasses to congregation members. Personalize the magnifying glasses for the people who order them.

2. Make name tags with the wood, leather straps, paintbrushes, paint and varnish. These name tags work especially well at camp outs, weekend retreats, or meetings with a nature theme.

Your Ideas and Variations

_____
_____
_____
_____
_____
_____
_____
_____
_____
_____

MAPS

140

The Church at Work
TOPIC: MISSIONS/OUTREACH

This exercise will help young people to understand the widespread witness of the Christian church. It will help them to see beyond their local church and to visualize the influence of the church in today's world. Following are three options for this exercise:

● **Witness in your state.** Place a large map of your state in your youth room. Secure a list of names and addresses of all the churches of your denomination within your state. On the map, stick colored pins to represent each church.

Have the young people write letters to the pastor and youth group of each of these churches. In their letters have them request a picture of the youth group or congregation.

As the pictures arrive, link them to the map location with a line or string. The impact of the witness will grow every week as more and more churches respond.

Depending upon the depth of the project, you can request more information from each church such as a description of the youth group, when the church was founded, etc. You also could visit several of the churches.

● **Witness in the United States.** Seek to contact one church of your denomination or another denomination in every state. Your denominational office can be helpful in obtaining addresses. Hang a large map of the United States in a visible location and enjoy watching the witness grow as you hear from all of the churches across America.

● **Witness in the world.** This project will help the group become acquainted with the world-wide witness of the mission program of your denomination. Place a world map in the youth meeting room. Secure from your national office names and addresses of leaders in churches around the world. Write to these churches and request information. Your youth group can adopt a project to help a church in another country: gather money, send clothes, etc.

These three projects will help your youth group members comprehend the importance of the church within their state, America and the world.

—Arlo R. Reichter

Variations

1. On a mission Sunday, present the project and correspondence to the church members.

2. Ask the congregations to send slides of their building and their members. Develop a slide show on God's love in action around the world.

Your Ideas and Variations

_____
_____
_____
_____
_____
_____
_____
_____
_____
_____
_____

141

Hearts for the World
TOPIC: HUNGER/PEACE

Here's a great program to raise your group's global consciousness.

Locate a large, world map and post it at the front of the meeting room.

Give each person a small paper heart (cut from red construction paper) and a straight pin. Better yet, go to a specialty shop and buy small, heart-shaped gummed stickers. Ask each person to meditate and decide what part of the world he or she presently feels most concerned for.

Ask your young people to brainstorm ways they can help these countries. For example, write to a congressman or congresswoman and voice concern over poverty; collect money or canned goods and donate to an organization such as Bread for the World, 802 Rhode Island Ave. N.E., Washington, D.C. 20018, (202) 269-0200.

If a young person expresses concern for his or her own town or state, contact agencies such as food services, senior citizen centers, nursing homes or welfare projects.

Close the session by having

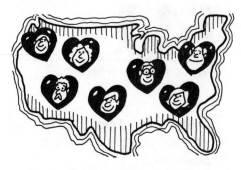

everyone step to the map and pin, or stick, the heart on the area of concern. Conclude with a song such as "He's Got the Whole World in His Hands."

—Lynn Potter

Variations

1. Cut hearts from red contact paper—for better "sticking" power.

2. Get a large blue ball or balloon. Use a marker to draw the continents on it. Play catch with the ball and sing "He's Got the Whole World in His Hands" or "It's a Small World" (**Clown Ministry**, by Floyd Shaffer and Penne Sewall, Group Books).

Your Ideas and Variations

_____
_____
_____
_____
_____
_____
_____
_____
_____
_____

MARBLES

142

The Crystal Ball
TOPIC: PLANNING/GOALS

All youth groups need a common goal, purpose and vision if they are to succeed and grow. This activity helps the kids to extend their vision and look into the future.

Give each person a clear marble. (You can buy these at specialty shops or discount stores.) Tell the kids that each marble is a miniature crystal ball, and that with its help, the group can catch a vision of where it needs to go, goals it needs to reach.

Ask the kids to gaze into their crystal balls and search for goals and visions for the youth group to aspire to; for example, enhancing peer ministry, student-adult ministry, student leadership, community outreach, etc. List these on newsprint.

Form small groups and assign each an area listed on the newsprint. Ask the small groups to continue to gaze into their crystal balls and brainstorm ways the youth group can attain these goals. Examples for community outreach could be visiting nursing homes, leading Bible studies for small children, gathering food for the city's needy people, etc.

Gather as a large group and establish group goals. Choose the top 12, most important ideas and schedule them in the youth group calendar. For example, this month visit a nursing home, next month sponsor an intergenerational potluck and fellowship night, the next month invite three youth groups from other churches to a special youth group meeting.

Keep the youth group alive and healthy by striving for the goals and helping others.

—Dave Mahoney

Variations

1. Challenge the young people to carry the marbles in their pockets or purses to remind them of the goals. Occasionally

offer an "award on the spot" to a person who can present a marble on demand. Award the person with a mini-pouch full of 10 clear marbles, or a pair of sunglasses with a slip of paper that says, "I've caught the vision."

Your Ideas and Variations

_____
_____
_____
_____
_____
_____
_____
_____
_____
_____
_____

MATCHES

143

A Symbol of Servanthood
TOPIC: SERVANTHOOD/OUTREACH

Use this easy, fun idea to stress servanthood. Tell group members that Christ came to serve—just as we should serve others.

Have each young person make a mop out of a match stick, tape, and string or yarn. Cut short pieces of string, and tape them to the end of a match stick. It really looks like a mop!

Let the kids use their mop as a bookmark. Have them place it in their Bible on Matthew 20:26-28, ". . . whoever would be great among you must be your servant, and whoever would be first among you must be your slave; even as the Son of man came not to be served but to serve, and to give his life as a ransom for many."

—J.B. Collingsworth

Variations

1. Plan a Bible study on servanthood; use these verses: Luke 16:13; 19:11-27; John 12:26; 2 Corinthians 4:5; 2 Timothy 2:24.

2. Make several mops and distribute them during service projects. For example, your group could sponsor a cleaning day for elderly members of your congregation. After they clean each house, they could give the resident a match-stick mop with a sign that says "Servants of Christ."

Your Ideas and Variations

_____
_____
_____
_____
_____
_____
_____
_____
_____
_____
_____
_____
_____

MITTENS

144

Candy Bar Relay
TOPIC: GAMES

Here's a fun relay that will satisfy each participant's sweet tooth.

You'll need several gift-wrapped candy bars (the more tape used on the wrapping, the better), several knives, forks and pairs of mittens. You also will need a cassette tape with lively music, a tape player, several large candy bars and several small candy bars.

Divide your group into teams of about six people. On a table, provide each team with a gift-wrapped candy bar, a fork, a knife, and a pair of gloves or mittens. The goal of each team is to be the first team to unwrap and eat the candy bar. Here's the catch: only the fork and knife may be used to unwrap the candy bar and the mittens must be worn by each team member.

Have one person control the tape player. When the music starts, the first person from each team runs to the table. The team member puts the mittens on and tries to unwrap the candy bar. That person works until the music stops. The music is turned back on and the next team member goes to the table and tries to unwrap the candy bar. Continue the process. The first team to unwrap and eat the candy bar wins. Award large candy bars to the winning team members and smaller ones to the remaining participants.

—Beth Dewey

Variations

1. For a healthier alternative, use oranges instead of candy bars. Follow the same procedures. Instead of unwrapping the candy bars, the students peel the oranges. Award oranges to the winners and orange juice to everyone for participating.

Your Ideas and Variations

_____
_____
_____
_____
_____
_____
_____
_____
_____
_____
_____
_____
_____
_____
_____

145

Helping Hand
TOPIC: HANDICAPPED

This lesson is about freeing handicapped people to feed themselves—helping them to be independent.

Divide into triads; give each group one pair of mittens, one hard-boiled egg and a small cup. One person in the group is to put on the mittens. The egg is placed in the cup and the cup is placed in the mittened hands. Give the following instructions: "The person with the mittens is your friend who has come to you with a problem. He or she needs to peel the hard-boiled egg so that no shell remains on it and place all the shells in the cup. Your friend may not remove his or her mittens. Discuss the problem briefly, then take affirmative action and help your friend. When your group finishes, remain where you are and quietly observe the other groups still working at their task."

In most groups you will find the unhandicapped persons peeling the egg and doing all the work. The less obvious solution, and the point of the task, is to enable the handicapped individual to become free to help himself or herself. This is best ac-complished if the two helpers remove the mittens from their friend's hands, thus freeing their friend to peel the egg. (The directions stated only that the person with the mittens could not remove them.)

This is a "tricky," yet fun way to illustrate the need to enable handicapped people to be independent.

—David Washburn

Variations

1. Introduce an activity to let the young people experience blindness during the next week. Each person picks a partner; one will be blindfolded while the other is his or her companion. Then switch the roles. Go to a shopping mall, out to eat, walk in the park—experience what an everyday activity would be like without sight. Record feelings and discuss them at the next meeting.

2. There are things a sighted person can do to aid the blind. The following pointers are designed for day-to-day situations you might encounter. Discuss these tips with the youth group members.

● Talk to the blind person. Don't think that because a person is blind, he or she also is deaf.

● Don't take the blind person's arm, let him or her take yours so that you, the sighted person, are leading, not pushing. To take a blind person's arm and push him or her along can be hazardous, especially when approaching stairs.

● As for the door, lead the blind person through. If the door opens in, tell the blind person on which side the door opens so he or she can put out a hand and you can continue walking through together.

If the door opens out, stay in front of the blind person, pull the door open, and tell the blind person the door is on the left or right. But if the blind person has a guide dog, it might not be necessary for the sighted person to help.

● To help a blind person enter a car, lead him or her to the car and put his or her hand on the doorhandle. Allow the blind person to open the door. This helps the person get his or her bearings.

● To go up or down stairs, don't try to count the steps. The logical thing is to say, "Here are stairs." Specify whether they go up or down.

As you, the sighted person, continue leading, your arm goes up and the blind person knows you're still going up stairs. Once your arm levels off, the blind person knows there are no more steps.

When descending steps, start down first, don't insist the blind person step down at the same time.

● To get on an escalator: When no one is waiting to get on, put the person's hand on the rail. He or she can then use his or her feet to find a step. Once the person is on, get on behind him or her.

● When you approach a table, take the person's hand and place it on the back of the chair and let him or her figure out where to sit.

● When seated for dinner, don't give commentary unless there's something strange about the place setting—if the dinner napkin is in the water glass. You don't need to say, "The fork's on the left, the knife and spoon are on the right and the plate's in the center."

● When the food is served, the sighted person can look at it like a clock, and say, "The meat is at 12 o'clock, the beans at 3, the roll at 6 and the salad at 9."

If the blind person asks, cut his or her meat, but wait for the blind person to tell you what he or she needs. Don't grab the plate and start cutting as if he or she were a 3-year-old.

● Behavior around guide dogs is important: Don't pet the dog!

● Try not to criticize the dog. The dog is not a machine. Dogs have personalities; like people, they also have idiosyncrasies.

● If you're walking with a

blind person and the dog takes off in the wrong direction, which means your blind friend also is going the wrong way, don't call the dog. There may be a reason the dog is going the wrong direction. If not, call to the person, not the dog.

Your Ideas and Variations

_____
_____
_____
_____
_____
_____
_____
_____
_____
_____

MONEY

146

Important Values
TOPIC: VALUES

What values did Christ uphold as important? What values do the youth group members regard as important? Let young people gain insight to these questions during this meeting.

Gather the youth group members and brainstorm a list of 10 to 20 values. List them on news-

print so everyone can see them. Values can include a quality education, good marriage, secure home, solid faith, etc. When the list is complete, pass out an equal amount of play money to each group member. Auction off the values to the highest bidder, collecting the money as you go along.

After the auction, discuss why certain values sold for such a high price. Why were some barely bid on? Ask the young people to share why they purchased the values they did. Explain to the kids that Christ does not see them as _valueless_ but as _invaluable_. End by deciding what Christ paid the highest price for—US!

—Steve Newton

Variations

1. Go to a grocery store or discount store and ask for a bunch of their price stickers. (Price stickers also can be purchased at most office supply stores.) Write on each one "You're priceless." Stick one on each of the youth group members after the lesson on important values.

2. Give the kids each a piece of play money and a marker. Have them write on the money "Jesus paid the price for my sins." Let the young people take the money home to use as a bookmark in their Bible.

Your Ideas and Variations

_____
_____
_____
_____
_____
_____
_____
_____
_____
_____
_____
_____

147

Making Wise Decisions
TOPIC: DECISIONS/RESPONSIBILITY

Christians have a responsibility to be discerning—to know whether or not to believe cer-

tain claims or buy certain items. The youth group members will learn more about this topic by participating in this lesson.

For this meeting, you will need ads for supermarket items. Choose ones with the most extravagant claims: "The best nutrition you can buy." Or, "More protein than any other." Gather cans and packages with the listing of ingredients on the label. You also will need one penny for each student.

Gather the youth group members and let them read the ads. Ask if they believe all that's claimed. Why or why not? Let them examine the boxes and cans. Explain that by law the ingredients must be listed in order of content. Items listed first are the largest percentage.

Say, "With ads and products, we can test and read the fine print. The products can make

any claim they want. We don't have to buy the product. You read in the paper that the funniest show of the century will be on television. You stay home and watch it. You're bored to tears. So what? You don't ever have to watch it again."

Now give each student one penny. Say that these coins represent $1,000 each. They're not much by themselves, but put them all together and it will be a large sum.

Ask two people to beg for the money by trying to convince everyone of the good that will be done with it. After the group asks questions of the two, vote on who to give the money to.

No matter how the kids vote, have the winner say, "Thank you. The truth is, I was lying to you. I'm from another country and I am taking this money back to my homeland. We will buy arms and ammunition and come back to destroy you."

Ask the students:

● Do you feel any responsibility? Why or why not?

● How could you have known?

● Should you feel guilty? Explain.

Say, "We do have a responsibility to check things out. People can come to you in the name of religion and ask for your money —your loyalty. As a Christian, it is your duty—part of your stew-ardship—to check it out, make sure of the claims."

—E. Jane Mall

Variations

1. Use Monopoly money instead of pennies.

2. Play a variation of the old game show "To Tell the Truth." Choose three people (whom your kids don't know) to come to a youth group meeting. Have them profess to be the same person; for example, "My name is Harold Bucks." Explain to the young people the profession of Harold Bucks. Let the kids ask the three gentlemen discerning questions such as "How did you choose your current profession?" "What is your educational background?" After several minutes of questioning, let the young people choose the real Harold Bucks. Then ask, "Will the real Harold Bucks please stand up?" See how many kids guessed correctly.

Your Ideas and Variations

_____
_____
_____
_____
_____
_____
_____
_____
_____
_____

148

Two Sides of the Same Coin
*TOPIC: DISCIPLINE/COMPETITION/
FAILURE*

Getting together to watch the Super Bowl each year has become a special event for many youth groups. This is an appropriate occasion to reflect on competition and achievement.

Distribute a coin to each person. Make the point that winning and losing are connected to each other—they are "two sides of the same coin." You cannot win without being willing to risk losing. If you become obsessed with winning you can become insensitive to others. Yet if you hold back for fear of losing you will never experience winning. Our competitive nature needs to be balanced just as the coin is balanced with each side being equal to the other.

Have your group reflect on Hebrews 12:1-2. Discuss these questions:

● What do you think these verses say about competition? about being willing to discipline yourself? about giving your best?

● How have you handled competitive situations in the past?

● How will you handle these situations in the future?

Pray together asking God to help each one make a commitment to seek a balance in dealing with competitive situations. Ask the group members to take their coin home as a reminder of their commitment.

—Chris Oehrlein
and Rich Weihing

Variations

1. Ask to borrow a church member's coin collection and bring it to a youth group meeting. Show the kids the coin collection, then talk about the two sides of a coin—heads and tails. Differentiate between the common meanings of such phrases as "heads you win, tails you lose" and "two sides of the same coin." Consider these questions:

● How is life like heads and tails? right and wrong? good and bad?

● Are all of our choices in life either right or wrong? good or bad? Explain.

● How is life like a valuable coin collection? How is it different?

—Russ Jolly

2. Develop a Bible study around Matthew 22:15-22. The Pharisees tried to trap Jesus with a question about taxes. Discuss how this passage relates to our lives.

3. Develop a Bible study around Mark 12:41-44. A widow

gave two copper pennies; Jesus said that she gave more than any other person that day. Discuss how this passage relates to our giving.

Your Ideas and Variations

_____
_____
_____
_____
_____
_____
_____
_____
_____
_____
_____
_____
_____
_____

MUFFINS

149

Muffin Sale
TOPIC: FUND RAISING

A fun fund raiser for any age or size of youth group is a Muffin Sale. Choose a day for the big sale. Ask each youth group member to bake one dozen muffins at home.

On the day of the sale, have the kids bring their muffins and one or two boxes of muffin mix

to the church. During the sale, have a crew of kids in the kitchen baking more muffins. The aroma of freshly baked muffins will fill the church and entice people to the sale table. Funds will grow with this mouthwatering idea.

—Bruce M. Nichols

Variations

1. Be creative with the muffin mixes—try whole-wheat, plain, buttermilk, blueberry, cherry or strawberry!

2. Plan a Muffin' Stuffin' Contest. Ask your pastor and a youth sponsor to come to the muffin sale—hungry. Place a can by each contestant. Label one can, "The Pastor"; label the other can, "The Youth Worker." Have people place donations in the can of the person they think will eat the most muffins. Allow 30 minutes for the hungry contestants to "stuff" their faces!

Your Ideas and Variations

_____
_____
_____
_____
_____
_____
_____
_____
_____
_____
_____
_____
_____
_____

MUSIC

150

Air-Band Night
_TOPIC: AIR BAND/VIDEO/ROCK MUSIC/
FELLOWSHIP_

Do you know what it means to lip-sync? Lip-sync is to synchronize lip movements to music. A group of kids lip-syncing and pretending to play instruments to music is called an "air band." Young people, gifted with a dramatic or musical flare, will gladly get into this act.

Divide your youth group members into smaller groups. Have them choose a favorite contemporary Christian song and devel-op an air-band number. Use these songs as part of a youth program or part of a Bible study. Your "band members" will have the benefit of internalizing the words, because it takes a great deal of practice to lip-sync well.

Here is another possibility. Invite some other church youth groups over for an Air-Band Night. Ask them to create numbers and wear appropriate costumes. Afterward, ask the kids to explain why they chose a certain song and what it means to them.

Have the youth pastors form a panel of judges. They can rate the acts on a scale of 1 to 10 in each of the following categories:

● **Lip-Sync Ability:** How "in sync" lip and body movements are to the music; does the group appear to be giving a live performance.

● **Costume:** Not essential, but will help the overall impression.

● **Showmanship:** The ability to entertain the audience with stage presence, eye contact, the use of the stage, props, etc.

● **Audience Response:** How much the audience is convinced and entertained by the act.

● **Clarity of Christian Content:** Important area, since the purpose is to glorify God and encourage the audience. A heavy metal song with obscure, unintelligible lyrics will not score well.

Have your panel of judges score each act individually and then tally the final scores. Award the multi-talented performers prizes such as Christian records and tapes.

—Leonard Kageler

Variations

1. Many teenagers fantasize about being in a music video. It is easier than you may think to produce a quality music video, for only the cost of the video-tape. Contact a cable TV company that serves your area. The Federal Communications Commission requires that cable TV companies provide free public access to their television studios and equipment. Some companies will even have a remote van available.

Use the air-band numbers the kids have developed. Be sure and write the companies that own the copyrights to the words and music of the songs. Most will appreciate your using their songs; some may charge you a fee.

Most cable companies will ask you to come for a two-hour training session prior to the scheduling of studio or remote van time. The cable company may provide one technician at the time of filming, while you provide the people to run the cameras. Many cable companies will duplicate your master tape, free of charge.

The tapes you produce could be sold as a fund raiser, or sent to other churches of your denomination as a ministry. A good-quality, 45-minute air-band show will be a real hit for a youth group program.

Arrange to have your video-tape aired on cable TV. Imagine the excitement this would produce in your group—and the outreach potential!

Your Ideas and Variations

_____
_____
_____
_____
_____
_____
_____
_____
_____
_____
_____
_____

151

Interpreting Rock Music
TOPIC: ROCK MUSIC/VALUES

Everyone in today's society is faced with countless choices and conflicting values. This activity allows the youth group members to compare contemporary values and Christian values.

Gather magazines, newspapers, paper, scissors, glue and pencils. Ask the youth group members to bring their favorite rock records to the meeting. You also will need a record player or tape player and copies of the following grid.

Tell the kids that much of the advertising that bombards us each day is aimed at persuading us to believe in a company or a brand name. Divide the participants into small groups and give each group paper, glue, magazines, newspapers and scissors.

Ask them to take a close look at the newspaper and magazine ads. Have them notice the values conveyed through the ads. Ask them to substitute theological words such as Christ, God, church or eternal life into the advertising slogans. For example, the slogan for Sears becomes, "There's more for your life with Christ." Ask the small groups to make collages of the new slogans and share them.

Move into a discussion on Christian values versus values presented in contemporary rock songs, by using the following grid. (Grid developed by Professor James B. Nelson, United Theological Seminary.) Discuss the six theological terms that are listed and encourage the kids to translate them into everyday terms (see the examples).

Theological Terms	Everyday Terms	Rock Song
God	What's most important?	
Human Nature	What are people really like?	
Sin	What is the root problem in the world?	
Salvation	What is the solution to the problem?	
Church	What is the group of people in which the solution takes place?	
Kingdom of God	What is the perfect world?	

Tell the young people that next they will listen to several rock songs and fill in the final column of the grid. Note that the idea is not to determine the faith of the performers; the focus is to identify the values that the songs represent.

In a recent session, my youth group and I listened to several songs and discovered that the most important things according to the songs were owning a Cadillac, having fun, earning lots of money and partying. Solutions to the problems were to rob a bank, print your own money and disobey your parents.

Discuss the values, problems and solutions that are stressed in the rock songs. Compare them to Christian values. With clear value statements like these, it isn't difficult to get a good discussion going.

—Walter John Boris

Variations

1. Use the same grid to evaluate videos, movies and television programs.

2. Ask the youth group members if they agree or disagree with the following statements. Have them give reasons.

● Record companies should provide ratings for each album's lyrics.

● Record ratings will keep people from buying the explicit albums.

● Wrapping lyrics or keeping them under the counter will drastically reduce sales.

● Listening to explicit music is a sin.

● People will buy more explicit records if they're labeled that way.

● Most people are embarrassed about buying explicit albums.

● Sexually explicit records aren't any different from explicit movies, television shows, books or magazines.

● Christians buy sexually explicit albums.

● Jesus doesn't care whether you listen to explicit albums as long as it doesn't affect your behavior.

Continue with a discussion using these questions:

● Who is at fault for violent and sexually explicit music—the record companies or the consumers? Explain. If people didn't buy explicit music, would companies, musicians and songwriters change? Why or why not?

● Why are parents concerned with what young people listen to?

● Does singing along with lyrics (even if you don't mean them) matter to God? Why or why not? Can Christians sing praise to God and not mean it? Explain. Which is worse?

● If only one song on an album has questionable lyrics, would you buy the album? Why or why not?

● Read Matthew 5:27-30. What is Jesus' warning in the passage? How does this apply to listening to explicit records? Will you go to hell if you listen to explicit lyrics? Why or why not? How do lyrics affect a person?

● Read 1 Corinthians 10:31. Can buying or listening to explicit music be done "to God's glory?" Why or why not?

● Read Deuteronomy 6:5-9. How is this opposite from listening to explicit music? How does what you hear and see affect your actions?

● What would you say to friends who buy explicit albums? What would Jesus say?

Your Ideas and Variations

_____
_____
_____
_____
_____
_____
_____
_____
_____
_____

152

Masks
TOPIC: SELF-IMAGE

Try this self-image reflection exercise for junior or senior high groups.

Set up tables and chairs in the meeting room. Bring a tape player or record player and a recording of "The Stranger" by Billy Joel. You'll also need paper and markers for each person.

As the kids enter the meeting room, give them some paper and markers and ask them to find a place at the tables. Begin a discussion on "hiding behind masks." Ask the kids if they

ever hide feelings such as sadness or inferiority. Ask, "Why do we keep certain emotions to ourselves? Why do we pretend to be someone different than we really are?"

Ask the kids to listen as you play "The Stranger." On their paper, have kids draw a mask that represents hidden things about themselves. For example:

Share the masks in small groups. The drawings help kids to open up and talk about their true feelings.

—Bruce M. Nichols

Variations

1. Give the youth group members each a piece of paper and a pencil. Begin a discussion on goals and ambitions. Ask, "What kind of person do you want to be? What qualities do you want to possess? What vocation do you strive for?"

Ask the kids to listen as you play "The Sky Is the Limit," by Leon Patillo. Have them draw or write anything that comes to their mind during the song. Discuss the papers and the fact that all things are possible with God.

Your Ideas and Variations

_____
_____
_____
_____
_____
_____
_____
_____
_____
_____
_____
_____

153

Musical Prologue
*TOPIC: GROUP BUILDING/
CHRISTIAN MUSIC*

Use this idea to promote group unity; to get the young people to meetings on time; to provide a relaxed atmosphere for the kids' visitors; and to popularize contemporary Christian music with your youth group.

Purchase the latest and best Christian tapes or records and secure a good, portable sound system. Twenty minutes prior to each youth group meeting, play the music, loudly! Tell the kids you're going to do this every week. (The adult sponsors will tolerate the loud music if they understand your purpose.)

It won't be necessary to play secular rock music at your meetings, because the kids will enjoy this positive alternative. They will discover that Christian rock music also has a great beat, and is fun to listen and dance to. Their friends who visit will love it too and ask, "Is this really a church?"

—Dave Mahoney

Variations

1. Once the kids are familiar with Christian artists, rotate responsibility for planning pre-meeting music. Let the kids play their favorite music for others to hear.

2. Play a variation of the game Name That Tune. Play a few notes of a Christian song and let the youth group members guess the title and artist. Award a Christian tape to the one who correctly guesses the most songs.

Your Ideas and Variations

_____
_____
_____
_____
_____
_____
_____
_____
_____
_____
_____
_____
_____

154

Rok Toks
TOPIC: MEDIA/ROCK MUSIC

In most youth groups there are young people who like heavy metal rock and others who like soft rock. There are some who enjoy synthesizer rock and some who like country western. During a group discussion on rock music, a problem occurs if a kid hates a song or group so much that he or she becomes obnoxious and disruptive.

The solution? Try what I have affectionately titled "Rok Toks" (Rock Talks). Instead of picking out one particular song and discussing its theme, pick a theme and tape excerpts from several different songs to create one song. A Rok Tok is a potpourri of short cuts taken from different artists and styles, recorded in succession. I usually choose segments from both Christian and secular albums. Kids tend to recognize the secular songs more, but the Christian songs provide answers instead of questions.

Creating a tape is affordable and can be done very easily, providing you have a record player with cassette recorder and a fair-size album collection. If you don't have the latter, you can borrow the albums from your young people. Since you won't be recording any song in its entirety, there will be no problem with violating existing copyright laws.

One Rok Tok I prepared was on suicide. Wanting to create a story effect, I began the Rok Tok with a segment from "Another Brick in the Wall" by Pink Floyd. Once the song played long enough to set the scene, I added several other segments that told a suicide story: "Don't Try Suicide" by Queen; "Suicide Boulevard" by Little River Band; "Jack and Diane" by John Cougar (in particular, the phrase, "Oh yeah, life goes on . . ."); as well as Christian songs "Jenny" by Steve Taylor and "Area 312" by Rez Band. I finished the tape with a segment from "For Annie" by Petra. Since this song deals with how we need to reach out to those who may be contemplating suicide, it served as an excellent discussion starter.

Every group I have used Rok Toks in has responded enthusiastically. Rok Toks are a refreshing new twist to the use of contemporary music—secular and Christian—within youth programming.

—Rick Chromey

Variations

1. Create a Rok Tok on "Money." Use the songs, "Money, Money, Money" by Abba; "Diamonds and Pearls" by Kansas; and songs from Christian artists such as First Strike and The Alwyn Wall Band.

2. Divide the teenagers into small groups. Have each group prepare a Rok Tok and lead a discussion on the chosen topic.

Your Ideas and Variations

_____
_____
_____
_____
_____
_____
_____
_____
_____
_____
_____
_____
_____
_____
_____

MUSICAL INSTRUMENTS

155

Kazoo Band
TOPIC: MUSIC/CHOIRS

Form a Kazoo Band with the members of your youth group. Divide into sections for soprano, alto, tenor and bass. Begin with the scale or simple tunes; then progress to hymns or even classical pieces. Be sure to schedule actual performances. A Kazoo Band provides great entertainment for all types of occasions—especially for little children.

For a kickoff performance, give a concert at the children's Sunday school. As a final number, play "Onward Christian Soldiers" and have the kids join your band in a follow-the-leader march to the refreshment table!

—Steve Newton

Variations

1. Make kazoos instead of buying them. Wrap a piece of wax paper around a comb—then hum through the comb teeth. The vibration of the paper against the comb sounds like a real kazoo!

2. Add other instruments to the Kazoo Band: cymbals, rhythm blocks, maracas, etc. Make joyful music to the Lord with this multi-instrument band.

Your Ideas and Variations

_____
_____
_____
_____
_____
_____
_____
_____
_____
_____
_____
_____
_____

156

Making a Worship Center
TOPIC: WORSHIP/GOD'S LOVE

Jesus knows our needs, worries, temptations and problems. Because of Jesus, we can come to God boldly and express our needs. It is no longer a throne of judgment, but a throne of mercy. There is help for the weak. In this meeting, the youth group members will learn Jesus Christ will meet their every need.

For this meeting, gather a harmonica and four tables. On the first table, place a piece of wood or paper, dried flowers, grass, twigs and glue. On the second table, place a clay pot, a small bag of potting soil and a

281

packet of vegetable seeds. On the third table, place two fairly large wooden sticks and a piece of rope or a leather thong. On the fourth table, place a pitcher, plastic cup, package of pre-sweetened Kool-Aid, water and crackers.

After group members arrive, start playing the harmonica. Play it very badly, and as loudly as you can. No doubt group members will groan or hold their ears. Say, "But I love the Lord so much! The Bible says to make a joyful noise unto the Lord. That's what I'm doing."

Play some more, then ask, "What's the matter? I'm sincere. Isn't that enough? What would you do? What talents do you have that are better than mine?"

Talk about the members' talents and how they would use them. Read and discuss Hebrews 4:14-16. Ask, "If we are weak and have no talent, should we just give up?"

Allow time for discussion, then say, "The Bible says God will meet all of our needs. If we don't have a talent in one particular area, he will provide something else for us."

Divide into four small groups. Assign each group to one of the four tables. Explain, "We need a beautiful worship center. I want you to make these four things: a beautiful marble altar;

a lovely picture to put on the altar; a golden cross; and communion wine in a chalice and wafers to represent the Bread of Life."

Leave the four groups alone to figure out what to do with the materials on their tables. When they are finished, the worship center should have: a nature picture made from dried flowers, a potted vegetable plant, a wooden cross, and a cup of Kool-Aid and crackers.

Ask, "Is this worship center acceptable? Can we worship God at this altar?"

Allow time for discussion, then say, "I asked for something grand, but you had to use what was at hand. Materials other than marble and gold were provided. How does God provide in your lives?"

Let the kids think of ideas such as:

● We need money—God gives us an opportunity to earn it.

● We need love—someone gives us a hug.

Conduct a worship service using the items group members made. Focus on thanking God for supplying all of our needs; then close with a feast of Kool-Aid and crackers.

—E. Jane Mall

Variations

1. At a retreat, assign four groups the worship center

needs: an altar, a picture, a cross, and communion elements. Rather than supplying the materials, give the groups 20 minutes to search inside and outside the building for ways to create these items. You'll be amazed at their creativity.

2. Set up the worship center outdoors. At the beginning of the service, give everyone five minutes to find something which is an invitation from God for worship. Then ask each person to share the item. For example, "The intricate veins of this leaf represent the paths of our lives. The entire leaf represents God's all-encompassing love as he watches over us. The leaf reminds us to worship our loving Father, because he cares for us so much."

After the insights are shared, invite the kids to arrange them in the center of the worship area. The items can be woven into the perfect mosaic that proclaims God's call to worship (**Creative Worship in Youth Ministry**, by Dennis C. Benson, Group Books).

Your Ideas and Variations

_____
_____
_____
_____
_____
_____

_____
_____
_____
_____
_____
_____
_____
_____

NAILS

157

Special Worship Services
TOPIC: EASTER/PASSION/GOOD FRIDAY/WORSHIP

Use these ideas to let your youth group members gain a deeper, spiritual meaning of the Easter season. They will experience sorrow and repentance on Good Friday—joy and victory on Easter.

Plan a Good Friday service for your youth group. Build a large cross out of 2×4s. Place this in the front of the meeting room. Gather various-size nails and a hammer. Dim the lights of the meeting room.

As the youth group members assemble for the service, give each one a nail. Ask the young people to ponder the nail as you say, "We all have been a part of the death of Christ. Our attitudes are no different from

those that killed Jesus: jealousy, envy, pride, anger, hatred and greed. We all have crucified Christ by these attitudes."

Ask the members to think of a sin they want to confess. Have them, one at a time, hammer their nail into the cross as a sign of their confession. Add to the somber atmosphere by pounding a hammer on an anvil in the background. As soon as all have finished, ask them to silently and reverently leave the room.

At the Easter morning service, give each person a long-stemmed flower such as a daisy as he or she enters the room. Announce, "Jesus Christ is risen. He is alive." Ask several guitarists to help lead an Easter song such as "Jesus Christ Is Risen Today." Ask the young people to bring life to the cross by hanging the flowers on the nails. This symbolizes Jesus' forgiveness of our sins—his victory over death. Sing more Easter songs, then display the beautiful cross for other church members to see.

Keep the cross year to year, leaving the nails in it. The cross becomes more rugged looking as the years pass; the services become more meaningful.

—L. Jim Anthis

Variations

1. Let your youth group plan these services for the entire congregation.

2. Keep the cross in a central spot in your youth room. Decorate the cross according to church holidays. For example, during the Christmas season surround the cross with red poinsettias; on Good Friday drape a black cloth over the cross; on Easter drape a white cloth over the cross and surround it with lilies.

Your Ideas and Variations

_____
_____
_____
_____
_____
_____
_____
_____
_____
_____
_____

NEEDLES

158

God's Elusive Presence
TOPIC: GOD

This game and Bible study illustrate that God is always present when we need him—even during the times when he seems hidden.

Before the lesson begins, hide a dozen sewing needles in the room. Make it tough: in cracks in the wall, in the chalkboard eraser with only the tip showing, stuck in the acoustical tile ceiling, etc.

Give each person a piece of paper and a pencil. Have the kids search the room for the needles. When they find the needles, they are to leave them in their places, and make a mental note of the hiding places. After about 10 minutes, bring the kids together and reveal the hiding places. Present a magnifying glass to the person who found the most!

Ask the group members to think about their feelings as they were searching for the needles. Did the experience remind them of times they were seeking God? Encourage discus-

sion.

Read Jeremiah 29:13 and ask, "How many of you have had an experience of seeking for, and finding God? Can you describe it to us?"

Read Psalm 105:1-4 and ask, "What do you think will happen to you if you seek God? How do you seek God?"

Read Matthew 6:33 and ask, "Does our task in seeking God go beyond the seeking itself? Explain."

Give each person a piece of paper and a needle. Ask the young people each to stick the needle to their paper and write, "Seek and you shall find" (Luke 11:9). Ask the kids to take the

paper home as a reminder of God's presence every moment, every day, in each one of our lives.

—James. D. Walton

Variations

1. Have everyone sit comfortably on chairs around the room. Ask the kids to close their eyes as you hide a needle. Find a spot for the needle so that everyone can see it without moving from their chairs. After it is "strategically" placed, ask the young people to open their eyes and look. When a person sees the needle he or she says, "I found it." The last person who finds the needle gets to hide it. Afterward discuss how we sometimes search for God in the wrong places, yet he is always within our sight.

Your Ideas and Variations

_____

_____

_____

_____

_____

_____

_____

_____

_____

_____

_____

_____

_____

_____

NEWSPAPERS

159

Eternal Life
TOPIC: DEATH/ETERNAL LIFE/ RESURRECTION

The Sadducees did not believe in life after death. The purpose of the Law was to preserve families from extinction. Their logic: If a woman married seven times, then in the next world she would have seven husbands. This meant that what was forbidden in this life would be okay in the next. Absurd!

They missed the whole point. Jesus told them that they were assuming that all conditions in the next life would be the same as they are here, and that's not true. In the next life there will be no marriage, no death; we will be like angels in heaven (Mark 12:18-27). Use this meeting to help the youth group think of life and death.

Gather a newspaper obituary, bones, dried flowers, funeral bulletin, handful of coins, incense to burn, and place them on a table. You also will need party items such as balloons, noisemakers, a fun record and a cake. Dim the lights and play somber funeral music.

As the class members enter, ask them to quietly walk around the table, view the items, then take their seats.

In a solemn voice say, "Mrs. Jones was a lively person. She was married for 40 years and raised three children. She was an active church member and a good wife and mother. This is all that is left of Mrs. Jones." (Turn to the table.)

Read and discuss Luke 20:27-47. Say that Mrs. Jones didn't leave a lot of material wealth. Some do. Ask if material wealth makes any difference. Then discuss these questions:

● What is the most important thing you can leave behind?

● As Christians, what is our hope for heaven? (For example, be with God; have a new body; have everlasting life.)

● Since no one has gone to heaven and then come back to tell about it, how can we be sure there is a heaven?

Then take everything off the table, turn up the lights, put on a party record and bring out party things. Give each person a balloon and noisemaker. Cut the cake and share. Then ask these questions:

● Is this wrong? Can we celebrate death? Why or why not?

● Is there a time when we cannot celebrate death? Explain.

Continue with the party, cele-

brating our lives on earth and our promise of eternal life.

—E. Jane Mall

Variations

1. Gather in a circle and have each person complete this sentence, "When I die, I want people to remember me as being . . ."

2. Discuss these questions with the youth group members:

● What is one word that describes your feelings of heaven?

● It has been said that earth is the real heaven or the real hell. Do you agree or disagree? Why or why not?

● What types of activities will we do in heaven?

● What does it take to get into heaven?

● Do you think St. Peter will meet us at the pearly gates? If not, how will we know we are in heaven when we get there?

Next, instruct the young people to find a partner with the

same color of eyes. The partners answer the following questions as the leader asks them. Allow a few minutes for each question.

● Mark 12:25 says, "For when they rise from the dead, they neither marry nor are given in marriage, but are like angels in heaven." What are angels in heaven like?

● Will we meet our family in heaven and have the same relationships?

● Isaiah 66:1 says, "Thus says the Lord, 'Heaven is my throne and the earth is my footstool; what is the house which you would build for me, and what is the place of my rest?' " Compare earth to a footstool. Why is it that way?

● Compare heaven to a throne. Why is it that way?

● How does thinking about heaven make you feel about problems on earth?

(The Youth Group Meeting Guide, by Rich Bimler, Group Books.)

Your Ideas and Variations

_____
_____
_____
_____
_____
_____
_____
_____
_____
_____

NEWSPRINT

160

Affirmation Event
TOPIC: AFFIRMATION/GROUP BUILDING

Let your youth group members give and receive affirmation with this activity.

For each person, you'll need a marker and a large 2-foot-by-3-foot piece of newsprint. Tape the pieces of newsprint to the walls of the meeting room. Write one person's name at the top of each piece of newsprint.

Give the kids 20 minutes to go to the different pieces of paper and write positive, affirming statements about the individual whose name is at the top. Each member should try to write on as many papers as possible, but *not* on his or her own. There will be wonderful statements such as "You are there when I need you," as well as funny statements like "You make me laugh—keep it up."

Each person can take his or her paper home and feel loved and encouraged by the positive things others see in him or her. Have the kids hang the posters in their rooms for daily affirmation.

—David Olshine

Variations

1. Form a circle. Give the group members five minutes to think how they will answer the following question: "If you could give each person in this group a gift (without thought of its actual feasibility), what gift would you give? For example, 'Because of your adventurous spirit, I want to give you a set of eagles' wings so you can soar to new adventures.' Or, 'Because you love to travel, I want to give you an airplane ticket with unlimited mileage so you can travel any time.' Or, 'Because you love to pray, I want to give you a giant, shady oak tree to sit under and pray to God.' "

Go around the circle and have each person share what gift he or she wants to give each individual and why he or she chose that gift (**Building Community in Youth Groups**, by Denny Rydberg, Group Books).

2. Form a circle, then distribute a paper and pencil to each person. Allow five minutes for each person to write seven qualities he or she admires about his or her parents.

Go around the circle and have each person share the qualities he or she admires. After one person has shared, have the group pick out two of the qualities in that person's parents that the individual also portrays in his or her own life. Ask the group members to describe and affirm a time the individual demonstrated those qualities (**Building Community in Youth Groups**, by Denny Rydberg, Group Books).

Your Ideas and Variations

_____
_____
_____
_____
_____
_____
_____
_____
_____
_____

161

Self-Acceptance
TOPIC: HOPE/SELF-IMAGE/ AFFIRMATION

This idea teaches young people the importance of self-acceptance and gives them hope for the future.

Give each group member a sheet of newsprint and one crayon. Read Ephesians 2:10. Tell them they are God's handiwork and are continually striving to become like him.

Explain, "Line three columns on the sheet of newsprint. Label the columns past, present and future. You'll have 20 minutes to

young people explain each of their columns of pictures. Allow time for members to affirm each other after they share. For example, a person could say, "Jim, I think you are an extremely positive and understanding person right now. In the future, I see you as a counselor, helping others through problems."

Assure the kids that God also sees the five positive things they've listed about themselves, and many more. Tell them to concentrate on the present and try to see how far God has brought them. By accepting themselves as they are now, emphasize how they can have hope for the future.

—Debbie Valleau

Variations

1. Ask the youth group members to choose songs that represent them in the past, present and future.

2. Rather than using newsprint, give each person three paper plates and a marker. Ask the young people to decorate the plates as clocks and label each one: past, present and future.

3. Give each person a pencil and a piece of paper. Have the youth group members each make a time line. Label the lower left-hand corner "birth" and the lower right-hand corner "death." Ask the kids to write in special events in their past and

think about these areas of your life. In the left column draw a picture symbolizing your past (sad or ugly face could represent an unhappy life; fire could represent a life of turmoil, etc.). In the middle column, draw a picture symbolizing the present (flower could represent peace; rocks—'My life is a little rocky right now,' etc.) and five things you like about yourself. In the third column, draw a picture symbolizing how you see yourself in the future (books could represent college, '$' could represent having a job). Begin your reflection."

Gather everyone at the end of 20 minutes for sharing. Have the ones they predict will happen in the future; for example, baptism, first day of school, first day of communion, first slumber party, straight A's, first date, high school graduation, college, marriage, etc.

Your Ideas and Variations

_____
_____
_____
_____
_____
_____
_____
_____
_____
_____
_____
_____
_____

NOVELTIES

162

Learning to Relax
TOPIC: MOODS/EMOTIONS

This exercise in "mood control" will increase teenagers' awareness of their moods and what to do about them. All you'll need are "mood stones" or "mood rings." (Mood rings were introduced on the market in the early '70s.) Try to find one mood stone for each member of your group. (Search at garage sales, Salvation Army stores or discount stores.)

On newsprint, write the 10 steps for dealing with stress. Post it on a wall. You also will need a piece of paper and a pencil for each person.

Gather the youth group members and explain mood stones by saying, "These stones vary, but many of them change colors from blue to green to brown to black, depending on how you're feeling. Black means you're highly agitated, nervous or stressed; brown means you're just a little shook up; if the stone is green, you're fairly calm; while blue means you're cool as a cucumber."

Let everyone hold the mood stone long enough to get a color reading. Ask everyone to remember his or her color. Next discuss things that upset, worry, or bother us—especially things we can do little or nothing about.

Read Matthew 6:25-34, then ask, "If Jesus gave his followers that advice, isn't this a pretty good indication that our fears, nerves and anxieties are not completely beyond our control? The study of biofeedback gives us clues about self-control techniques as well as offering us the opportunity to improve our obedience to Jesus' words. Here's a 10-step program for obeying him in this area of your life." Call the students' attention to the newsprint; go over each of the 10 steps.

1. When you feel nervous or upset, use the mood stone to discover your stress level.

2. Stop what you're doing and remember Jesus' words in Matthew 6:25-34; he told you not to worry needlessly.

3. Pray a short prayer, asking Jesus for help in calming yourself. Thank him for giving that help.

4. Read Psalm 23. It's the one that begins, "The Lord is my shepherd . . ." Pause after each idea and try to visualize it. Notice your breathing pattern while reading and thinking. Try to make each breath come from the bottom of your stomach.

5. Use the mood stone again. You'll probably discover your mood has improved, but keep going. Now you're in the right frame of mind to do something about your problem.

6. Take a sheet of paper and write a clear description of your problem at the top.

7. List all the solutions to your problem you can come up with.

8. Add "accept it" to your list if it's a problem you can do nothing about.

9. If there is something you can do, plan a strategy. Make your strategy detailed enough that you can take one step at a time.

10. Begin taking those steps.

Distribute paper and a pencil to each person. Give the kids 15 to 20 minutes to think of a problem and try to work through it using the 10 steps. Discuss the process when everyone is finished.

The mood stone exercise will draw teenagers' attention to Jesus' words about needless worry. With practice, they may learn how to cope in stressful situations. The important thing to remember is Jesus doesn't want us to be anxious, up-tight, stressed-out people; there are techniques to help us obey his wishes.

—Walter Mees

Variations

1. If you can't find mood stones, look for a product called "Stress-less: Biofeedback Stress Control System." Write for information to Allied Research Corp., 336 Old Hook Rd., Westwood, NJ 07675, (201) 664-8500.

2. Give the youth group members each a piece of paper and a pencil. Ask them to write down these verses and keep the paper. Instruct them to read the verses whenever they feel stressed or worried: Psalms 46:1-3, 10; 56:11; 61:8; Matthew

6:25-34; Luke 12:32; John 14:1, 27.

Your Ideas and Variations

_____
_____
_____
_____
_____
_____
_____
_____
_____
_____
_____
_____

163

Wacky Wallwalker Races
TOPIC: GAMES

This is a really fun event to use in your youth group.

For your next meeting, ask the kids to bring "Wacky Wallwalkers" that come in certain kinds of cereal boxes. These wonderful, rubbery creatures climb down the walls like eerie spiders.

Mark a spot on the top of the wall as the starting line and another line toward the bottom as the finish. Tell the contestants that when you yell "go" they are to throw their Wacky Wallwalkers above the starting line.

The first Wallwalker to cross the finish line wins. Compete for the best time. Determine the top three winners and award prizes. How about a box of cereal for each winner?

You also can have the contestants name their Wallwalkers and invent stories about their lives. Have the kids introduce their "friends." For example, "This is Wally Wallwalker. He has lived for several weeks in a stuffy home. He never is hungry—he always has more than his share to eat. Wally really wants to stretch his legs now that he's on his own and out of his box."

Enjoy the wacky introductions as well as the wacky race!
—Jeffrey A. Collins

Variations

1. If you can't find enough Wacky Wallwalkers, ask your young people to go to a discount

store and buy a Slinky. Race the Slinkies down the steps of your church.

2. Raid the church nursery toy box or have the youth group members search their little brother's or sister's closets. Make sure every person has a wind-up toy—then host "The Great Toy Box Derby."

Your Ideas and Variations

_____
_____
_____
_____
_____
_____
_____
_____
_____
_____
_____
_____

PAINT

164

Bible Murals
TOPIC: BIBLE STUDY/MURALS/
    CREATIVITY

The purpose of the mural is to teach a specific Bible story or concept while having fun through the creative process.

You'll need flat, white house paint, a paint roller, various colors of tempera paints, 2-inch brushes, smaller brushes for detail work, paper, pencils and a Bible.

Discuss these considerations with the youth group and the appropriate officials before you begin your Bible Mural.

● What size is the proposed mural?

● When will it be completed?

● Will it be relatively easy to clean up after each painting session?

● Will the project cause others any inconveniences?

● Is the space in a location where you can work on the mural at any time?

● How often, if at all, will the mural be changed?

● Discuss any other items that may be unique to your group or church.

Gather the youth group members and list their favorite Bible stories. Then take a vote for the all-time favorite. Once a story is chosen, say that they are going to have a chance to create a mural to portray the story.

Distribute paper and pencils and ask the young people to sketch rough ideas on how best to illustrate the story. For example, someone could draw Jesus in the temple surrounded by older "learned" men. Around the temple could be crowds of people, animals, trees, etc. In one corner could be Mary and Joseph asking, "Have you seen Jesus?" Go over all of the sketches and agree on one to enlarge for the mural.

Use large brushes or rollers to cover the surface with a flat, white house paint. After it dries, begin painting the mural. Obviously, some group members will not feel comfortable using a brush. Let them ease into the project. There are many other jobs that they can do such as mixing colors.

This project gives the group members a sense of accomplishment, an opportunity for fellowship and is a learning experience. The mural also is a source of inspiration for those who see it.

—Steve Roberts

Variations

1. Paint the wall mural on butcher paper. Display the finished work in the youth room or on a wall in the church. Let the whole congregation enjoy the art masterpiece!

—Steve Newton

2. Decorate the walls of the youth room to represent your group. Paint the wall with symbols, names and special events that characterize the current youth group. For example, "Re-

member the talent show of 19____?" Or, "In 19____, the seniors were in charge of the best submarine-sandwich-eating contest." (Paint a large submarine sandwich on the wall.)

Do a good job, and keep up the tradition. As the years go by, let each group add their names, activities and special events. The wall painting creates nostalgic feelings for the past; yet it also promises hope for good things to come in future youth groups.

—Bruce M. Nichols

Your Ideas and Variations

_____
_____
_____
_____
_____
_____
_____
_____
_____
_____

165

Colorful Ideas
TOPIC: DISCUSSION STARTERS

Never throw away old "stuff" like paint charts. You'll be surprised at their uses!

Go to a paint store, home decorating shop or discount store.

Ask them to give you their old paint charts. Cut up a paint chart into squares then use the squares as follows:

Glue them to name tags and allow the kids to choose their own colors. Divide the kids into groups by colors. Then ask questions for small group discussion such as:

● Why did you choose your color?

● What mood does your color represent?

● What moods or feelings could the other colors represent?

● Think of how you are feeling now. What color represents that feeling? Explain.

Another idea is to use the paint chart squares for an object lesson. Pass out one paint square to each person. Say, "Sir Isaac Newton, the discoverer of gravity, was conducting an experiment on light. By passing sunlight through a prism, Newton demonstrated that ordinary sunlight is actually made up of an infinite number of spectrum colors. The sum of the diverse colors is responsible for light. You hold in your hand a color. As a member of the body of Christ, you are indispensable. Our effectiveness as a unit would be diminished without your cooperation and participation. Add your color to ours in this effort. You are important!"

Have all of the participants glue their color squares to a piece of posterboard. Label the top of the poster: "We are one!"

I'll bet you never guessed that paint chart squares could be so useful!

—Dave Mahoney

Variations

1. Give each youth group member a paint chart. Have the kids label their chart, "Ways to Brighten My Life." Ask them to write on each paint square a goal they feel would enhance their life. For example, "Go out to eat once a week with a friend." "Talk to my parents each night." "Read one chapter in the Bible each day." "Slow down."

2. Supply paper, paintbrushes, scissors, glue, fabric scraps, paint charts, crayons and paints. Have the young people create "Color Collages." Have them glue different-colored squares and fabric scraps to the paper, then use crayons and paint to splash on additional colors. Study the blinding brightness of God's love and forgiveness. Read and discuss these verses: Romans 5:1-11; 8:38-39; 1 John 1:8-9; 3:1, 16-18; 4:16-21. Or study Paul's blinding conversion in Acts 9:1-31.

Your Ideas and Variations

_____
_____
_____
_____
_____
_____
_____
_____
_____
_____

166

Finger Paint and Theology
TOPIC: GOD/CHRISTIAN SYMBOLS

Christian terms can be intimidating to young people. Terms like "sin," "saved," and "righteousness" can bring discussion

to a halt. Finger painting can provide a means of expressing and exploring these concepts.

Design a meeting to let the youth group members explore religious language and express feelings through finger painting. You'll need finger paints of various colors, paper, water, towels, newspapers, classical music and a record player. Cover a table with newspapers and set up the finger painting materials.

When the young people arrive, ask them to select some religious terms that are particularly difficult to handle. Allow time for discussion on why these terms are hard to understand. Ask the kids to each choose one

term and think of how they could portray it using finger paints. For example, sin could be symbolized with black paint and bold, zigzag strokes.

Gather the participants around the table. Have them use the materials to create a finger painting of a religious term. Turn on some classical music and allow the creative expressions to flow. When everyone is through, share and discuss the creations. Dry the paintings and give them titles.

Your youth group can explain their creations to the elementary Sunday school classes and help them do the same process. Share the fun!

—Karen Darling

Variations

1. Choose two types of music: somber, slow, melancholy; happy, joyful, upbeat. Play the somber music first and let the youth group members finger paint according to their mood. Then play the joyful music and finger paint accordingly. Compare the two paintings; discuss how music affects our moods.

2. Roll out some butcher paper and give everybody a paintbrush. Play several types of music (classical, country, jazz, etc.) and have the kids paint according to the moods that the music creates. After several minutes, have the artists stand

back and admire their "mood mural."

3. Try finger painting with various flavors of pudding. The clean up is easy—the kids simply lick their fingers!

Your Ideas and Variations

_____
_____
_____
_____
_____
_____
_____
_____
_____
_____
_____
_____
_____

PANTY HOSE CONTAINERS

167

Spreading Christmas Joy
TOPIC: CHRISTMAS/ELDERLY/ OUTREACH

When it's time for a Christmas work project, collect some egg-shaped panty hose containers. Gather some string, glitter, glue, a few permanent markers—and you're all set.

Let the young people decorate the containers with Christmas

designs, pictures and messages. Glue the string to the top of the container and, before you know it, your group can deliver some very original Christmas ornaments to your church shut-ins.

Deliver the ornaments and serenade the shut-ins with favorite Christmas carols. This activity is sure to spread Christmas joy to all involved.

—Denise Turner

Variations

1. Decorate the panty hose containers as ornaments for an Easter egg tree.

2. Plan an Easter egg hunt for the Sunday school children. Place a coupon for a free Bible in an egg-shaped panty hose container; wrap it in aluminum foil. Hide the "silver egg," along with candy eggs and hard-boiled eggs; present a Bible to the finder of the silver-coated prize!

Your Ideas and Variations

_____
_____
_____
_____
_____
_____
_____
_____
_____
_____
_____
_____
_____
_____

PAPER

168

Communication Drawings
TOPIC: COMMUNICATION

This game is an excellent way to introduce a study on communication. Gather pieces of paper, pencils, and magazine ads that depict common household items such as a blow-dryer, sofa or stereo.

Choose a person to be the "artist" and give him or her a piece of paper and a pencil. Show one magazine ad to the group (not to the artist). The group members must describe the chosen picture to the artist without actually saying anything about it. They may direct pen movement and give other directions such as, "Draw a line straight down the page. The line should be on the far left side of the paper. On the far right side of the paper draw a parallel line."

Once the artist identifies the picture, choose a new artist and a new picture. Then discuss the activity using these questions:

- How did the artists feel?
- Did anyone "take over" the descriptions? Explain.
- Did anyone feel left out of the descriptive process? Explain.
- Were some of the directions difficult to understand? Give some examples.

This game is sure to stimulate good discussion and make the kids aware of the importance of clear communication.

—Mitchell M. Olson

Variations

1. Try the activity once, allowing the "artist" to ask clarifying questions about the directions; try the activity a second time and don't allow clarifying questions. Discuss how clarifying questions facilitate clear communication.

2. Ask the youth group members to be the "artists" and give them each a piece of paper and a pen. Show an ad to one person (not the artists). Have him or her direct the pen movements.

Choose the artist's rendition that most resembles the ad. Give the artist the "Silver Pen Award" (a pen wrapped in aluminum foil).

Your Ideas and Variations

_____

_____

_____

_____

_____

_____

_____

_____

_____

_____

_____

_____

169

Computer Banners
TOPIC: CHRISTMAS/OUTREACH

Have the youth group members create banners of good will or good cheer for shut-ins. They can be "Merry Christmas" banners, "Happy Birthday" banners, or banners for any special occasion.

Find a member in your congregation who has a computer and a printer. Ask the member to help you print the banners (using a software program that enables you to create pictures and letters). Then gather the

youth group members to color
and sign them.

Plan a banner-delivery day. If
the banner delivery is for Christmas, sing Christmas carols to
the shut-ins; if the banner delivery is for a birthday, sing "Happy Birthday." Stay and visit
awhile—show the people that
they are remembered and loved.

—Mitchell M. Olson

Variations

1. Create banners to introduce a play. Roll out the title,
then let the action begin!

2. Design banners with a retreat theme or meeting topic.

3. Use other software programs for cards, coupons or bulletin boards. The ideas are endless!

Your Ideas and Variations

_____
_____
_____
_____

_____
_____
_____
_____
_____
_____
_____
_____
_____
_____

170

Erasing Sin
_TOPIC: RECONCILIATION/SIN/
REPENTANCE_

Focus a youth group meeting
on sin and forgiveness. All you'll
need is paper, pen and pencil
for each person.

Distribute paper and ball
point pens and ask the young
people to begin writing their autobiography. Explain that an autobiography is the story of your

life written by yourself. After 10 minutes, ask the kids to stop and review what they've written so far. See if any errors were made in writing. Say, "We can't write or live our lives perfectly—the reality of sin is that we are alienated from God, from others, and from our true selves. From a worldly view, sin and death are similar to the pen—it seems we have permanent ink only. But the Gospel proclaims forgiveness, and in that respect, life is more like a pencil and eraser. 'If we confess our sins, he (God) is faithful and just, and will forgive our sins and cleanse us from all unrighteousness' (1 John 1:9)."

Have the group members continue writing their autobiographies with pencils as they experience the freedom of forgiveness. Ask volunteers to read these verses on forgiveness: Nehemiah 9:17; Psalm 130:4; Matthew 26:28; Romans 4:7; Ephesians 4:32.

Share the autobiographies, then conclude the meeting with a prayer thanking God for erasing our sins.

—Lynn Potter

Variations

1. Combine the autobiographies into one book. Title the book "All About Us"; design a cover and let everyone sign it. Give a copy of this book to each

of the youth group members as a keepsake of their year together.

2. As a closing "amen" activity, have the young people shout, "Jesus erases all of our sins!" Then, give the kids each an eraser to take home with them as a reminder of Jesus' forgiveness.

Your Ideas and Variations

_____
_____
_____
_____
_____
_____
_____
_____
_____
_____
_____
_____

171

Gentle Thursday
TOPIC: OUTREACH/CAMPUS MINISTRY

Show college students you care by planning a "Gentle Thursday" once a month. Our youth group members sponsored a Gentle Thursday at a local college—you could do the same. If you don't have a college in your town, secure permission from a local high school and show a little compassion, love and interest in those students.

Our youth group members bought red contact paper and cut out hearts. They used a black marker and wrote on each heart, "Have a Gentle Thursday."

We went to the local college campus and passed out hearts and did extra special things for people. For example, we helped students carry their books, we told people to have a great day, etc. Some of our young people wore T-shirts printed with, "Have a Gentle Thursday."

One Thursday, we rented a cotton candy machine from a local rental company and gave out cotton candy. We also distributed "sweet" sayings with the candy such as "Jesus loves you" and "Do unto others as you would have them do unto you."

Gentle Thursday is a wonderful way to help your youth group members reach out to others in your community.

—J.B. Collingsworth

Variations

1. Sponsor a Gentle Thursday at a shopping mall, grocery store or nursing home.

2. Change the name to Servant Sunday and sponsor the activity after a church service.

Your Ideas and Variations

172

The "Haves" and the "Have Nots"
TOPIC: POVERTY/JUSTICE/WORKCAMPS

"Righteousness" is a term not often used in our speech today. Yet Jesus tells us in the Sermon on the Mount that we are to "hunger and thirst after righteousness." This simulation game will enable young people to struggle with the meaning of this verse and to be challenged to take action.

This activity was created for use on the night before the first day of a workcamp. However, it is appropriate to use any time to confront young people with the inequity in our world and to challenge them to use whatever resources they have to work for justice.

Gather enough construction paper, Popsicle sticks, paper clips, tape, scissors, glue sticks, pipe cleaners, wire, and crepe paper to make a packet for each team of five to six young people. Prepare the packets unequally so that some teams have bright-colored construction paper and plenty of supplies to easily construct a house while others have dull-colored paper and few supplies. Be sure some teams do not have scissors or tape. You also will need pencils, index cards, matches and a candle.

Divide the participants into teams. (If you are using this during a workcamp, use the same teams as the groups working on houses.) Tell them the object of this game is to build a house to the best of their abilities in a 20-minute time period. Do not give any additional instructions! Give each team a packet which they are not to open until you say to begin. After each team has a packet, begin the game.

After the 20-minute period, stop the game. Each team answers the following questions:

● **For the "Have" teams:** What were your thoughts and feelings during this game? Did you share your materials with any other team? Did any of you think of helping another team? Did you want to share? Did you feel guilty that you had so much when other teams had so little?

Did you make a deal with any other team to trade materials or construction ideas?

● **For the "Have Not" teams:** What were your thoughts and feelings during this game? Did you ask for materials or ideas for construction from any other team? Did you think about or try to steal materials from other teams? Did you consider just giving up? Did you decide not to ask for materials or ideas from other teams because you wanted to prove you could do it yourself? Did you consider joining together with other "Have Not" teams to combine your materials to construct a better house?

● **For all teams:** According to **Webster's New World Dictionary**, "righteous" comes from combining the words "right" and "wise." It means, "acting in a just, upright manner; doing what is right; virtuous; morally justifiable [full of righteous anger]." How does this game relate to Matthew 5:6? What would it mean for the "Have" teams to act with righteousness? What would it mean for the "Have Not" teams to act with righteousness? What do you think is the good news of this verse for the "Haves"? the "Have Nots"?

Place all the completed houses in a circle around a lighted candle. Gather all the teams together and sit in a circle around the houses. Have each team share their feelings and answers to the reflective questions.

Conclude with the following worship experience, which focuses on making our community more righteous. Ask a young person to volunteer to read the parts not designated as "unison." Dim the lights.

Call to Worship and Praise

Leader: "Rejoice in the Lord, O you righteous! Praise befits the upright. Praise the Lord with the lyre, make melody to him with the harp of ten strings! Sing to him a new song, play skillfully on the strings, with loud shouts" (Psalm 33:1-3).

Sing upbeat songs about cooperation and togetherness such as "We Are the Family of God." (**Songs,** by Yohann Anderson, Songs and Creations, Inc.)

Words of Confession

Unison: "Dear God, we're afraid of this upcoming event. We fear we might not have the strength or courage to complete our work projects. Help us through this trying time. Make us strong."

Prayer of Forgiveness

Leader: "Dear God, we thank you that you love us no matter how great our doubts and fears. We know that you are here with us right now, guiding us in this workcamp. We celebrate your forgiveness and your love! Amen."

Hear God's Word

Leader: "Blessed are those who hunger and thirst for righteousness, for they shall be satisfied" (Matthew 5:6).

We Respond

Leader: "Each of us has the power to choose how we will use the resources God has given us to make our community more righteous. Write on the card you receive what you will do to support this workcamp."

(Substitute "make our community more just" for "support this workcamp" if needed. Distribute index cards and pencils. After each person has finished writing, build a bridge with the cards to connect the houses in the center of your circle. Invite each person to read his or her card aloud before adding it to the bridge structure. Have an adult leader go first. Fold the first cards in half and stand on the ends to make "supports" for the bridge. Then place the remaining cards flat on top of the supports to complete the bridge.)

Unison: "It is you. It is me. Each of us a separate person, yet choosing to join together for the same purpose: to make a difference; to use what we have to work toward the elimination of poverty housing in our community; to act with righteousness! Amen!"

—Kathi B. Finnell

Variations

1. Save the construction-paper houses. At the end of the work-camp, have the kids look at the paper houses and compare them to the work projects. Discuss whether the workers felt they had all of the necessary skills and equipment to repair the homes in the community. Ask how obstacles were overcome and how God works for good in all things.

Your Ideas and Variations

_____
_____
_____
_____
_____
_____
_____
_____
_____
_____

173

L.O.V.E.S. Month
TOPIC: VOLUNTEERS/AFFIRMATION

"L.O.V.E.S. Month" is a special way to let your volunteer staff know how much your youth group appreciates their ministry. L.O.V.E.S. stands for **L**oving **O**ur **V**olunteers for **E**xceptional **S**ervice.

Have the young people choose a month and proclaim it L.O.V.E.S. Month. (February is an ideal month, but any month will do.) On each Sunday of that month, honor and express love and appreciation for a different group of volunteers. The first Sunday could be for youth group sponsors, the second for Bible school teachers, the third for youth coaches, the fourth for children's church workers, and so on. Make sure all of your volunteers are recognized.

Have the youth group members make heart-shaped pins or stickers by cutting hearts out of red contact paper. Write each volunteer's name on a heart. You also could make hearts out of red construction paper and use straight pins to pin them on the volunteers' clothing.

Recognize volunteers each Sunday by asking them to stand at a special time during the worship service. Have group members give the heart-shaped pins to the volunteers. Encourage the kids to seek them out for handshakes, hugs, or a few words of encouragement.

Publicize L.O.V.E.S. Month in newsletters, bulletins and on posters. Clearly indicate which volunteers are being recognized each Sunday. By the end of the month, your volunteers will have no doubts as to how much they and their ministry are appreciated.

—Tommy Baker

Variations

1. Highlight the end of the month by holding a banquet or special dinner for your volunteers. For dessert, serve a heart-shaped cake complete with pink frosting and red hots for the "red-hot, exceptional volunteers!"

2. Use this same idea to celebrate other special occasions: birthdays, anniversaries, Mother's Day, Father's Day, high school graduation, etc.

Your Ideas and Variations

_____
_____
_____
_____
_____
_____
_____
_____
_____
_____
_____
_____
_____
_____
_____

174

Palm Trees
TOPIC: DECORATIONS

Plan a Hawaiian luau for your youth group. Include all the fun things such as Hawaiian music, dancing, mouthwatering fruit and delicious fruit drinks. Add an extra-special touch by decorating the room with palm trees. Here's how.

Tape several wrapping paper cylinders end to end to form an 8-foot trunk. Form branches out of reshaped coat hangers covered with brown crepe paper. Tape the branches to the top of the trunk. Make palm fronds out of green construction paper or green crepe paper. Tape the palm fronds to the branches. Prop up the tree by sticking the base in a large pot filled with soil.

There you have it. Your very own swayin'-in-the-breeze palm tree. Aloha.

—Tim Pontius

Variations

1. Plan a Banana-Eating Contest. See who can eat the most bananas, or see who can eat one banana in record-breaking time. This race is especially funny when you give each of the contestants a glass of 7-Up to

drink after they eat their banana.

2. Divide the kids into two groups. Give each group a coconut, a hammer and a screwdriver—then host The Great Coconut-Cracking Contest. The teams race against each other to see who can be the first to crack open and eat their coconut.

Your Ideas and Variations

_____
_____
_____
_____
_____
_____
_____
_____
_____
_____
_____
_____

175

Personalized Place Mats
TOPIC: DISCUSSION STARTERS

All youth group leaders can use new ideas to start discussions. Personalized Place Mats are great discussion-starters, and they help the kids get to know each other better. These place mats work especially well during meal times at retreats.

Give each youth group member a piece of construction paper and a marker. On the paper, have the kids answer questions according to the theme of the retreat. Or you can have the kids answer questions such as these:

- Where were you born?
- Where were you raised?
- Share some funny stories about your childhood.
- What schools did you attend?
- What did you like about the schools?
- Who was your best friend in grade school?
- What do you like to do in your spare time?
- Do you have any hobbies?
- Whom do you most admire (past, present, real or fictional)? Why?
- Describe your idea of the perfect holiday.

Cover the place mats with clear contact paper so they will last longer. Set the tables using these creations. When the kids come in to eat, have them sit by someone they don't know very well. Have the partners discuss the questions while they enjoy their food. A great way to make use of meal times!

—Mary Kay Fitzpatrick

Variations

1. Make place cards by using the same materials. Simply cut

the construction paper into 6-inch-by-6-inch squares. Have the kids fold them in half and write their name on one side. Over the rest of the card, have them answer questions about themselves.

2. Make centerpieces. Divide the young people into small groups and give each group a large piece of construction paper and several markers. Have the kids in each group design a centerpiece with their names and answers to the questions.

3. For your next retreat, ask kids to bring a recent picture of themselves. On 11×17 pieces of paper, make copies of the following place mat and distribute them to the participants. Have them answer the questions, tape their picture in the upper-left corner, and cover it with clear contact paper. Shuffle the place mats and set them at different locations for each meal to encourage the kids to make new friends.

—David Washburn

Your Ideas and Variations

_____
_____
_____
_____
_____
_____
_____
_____
_____
_____
_____
_____
_____
_____

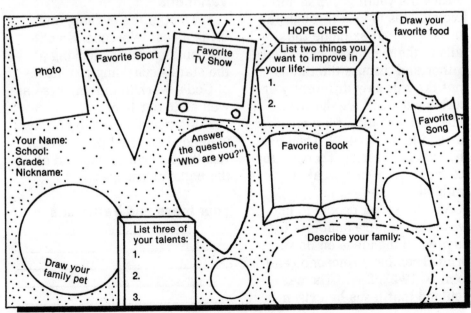

176

Unless I See
TOPIC: FAITH/BIBLE STUDY

This Bible study focuses on Thomas, the disciple, and Christ's active role in our lives.

Distribute a piece of paper to each youth group member. Ask the kids each to make a telescope by rolling the paper into a cone. They can adjust the "lens" to get a wide or narrow view.

Say, "Sometimes we walk through life without really noticing the things around us. Sometimes we need to narrow our view and look at things more closely."

Give the youth group members five minutes to look through the telescopes and examine the details of the meeting room. Then gather and discuss the things that the kids saw differently or perhaps noticed for the first time. Ask a youth group member to read John 20:24-29. Then ask the kids to describe Thomas; for example, skeptical, weak in faith, etc.

Ask the young people to list ways that we are doubters today; write the ideas on newsprint. Then have someone read John 20:19-23. Say, "Thomas doubted that Jesus had risen,

but that wasn't his real problem. His real problem was that he didn't look for the signs of the Resurrection in the right place; for example, on the faces of the other disciples. The other disciples were no longer afraid, but filled with joy."

Give the members each a marker and ask them to write on their telescopes the answers to these questions:

● Where do you see Christ's love in your life?

● How can you help others to see Christ's love?

Share the ideas written on the telescopes, then have the kids keep them as reminders to look for Christ's love in everyday blessings.

—Nancy Going

Variations

1. Meet in the evening and bring a real telescope. Go outside and take turns looking at the stars—sparkling reminders of God's work in the universe as well as in our lives.

2. Make binoculars by taping together two toilet paper rolls. Use the binoculars instead of the paper telescopes.

Your Ideas and Variations

_____

_____

_____

_____

_____

—————————————
—————————————
—————————————
—————————————
—————————————
—————————————
—————————————
—————————————

PASTA

177

Judgment
TOPIC: CHRISTIAN UNITY/JUSTICE

Salvation comes to us through a personal relationship with our Lord—in our knowledge of him. The hour of judgment will bring many surprises.

For this meeting, you'll need several world almanacs (they do not have to be current) and pasta cookbooks. On a tray, place many kinds of uncooked pasta such as noodles, macaroni and spaghetti.

In small groups, look through the world almanacs. Take note of the many different kinds of people, places, religions, colleges, languages, etc. Talk about the places young people have visited or hope to visit.

Bring out the tray of pasta. Let group members look through the pasta cookbooks. Ask them

to tell their favorite pasta, how they like it cooked, etc.

Read and discuss Luke 13:22-30. Talk about how the day of judgment will be full of surprises.

Tell the group you think the only really good pasta is linguine with clam sauce, but your neighbor only cooks macaroni and cheese. Ask other ways we differ from each other. For example, different ways of studying for a test, doing chores, asking for a date. Ask, "Who's right and who's wrong?"

Allow time for discussion then say, "I say linguine is best and my neighbor says macaroni is best, but we both produce the same thing: a nourishing meal our families enjoy. So it is with Christians. We all love the same Lord, but we have different ways of expressing our love. Some kneel, some wave their

arms and shout. Who can say which is right or wrong? Or even best? Only God knows. We have no right to judge."

—E. Jane Mall

Variations

1. Ask the kids to bring their favorite pasta recipes to class. Discuss why the recipes are their favorites, then proceed with the lesson.

2. Follow the discussion by serving a hot meal of scrumptious spaghetti and meatballs.

Your Ideas and Variations

_____
_____
_____
_____
_____
_____
_____
_____
_____
_____
_____

PERFUME

178

The Scent
TOPIC: CROWDBREAKER

Need a unique way to divide your kids into groups? How about using perfume?

You will need a number of distinct smelling perfumes—one for each group you intend to form. Disguise the different perfume containers.

Spray or dab perfume on each young person and be sure that he or she doesn't see the bottle. Be careful not to get perfume in a person's eyes or on a person's clothing. Keep a master list of who was sprayed with what perfume.

The fun part for the kids is sniffing out their group. Everyone uses his or her sniffer to find people wearing the same perfume.

A crazy idea? The young people won't forget the experience for some time. In fact, they'll probably talk about it at school. Activities like this one help the kids let others know that they are active in a church youth group. Alas—a new evangelism technique!

—Arlo R. Reichter

Variations

1. Use this activity to lead into a Bible study on Matthew 26:6-13. In this passage, the disciples become indignant when a woman anoints Jesus with an expensive ointment.

2. Bubble Gum Crowdbreaker is another way to divide your kids into smaller groups. Selectively distribute different-col-

ored bubble gum and ask the group members to chew only the gum you've provided. If you want three small groups, hand out three colors; if you want four small groups, hand out four colors; etc.

To split into the groups, ask kids to blow bubbles and get together with other kids who have the same-colored bubbles.

If you later want to further divide the groups, have a bubble-blowing contest. Pass out more gum to group members who have discarded their original wads (colors don't matter at this point). Choose the three kids who blow the largest bubbles to form a group; choose the three kids whose bubbles pop first to form another group; and continue this process until everyone belongs to a new small group (**Try This One . . . Strikes Again**, Group Books).

Your Ideas and Variations

_____
_____
_____
_____
_____
_____
_____
_____
_____
_____
_____
_____

PHOTOGRAPHS

179

High School Photos
TOPIC: POSTER

Capture everyone's attention and give the adult sponsors an opportunity to remember "the good ol' days" by making this unique poster.

Ask your adult sponsors and the pastor to bring one or two of their high school pictures. The older your staffers are, the more fun your group will have posting these pictures.

On a large piece of posterboard, tape or glue the pictures. At the top write "Guess Who?" Hang the poster in your youth room.

For fun, let the kids make yearbook descriptions for each picture. For example, "Tim Smith. Involved in drama club and speech club. Enjoys potlucks and going out for sodas. Voted as most likely to become a full-time youth group sponsor."

Combine the descriptions, make copies and give one to each of the sponsors!

—Leonard Kageler

Variations

1. Ask the young people to give you one of their baby pictures before the next youth group meeting. Number each picture then pin them to a bulletin board. When the kids arrive, give them a piece of paper and a pencil and have them guess the names of the babies. Use this activity as a springboard to a discussion on 1 Corinthians 13:11. Ask these questions:

● What does it mean to "give up childish ways"?

● How can you "give up childish ways" with regard to spirituality?

● How can you "grow up" in your faith?

—Rhonda Olshine

2. Collect baby pictures of various church leaders such as the ministers, board chairmen,

choir directors, organist, etc. Mount the pictures on a bulletin board and number them. On the top half of a sheet of paper, list the numbers and leave spaces for people to write their guesses. At the bottom, randomly list the names of those pictured. Make copies and sell each sheet for $2. Announce the winner in the church bulletin or newsletter.

—Gail Alston

Your Ideas and Variations

_____
_____
_____
_____
_____
_____
_____
_____
_____
_____

180

Picture Captions
TOPIC: HUNGER

Help your youth group create an art gallery about world hunger. Choosing and writing captions for pictures of starving people will motivate the kids to do something about world hunger.

Gather three or four large cardboard boxes, plain-colored paper, construction paper, tape, markers, about 10 8×10 pictures depicting world need. Inquire at your denominational relief organizations or one such as UNICEF, 331 East 38th St., New York, NY 10016, (212) 686-5522.

Ask the kids to stack the boxes on top of each other (largest on bottom, smallest on top) to form a kiosk (multi-sided billboard). Tape the boxes together. Instruct them to cover all sides of the boxes with plain-colored paper; then mount the pictures on construction paper and glue them attractively on the kiosk.

Next, ask the young people to select an appropriate, thought-provoking caption for each picture that will inform people about world need. Encourage the kids to examine each picture carefully and use their imaginations. A picture of a mother and child outside of their home could be captioned, "Most families live in homes about the size of our toolsheds. The homes are small, ramshackle shanties."

Once the kiosk is finished, place it in the middle of the narthex or hallway so it can be shared with the congregation. Collect money, clothes and food and donate these to relief organizations. Help make others aware of the hungry and needy people of the world.

—Brethren House Ministries

Variations

1. With permission, display the kiosk at a shopping center, mall or school. Distribute hunger literature and collect money to donate to world hunger organizations.

2. Change the pictures and captions at regular intervals. Emphasize different countries' needs or different missionaries' needs.

Your Ideas and Variations

_____

_____

_____

_____

_____

_____

_____

_____

_____

_____

PICTURES

Framed Pictures
TOPIC: PUBLICITY/AFFIRMATION

Want to affirm your youth group members with a unique gift? Give them each a framed picture of their favorite things.

Look for pictures of the teenagers' favorite athletes, movie stars, animals, Christian music groups and performers. From your local newspaper, cut out articles and pictures that feature the youth group members in school or community events.

Arrange the pictures as a collage on a piece of cardboard. Leave at least a 1-inch border around the sides. Cover the border with a variety of items such as strands of different colored yarn, glitter or sequins, or patches of leather or fabric.

Framed Pictures are affordable projects that let your young people know that you care.

—Linda R. Hazzard

Variations

1. Gather several youth group members and form a "Framed Picture Patrol." Have them keep track of youth group members who are sick, inactive, or who

will be celebrating birthdays. Have the patrol put together the pictures.

2. Take orders for custom-made pictures from members of the congregation. Charge a small fee to make money for the youth group and deliver them with a smile!

Your Ideas and Variations

_____
_____
_____
_____
_____
_____
_____
_____
_____
_____
_____
_____

182

Gossip
TOPIC: GOSSIP/COMMUNICATION

Everyone has experienced gossip in one form or another. This lesson will help youth group members better understand why people gossip and how to avoid it.

You will need a picture of a skeleton to hang up in front of the room. Many discount stores sell cardboard skeletons, especially around Halloween. You also will need a magazine picture of a man or woman, pencils and paper.

Ask the youth group members what the phrase "skeletons in the closet" means. Discuss the idea that everyone has personal things they don't want others to know or talk about. Everyone has skeletons in the closet.

Gather everyone in a circle and play a game of gossip. Whisper the following in a person's ear: "Did you hear that Susie went out with Sam last Friday night? They stayed out until 3 a.m. Her parents won't let her see Sam again."

Have the kids pass the gossip around the circle until the last person tells the first person what he or she heard. Discuss:

● Were some facts exaggerated? Which ones?

● How did the story change?

● What caused the change?

● Why is it important that we don't spread around news about others?

Distribute paper and pencils and ask each member to look at the magazine picture of the man or woman. Have the teenagers each write a one-sentence bit of gossip about the person in the picture. For example, "Did you know that John might be fired because he's late to work every day?" Have the members read their juicy tidbits in a whisper—pretending to gossip. Then discuss these questions:

- Since you don't know the person in the picture, can what you say about him or her be true?
- How can this be compared to gossip about a friend?
- When we hear about a friend's problems, should we tell others? Why or why not?
- If we had unpleasant or embarrassing experiences, would we want others to know? Explain.
- How can we keep others from knowing about our problems—our intimate skeletons?
- How can we protect our friends' most personal skeletons from getting out? In other words, what's the best way to stop gossip?

Read and discuss Leviticus 19:16; Psalm 34:13; Proverbs 18:8; 1 Timothy 5:13. What does the Bible tell us about gossip?

Close with a prayer asking God to help us treat our friends' skeletons like we want ours treated. Help us keep all skeletons in the closet for the next month, and the next and the next.

—Janet R. Balmforth

Variations

1. Have the kids check what the Bible says about gossip by reading these verses: Psalms 5:9; 12:3; 52:2; 109:2; 120:2; Proverbs 17:4; 25:3; Jeremiah 9:8; James 3:6.

Then have the kids find out ways to control the tongue by reading these verses: Psalms 141:3; Proverbs 10:19; James 1:26.

2. Illustrate how messages get scrambled by playing this game. Form teams of six people. Instruct each team to sit in a line, one person behind another, and take a vow of silence for the game. Give the first person in each line a pencil and a piece of paper. Then show the last person in each line a simple hand-drawn picture of an object such as a house, cat or car. That person must use his or her finger to draw the object on the back of the person in front of him or her, and so on. When the drawing reaches the first person in line, he or she must draw it on the piece of paper. Have judges determine which team's picture most resembles the original (**Try This One . . . Strikes Again**, Group Books).

Your Ideas and Variations

_____
_____
_____
_____
_____
_____
_____
_____

_____
_____
_____
_____
_____
_____

183

Images of Christ
TOPIC: CHRIST

Artists and musicians have attempted to portray Jesus Christ since the early beginnings of our faith. Being from a poor family, and also part of a culture that forbade portraits, Jesus never sat for his portrait. Thus the attempts to picture him have always been the interpretation of various artists. These reveal as much about the faith of the artist, and the time period in which he or she lived, as about Jesus. This session provides an opportunity for young people to form and share their image of Christ. This experience also allows young people a creative way to understand the process of interpreting the Bible.

Hang reproductions of various paintings of Jesus around the meeting area. The picture file of your Sunday school should have a good selection that comes with the teachers' packets of materials. Your local library may have reproductions of some of the masters' portrayals of Christ, such as Rembrandt's and da Vinci's. Art books (especially coffeetable books) are good sources, as are some magazines, such as National Geographic. Find examples of the following art:

- Byzantine
- Medieval
- Renaissance
- African and Asian
- Dutch
- 18th and 19th century
- Contemporary

As the youth gather for the meeting, play various kinds of Christian music—everything from Handel to Rez Band. Introduce the topic by asking the young people how they think Jesus looked. How do we know—or do we? Explain that whatever we know about Jesus' physical appearance is conjecture, merely artists' interpretations. There are hundreds of these interpretations, just as in music. Discuss the differences between Christian rock and classical works.

Invite the youth to walk around the room and look at all the different pictures. Have each member stand by his or her favorite interpretation. Go around the room and let each person tell why he or she chose that particular rendition. Ask each group member: "What is the artist trying to express about Christ in the picture? Does the portrayal seem true to the Gospel? How does the work help the viewer better know Christ?"

If time allows and the group is interested, you might have various types of art materials on hand and let the members try creating their own interpretations. Suggest the kids try mediums other than paint or pen. You could have available: clay; materials for collages (magazines, paints, etc.); and fabrics for making banners. Ask each young person to offer a prayer of thanksgiving for God's gifts in the arts, for endowing us with creative gifts for ministry. Close with a song of Christ such as "Lord of the Dance."

—Ed McNulty

Variations

1. There are a number of excellent short films that present unusual images of Christ. One of them can be shown in conjunction with the session. Or, you can arrange to show them in a Lenten series (though not just during Lent); call it "Images of Christ." Here are some images of Christ and films that portray them:

● Image of Christ as a clown—The Floyd Shaffer clown films, **The Mark of the Clown, A Clown Is Born** and **That's Life**.

● Image of Christ as a street sweeper and builder of community—**Oh Happy Day**.

● Image of Christ as a nonconformist—**The Man Who Had To Sing**.

● Image of Christ as an old beggar—**The Rocky Road**.

● Image of Christ as a carpenter—**It's About This Carpenter**.

● Image of Christ as a troubadour—**A Fuzzy Tale**.

● Image of Christ as a dishwasher—**The Jesus Roast**.

All of the above films may be rented from Mass Media Ministries, 2116 N. Charles St., Baltimore, MD 21218 (301) 727-3270.

For an unusual exposition of this theme, see the two-screen slide/tape presentation "Images of Christ," available from Visual Parables, c/o First Presbyterian Church, 49 S. Portage St., Westfield, NY 14787 (716) 326-2643.

Your Ideas and Variations

_____
_____
_____
_____
_____
_____
_____
_____
_____
_____
_____
_____
_____

184

**Jesus Knocking
at the Heart's Door**
TOPIC: BIBLE STUDY

Here is a neat group exercise
to open a Bible study series.
This exercise illustrates the idea
that we can study the same Bible scripture many times, yet receive something new and fresh
each time.

Buy the wallet-size picture of
Jesus which shows him standing
and knocking on a wooden door,
entitled **Christ at Heart's Door**
(available from Kriebel & Bates,
Inc., 6888 Hawthorne Park Dr.,
Indianapolis, IN 46220 (317)
842-8440). You'll need one for
each teenager.

Gather the kids in a circle.
Pass out the pictures and say to
the group, "This picture is often
called 'Jesus knocking at the
heart's door.' The artist who
drew this picture had to think
about, then paint every detail.
Nothing is here by accident. We
are going to go around the circle
and share one thing we see in
this picture that tells us something about Jesus or about ourselves." You can expect the
group to point out between 30
and 45 details.

When no one else has any-
thing new to say about the pic-

ture, close the exercise with a
lesson on how to study the Bible.
Include the following points:

● The scriptures were written
to disclose Christ. Any valid
study must begin and end in
him.

● The key to knowing God's
Word is to read and study the
scriptures—always looking for
new insights.

● We can learn something
new each time we study a passage. Just when we think we
can't, we gain a new insight and
learn that there is always more
to his Word than meets the eye.

—Rickey Short

Variations

1. Present various artists' ren-
ditions of Jesus. Ask the young
people to look for details and
compare the pictures.

2. Give the kids each a Bible
passage, piece of paper and
crayons. Ask them to be "artists
for the day" and create their
own rendition of the passage.

Your Ideas and Variations

_____
_____
_____
_____
_____
_____
_____
_____
_____
_____

PILLOWCASES

185

A New Use for Old Pillowcases
TOPIC: GAMES/FUN

Don't throw away those old pillowcases—make jerseys out of them to identify your team players on the field.

Each youth group member will need an old, plain-colored pillowcase. Ask members of your congregation to donate them or ask your youth group members to bring an old pillowcase from home.

At a youth group meeting, give each person a pillowcase, several permanent-ink markers and scissors. Divide the kids into two groups and say that they are going to make jerseys—pullover shirts worn by athletes for identification.

Ask each group to think of a team name such as "The Saints" or "The Crusaders." Ask the kids each to choose a different number and write the number on the front and back of the pillowcase—along with their team name. Next, have the youth group members cut out holes for their necks and arms.

To get immediate use out of the jerseys, have the kids put them on and play a team sport such as football, soccer, hockey or baseball. Store the jerseys in your youth room and use them

over and over again.

—Tim Pontius

Variations

1. Use old pillowcases to store equipment such as balls, ropes, blindfolds, etc.

2. Cover and store sleeping bags with old pillowcases. The pillowcases keep the sleeping bags clean, and they keep the sleeping bags from unrolling. The pillowcase coverings also are easy to grip when loading and unloading the vehicles during youth group trips.

3. Make pillowcase people for talent shows, announcements, or just for fun. Design a large face on a white pillowcase. Ask a person to place his or her arms on top of his or her head. Then cover the person with the pillowcase. Button a shirt or jacket around the person's waist. The pillowcase person looks hilarious—a large head on a miniature body.

Your Ideas and Variations

_____
_____
_____
_____
_____
_____
_____
_____
_____
_____

PINGPONG TABLES

186

The Bible and Hungry People
TOPIC: HUNGER/POVERTY/JUSTICE

Help young people learn what the Bible tells us about hunger that stems from poverty and injustice. Capitalize on teenagers' desire to have fun and do something different; consider messages of scripture passages and then play pingpong—with meaning.

You'll need a pingpong table, paddles, ball, plain paper, tape, markers, yardstick, glue, scissors, Bibles, Bible commentaries, pictures of hungry people from world relief literature, newspapers or magazines.

Cover the pingpong table with

	Who said it?	What does it say to us?
Deuteronomy 15:11		
Proverbs 29:7		
Proverbs 14:21		
Psalm 146:5-9		
Psalm 147:6-11		
Isaiah 58:10		

	Who said it?	What does it say to us?
Luke 9:13		
Acts 2:45		
Acts 4:32		
2 Corinthians 9:7		
2 Corinthians 8:2, 3		
1 John 3:17, 18		

the plain paper. Draw the following grids or charts on the paper—Old Testament on one side of the net; New Testament on the other.

Divide the young people into two teams. Have them consult the Bible and commentaries to complete the grids. Adults may assist if needed, but there are no right or wrong answers for the "What does it say to us?" sections.

Then have the young people cut pictures of needy people from hunger literature, newspapers or magazines, and glue them on open areas of the table top. Once the table is covered with the grids and pictures, let group members take turns playing pingpong.

After a while, ask the group members to sit in a circle. Remove the net and turn the table on its side, facing the group. Discuss these questions:

● What were your feelings when rough areas made the ball bounce erratically and interfere with the game?

● Did the words and pictures affect your concentration?

● How did you feel about playing a game as you looked at pictures of starving people? Were your reactions positive or negative? Explain.

● As an observer, how did you feel as you watched the game? How do those feelings apply to the world today?

● What does this experience say to us about the affluent Western world enjoying life and "playing games," while people are starving on the other side of the world?

—Brethren House Ministries

Variations

1. Don't throw the paper away. Display the pingpong table top in the church foyer and collect money to give to world hunger organizations. Ask your denominational office what areas could use help, or contact an interdenominational organization such as Bread for the World, 802 Rhode Island Ave. N.E., Washington, D.C., 20018 (202) 269-0200.

For a small fee, you can join Bread for the World and receive a quarterly newsletter that lists areas where you can become directly and immediately involved. The newsletter contains ideas such as writing letters to congressmen and congresswomen regarding bills before Congress. Help all congregation members become more aware of world hunger and the need for their help.

Your Ideas and Variations

_____
_____
_____
_____
_____

_____
_____
_____
_____
_____
_____
_____
_____
_____

PIPE CLEANERS

187

Pipe Cleaner Sculptures
TOPIC: CHRISTIAN SYMBOLS

Use pipe cleaners to create meaningful sculptures of spiritual concepts.

Choose a topic such as the gifts of the Spirit or the Beatitudes. After sufficient discussion, give a handful of pipe cleaners to each member of the youth group. The kids should create a pipe cleaner "sculpture" to illustrate the spiritual concept.

One young person used the pipe cleaners to make three intersecting rings—they symbolized the Trinity. Another person sculpted a manger and a heart—they symbolized God's love for us at Jesus' birth.

You'll be surprised at the creative sculptures and their pow-

erful messages!

—Steve Newton

Variations

1. Make a "sculpture mobile" by attaching several pipe-cleaner sculptures to a clothes hanger. Display the mobiles in the youth room.

2. "Sculpt" from other items such as clay, paper clips or colored telephone wire (get this from your local telephone company).

Your Ideas and Variations

_____
_____
_____
_____
_____
_____
_____
_____
_____
_____
_____

PIPING

188

Giant Banana Split
TOPIC: FUN/CROWDBREAKERS

Have you ever planned to make a giant banana split, but couldn't talk the hardware store manager into loaning you the necessary guttering? Try this as an inexpensive alternative.

Get some 4-inch PVC (poly-vinyl-chloride) pipe from people who have recently remodeled or from a building supply store (ask for weather-damaged pipe).

Purchase a piece the length you want your makeshift banana-split dish to be. Use a hand-saw to cut the pipe lengthwise. Wash the pipe. Tape the pipe to a table, line it with foil, and add the various ingredients to make your ice cream sensation.

Our youth group recently made a 120-foot banana split. What a monster! We ate every last drop!

—Dave Mahoney

Variations

1. Use this unique container for youth group refreshments. One week serve nachos, another week serve popcorn or caramel

corn, etc.

2. Secure the ends of the pipe with lots of tape and aluminum foil. Fill it with a beverage, then give everyone a straw and guzzle up!

Your Ideas and Variations

_____
_____
_____
_____
_____
_____
_____
_____
_____
_____
_____
_____
_____
_____
_____
_____
_____

189

Good News Pizza
TOPIC: HUNGER/EVANGELISM

Use this activity to illustrate the need for Christians to share the gospel with their friends. So many times we go to church and are fed the Word of God, then we keep it to ourselves—never sharing with others.

Before the meeting, buy a pizza and keep it warm in the oven to serve at the end of the meeting. Don't let the kids know it's there. Arrange to have a local vendor deliver another

pizza, with all the trimmings, during your meeting. Distribute the mouthwatering slices of pizza to just the kids sitting closest to you. Continue to give out the pizza to those kids until it is all gone. There will be many loud protests from the other members!

Ask a young person to read Matthew 14:13-21 where Jesus feeds the 5,000. Compare Jesus' actions with the pizza experience. Note that Jesus fed everybody and there was food left over; the pizza was fed only to a few. Ask how the "full" kids feel. Then ask how the ones who didn't get pizza feel. Say that we are to have concern for *all* people. When we hear God's Word at church, we need to share it with our friends, family, at school and at our jobs.

After the point is made, bring the pizza out of the oven for the rest of the members. This activ-ity touches the kids' taste buds and makes a lasting impact.
—Randy Gross

Variations
1. Use this lesson to emphasize world hunger. Note that a few countries are well-fed if not overfed, while millions of people are starving. Discuss possible ways to help this situation. Offer your help with community agencies or world hunger agencies such as Bread for the World, 802 Rhode Island Ave. N.E., Washington, D.C., 20018 (202) 269-0200.

Your Ideas and Variations
_____
_____
_____
_____
_____
_____
_____
_____
_____
_____

PLATES

190

Prayer Wheel
TOPIC: PRAYER

Prayer is more than just talking to God. This activity helps group members understand the many forms of prayer.

Give each person a white paper plate, marker, small metal clasp and some string. Tell the kids to divide the underside of the plate into eight sections and list each form of prayer as follows:

Have the youth group members insert the metal clasp in the middle of their plate and spread the prongs on the other side. Tie the string around the two spread prongs. (The string is used as a hanger for the Prayer Wheel.)

Discuss each form of prayer, read the accompanying scrip-

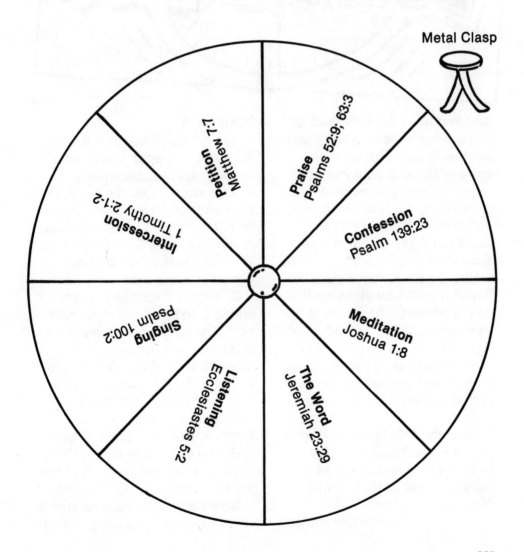

Metal Clasp

ture and have the kids think of ways to incorporate each prayer form each day. For example, one day the kids could say a prayer of praise—concentrating on thanking God for his majesty and power. Another day they could say a prayer of confession—focusing on their sins and asking for forgiveness. Another day they could focus on meditation. They could find a quiet spot, get comfortable and allow 10 to 15 minutes to just listen to God. Encourage the youth group members to give several examples and ideas for each form of prayer.

Have the kids take the Prayer Wheel home, hang it on their bedroom wall and use it as a reference tool in their prayer life.

—Debbie Valleau

Variations

1. Give the youth group members each a paper plate and a marker. Have them write a prayer concern on the plate. On the count of three, have them toss the plates into the air then catch one other than their own. Have the kids pray for these concerns during the next week.

2. Turn a delicious pie into an edible prayer wheel. Bake several pies and cut them each into eight pieces. (The number of pies you'll need depends on the number of kids in your group.) Tape a slip of paper to a toothpick and label it one of the forms of prayer. Stick the toothpick into one of the slices. Continue this process until all of the prayer forms are represented.

Give the youth group members each a piece of pie. Let them eat their slice and keep the tooth-pick as a reminder to focus on this form of prayer in the up-coming week.

Your Ideas and Variations

_____
_____
_____
_____
_____
_____
_____
_____
_____
_____
_____

POST CARDS

191

Picture Post Cards
TOPIC: PUBLICITY

Everybody likes to look at picture post cards. Create a unique post card—with a picture of your youth group.

Take a picture of your youth group, then contact a photo store. Ask the store to use the picture and make post cards for your group. Send the post cards to visitors, to kids who miss a meeting or activity, or to youth group members who are celebrating a birthday or other special occasion.

Let your young people know your whole group cares about them.

—Tim Pontius

Variations

1. Enlarge a picture of your youth group into posters. Sell these to the kids and their families. You also can decorate your meeting room with these posters.

2. Have all of your young people who attend a youth group meeting pile on the sofa. Take a photo of the group, preferably with an instant-print camera. Hang the photo over the sofa and include the date and total number of kids who were present.

Your group members will soon be talking about breaking the sofa-stuff record.

Your Ideas and Variations

_____
_____
_____
_____
_____
_____
_____
_____
_____
_____

192

"YES" Cards
TOPIC: PUBLICITY

Big events need lots of publicity. Here is a new idea to try.

Before your next big event, have a local printer reproduce a number of the following "YES" cards. The bigger they are, the better; however, they should at least be the size of a post card.

(Name)
will attend the Youth Kickoff
September 7
First Church of Christ

Mail a "YES" card to youth group members and to those who have visited your group. In group meetings preceding the event, distribute extra "YES" cards for the group members to give to their friends. Instruct the kids to bring their "YES" card with them to the event.

Collect the cards at the event. Form a chain by joining the cards with masking tape. Place a poster at the top of the chain that says, "Yes! We're glad we came!"

—Doug Newhouse

Variations

1. The "YES" cards may be used throughout the year in youth group meetings. Send them to members who have missed a meeting. Leave the bottom blank and write the member a short note, asking him or her to return to the meetings and bring his or her "YES" card. Keep building onto the chain

throughout the year. You'll be surprised how it grows!

Your Ideas and Variations

_____
_____
_____
_____
_____
_____
_____
_____
_____
_____
_____
_____

PRODUCT SAMPLES

193

Crazy Awards
TOPIC: AWARDS/GAMES

Every grocery store or drugstore has a section of "samples"; small portions of shampoo, soap, deodorant, toothpaste, hair conditioner or mouthwash. Before your next retreat, buy several of these sample products and give them away as awards. Try to purchase them ahead of time on sale. Here are some ideas:

● **Shampoo:** Attach a sign that says, "Head and Shoulders above the rest."

● **Toothbrush/toothpaste:** Award for kids who forgot theirs. Or attach a note that says, "Brightest smile."

● **Mouthwash:** Attach a sign that says, "Best discussion participant. Confidently presents new ideas and opinions."

Be creative and inventive in awarding the prizes!

—Mitchell M. Olson

Variations

1. Award a bottle of lotion to a person who "softens argu-

ments with soothing comments."

2. Attach the following note to a deodorant stick: "Daily application of (name of person) keeps the youth group fresh and ready for action!"

Your Ideas and Variations

_____
_____
_____
_____
_____
_____
_____
_____
_____
_____
_____
_____
_____

194

Listening to God
TOPIC: LISTENING

Help the kids realize the importance of listening—to others and to God.

You'll need a Q-Tip for each person and a recording of the following sounds: a car starting, a door slamming, water dripping, a vacuum cleaner running, etc.

Divide the teenagers into small groups and have a contest. Play the recorded sounds and see how many each group can identify. Award the winning team a box of Q-Tips.

Then discuss the importance of listening to each other. What makes a good listener? Talk about the importance of listening to God. How do we hear God? Ask the kids what the following verses tell us about listening: Psalm 115:6; Isaiah 6:9; Matthew 7:24-27; 11:15.

Give everyone a Q-Tip to use as a bookmark in their Bibles. Say that the Q-Tip should remind them of the importance of listening—especially listening to God.

—Lynn Potter

Variations

1. Attach a note to the Q-Tip that says, "Listen to God."

2. Give each person construction paper, glue, a handful of Q-Tips and a marker. Tell the kids to spell the word "LISTEN" by gluing the Q-Tips onto the construction paper. On the bottom of the paper have them write, "Be still and know that I am God" (Psalm 46:10).

Your Ideas and Variations

_____
_____
_____
_____
_____
_____
_____
_____
_____

QUESTIONNAIRES

195

Created in the Image
TOPIC: PEER INFLUENCE/SELF-IMAGE

In the search for identity, it's valuable for young people to understand how their self-image is influenced by the important people in their lives. The purpose of this session is to help the young people identify people who affect their self-image in both positive and negative ways.

Gather a pencil and a copy of the following worksheet for each person.

Who Am I?

1. How would you answer if a stranger asked, "Who are you?"

2. How would your best friend describe you?

3. How would your mother or father describe you?

4. How would your brother or sister describe you?

5. How would your favorite teacher describe you?

6. How would your boyfriend or girlfriend describe you?

7. How would God describe you?

Pass out the worksheets and allow the young people enough time to fill them out. Then gather in small groups to discuss insights gained from the experience. Have the young people compare their answer to the first question with the characteristics they listed on the rest of the worksheet.

Read Genesis 1:26-31 and Colossians 3:9-15. On the back of their worksheets, ask the youth group members to each write a paragraph or poem on what it means to be created in the image of God.

Ask the young people to take the sheets home and keep them in their Bibles. During their daily devotions, have them reflect on how special they are because they are created in God's image.

—Walter John Boris

Variations

1. Give the youth group members each a handful of clay. Let them create anything at all: a ball, cross, car, person, etc. Compare this experience to Genesis 2:7—God made Adam out of a lump of clay. Say that each one of us is a unique creation; just as each student's clay object is unique and special.

Your Ideas and Variations

_____

_____

_____

_____

_____

_____

_____

_____

_____

_____

_____

_____

_____

196

Getting to Know You
TOPIC: INTERVIEWS/CROWDBREAKERS

Here is an activity that is more than a crowdbreaker. This activity helps the youth group members get to know each other by asking fun interview questions.

As the group members arrive, give them a pencil and the following interview sheet. Say to the kids, "Find a different person to interview for each question. Share your names and how long you have been part of this church. Then, ask one of the questions. When you have completed your interview, ask the interviewee to sign the question he or she answered. When you have 20 signatures, you're free to ask your own questions."

Interview
1. How did you feel your first day in junior high school?

_____

2. What do you like best about your family?

3. If you could have any kind of pet, what would you choose and why?

4. What do you admire most in your best friend?

5. What unique talent or skill do you have that no one knows about?

6. What is your favorite teacher like?

7. What movie do you like best and why?

8. When you want to be alone, where do you go?

9. How would you describe the perfect vacation?

10. How do you get along with your parents?

11. What is the greatest achievement in your life?

12. What are your plans after high school?

13. Where do you hope to be living and what do you hope to be doing 15 years from now?

14. Are you going to have children some day? Why or why not?

15. What is your greatest fear in life?

16. What sports do you play?

17. What jobs do you do to earn spending money?

18. What is your favorite music?

19. What is the most exciting book you have ever read?

20. What do you like best about yourself?

(A copyrighted resource from **Youth Ministry Cargo**. Permission granted to copy this interview for local church use only.)

You can adapt this interview sheet to a holiday mixer for your youth group. Use the following idea:

A Christmas Interview
1. What did you like best about winter when you were a child?

2. What happened on your most memorable Christmas?

3. What is the recipe of your favorite Christmas cookie?

4. Do you still believe in Santa Claus? Why or why not?

5. What kind of Christmas decorations did your family have when you were growing up?

6. What was the one Christmas gift you felt the most ex-

cited about giving someone?

7. What kind of Christmas tree do you like best? Why?

8. What Christmas tradition has the most meaning for your family?

9. What is the best time to open presents, Christmas Eve or Christmas morning? Why?

10. What is your choice for the "best ever" Christmas song? Why?

11. How did you feel your first Christmas away from home?

12. Will you describe your special Christmas ornament?

13. What Christmas gift, that you received, meant the most to you?

14. What Christmas worship service stands out in your memory?

15. Who performs on your favorite Christmas album?

16. What are three smells that remind you of Christmas?

17. What is your nomination for the "official food" of Christmas?

18. Were you ever in a Sunday school Christmas program? What part did you play?

19. What did you do on Christmas five years ago?

20. If you were granted one wish for a perfect Christmas for your family, what would it be like?

Use these interviews at retreats, lock-ins, parties, or special intergenerational events. Not only do the interview sheets encourage people to talk with each other, they offer a safe context for deeper sharing.
—Walter John Boris

Variations

1. Adapt the questionnaire to any topic such as Easter, Halloween, Thanksgiving, back to school, vacation memories, favorite friends, etc. For Thanks-

giving you could ask questions such as, "What is your favorite Thanksgiving dessert?" "What is your most special Thanksgiving memory?" For a back-to-school questionnaire you could ask, "Do you remember your first day of school? If so, describe it." "Who was your favorite teacher and why?" "Who was your best friend in elementary school? Describe him or her."

2. Give the kids each a questionnaire and have them interview a member of their family. Better yet, have them ask the questions during a family meal—the questionnaire stimulates fun discussions!

Your Ideas and Variations

_____
_____
_____
_____
_____
_____
_____
_____
_____

197

On Schools and Rules
TOPIC: AUTHORITY/RULES/SCHOOLS

The following ideas grew out of requests from youth group

members to talk about the pressures that they face at school. School is a big part of young people's lives. It also is one of the greatest sources of stress that they face.

For this meeting, you will need several new, unsharpened pencils; two paper bags; sharpened pencils; copies of the questionnaire; 3×5 cards; bowls; spoons; and ingredients to make ice cream sundaes.

Start this program by playing Pencil Pusher Relay. Designate a starting line at one end of the room. At the other end, place two opened paper bags. Divide the group into two teams and give each team a new, unsharpened pencil. Tell the kids, "The object of this relay is to balance the pencil on your nose (it can lean on another part of your face as long as it is touching your nose) and carry it that way to the other end of the room. Drop it into the paper bag, then pick up the pencil in your hand, run back to the starting line and pass it on to the next player. The first team to have each player successfully run the course wins." Run the relay then award appropriate prizes such as new, unsharpened pencils for each team member.

Next, introduce the story on the next page, written by a very absent-minded author. He forgot several key words and now

needs help to finish the story.
Ask your group to give you
words to fit the descriptions in
parenthesis after each blank
space. When you have filled in
all the blank spaces, read the
story out loud. The results are
hilarious!

A Day at School

One day as _____ (girl's name) was walking to school, she met
a great big, hairy _____ (animal) near the old _____ (place).
Not knowing what else to do in such a situation she quickly began
to _____ (type of physical activity). When she finally arrived at
school she was late and in her hurry she tripped on the bottom stair
and sprained her _____ (part of the body). Without hesitation,
_____ (boy's name), seeing her in distress, threw down his books
and picked her up in his big strong arms, and carried her to the
nurse's office. The nurse put on a _____ (adjective) bandage and
sent her to class. But before she got to the classroom there was a fire
drill and everyone went to _____ (place). After studying the eating
habits of _____ (nationality) bingo players, it was time for lunch.
Today the cafeteria was serving mashed _____ (kind of food) with
_____ (another food) sauce. But they ran out of spoons, so she
had to eat it with a straw. After lunch they had a _____ (social activity) in the bathroom, needless to say. In study hall, the boys were
making paper _____s (plural noun) and throwing them out of the
windows, while two kids talked about _____ (noun) wrestling in
_____ (country). _____ (repeat girl's name) preferred to
study _____ (subject at school) with _____ (repeat boy's
name). She wondered if she would ever finish grade _____ (number
from 1-10); after all she turns 23 next month. After school, she
watched _____ (TV program) on TV and ate popcorn in the
_____ (part of the house) while doing her homework, and then
turned in early because tomorrow was another day at school.

After the story, give a pencil
and copy of the questionnaire on
the next page to each group
member. Allow several minutes
for them to complete it.

340

On Schools and Rules

1. What do you like the most about school? (person, subject, extra-curricular activity, etc.) _____

_____

2. What do you dislike about school? _____

_____

3. If you could change anything about school, what would it be? ____

_____

4. Who is your favorite teacher? _____ Why? _____

_____

5. Are most of your teachers people who you would like to be like? __
Is that important? _____ Why? _____

_____

6. Do you feel that you learn enough in school to prepare you for life? Explain. _____

_____

7. Do you feel pressured to be something that you don't want to be at school? _____ By whom? _____
In what ways? _____

8. Are you free to practice your Christian faith at school? _____
Why or why not? _____

_____

Is that important to you? _____ Why? _____

_____

9. Does competition exist between you and your classmates? _____
Is this healthy or unhealthy? _____

_____

10. Do you feel that you lead a stressful life with regards to school? Explain. _____ _____

_____

Discuss the questionnaire then ask several volunteers to read these verses: Matthew 6:25, 34; 10:19; Romans 12:2; Philippians 2:3; 2 Timothy 1:7-8; 1 Peter 3:15. Ask how each of these verses applies to the youth group members' lives. What advice does God give?

Give everybody a 3×5 card. Ask the participants to write the following verses on the card: "Therefore I tell you, do not be anxious about your life, what you shall eat or what you shall drink, nor about your body, what you shall put on. Is not life more than food, and the body more than clothing? Therefore do not be anxious about tomorrow, for tomorrow will be anxious for itself. Let the day's own trouble be sufficient for the day" (Matthew 6:25, 34).

Have the young people take the cards with them to school. Whenever they feel the pressures build, encourage each of them to look at the card and know that God loves them. He doesn't want them to worry or be anxious. God cares for each person.

Serve refreshments cafeteria-style. Have the students start at one end of a table and build a sundae as they move to the other end. First the ice cream, then the nuts, then some candy, then some whipped cream, and finally a cherry on top!

—Jeffrey A. Collins

Variations

1. Play a variation of Simon Says called Teacher Says. One person is chosen as the teacher and told to stand in front of the others. The teacher gives directions to the students, which they must follow. The kids must follow all directions that are prefaced with, "Teacher says . . ." The kids must not follow directions that are not prefaced with that statement. If they do, they must sit down. The winner is the last one left standing—the one who listened the best.

2. Create a continuum in your room. Ask the kids, "Which of the following two words best describes your experience with school?" Assign one end of the room as one word; assign the opposite end of the room as the other word. Use these words and allow time for discussion after each choice (**Building Community in Youth Groups,** by Denny Rydberg, Group Books).

forget/remember
rain/sunshine
tough/gentle
beginning/end
together/apart
closed/open
hammer/nail
listener/talker
peace/anxiety
hearer/doer
helping/watching
creative/traditional
self-oriented/others-oriented
future/present
activities/knowledge
sprinter/jogger
leader/follower
giver/taker
aggressive/passive
research/recreation
old/new
world/local

Your Ideas and Variations

_____

_____

_____

_____
_____
_____
_____
_____
_____
_____
_____
_____

198

Work! Who Needs It?
TOPIC: BIBLE STUDY/PART-TIME JOBS/
PRIORITIES

Most youth groups have members with part-time jobs. This Bible study will help youth group members evaluate work.

Each person will need a Bible, pencil and copy of the Work Survey. You also will need an overhead projector.

Distribute the Work Survey and a pencil to each group member. Allow time for the kids to complete the surveys; then share results.

Work Survey
1. Do you have a part-time job? If so, where do you work?

2. Why did you get this job? How long have you had it?

3. Have you had other jobs? If so, where?

4. If you don't have a job, why not?

5. If you aren't working now, but had a job in the past, why did you give it up?

6. Do you feel you are paid well? Why or why not? How much do you think you should be paid?

7. What do you do with the money you earn? Approximate what you spend in various areas such as on clothing, for entertainment, saving for a special purchase.

8. What sacrifices have you made by working? What have you given up?

9. What is your parents' attitude toward your working?

10. If you could pick one job and do it for the next 25 years, what would it be? Why did you choose this job?

(A copyrighted resource from **Youth Ministry Cargo**. Permission granted to copy this questionnaire for local church use only.)

_____

After reviewing the results of the survey, see what the Bible has to say about working. Read the following verses and discuss the questions.

● Read Luke 10:38-42. Who was the "worker"? How would you describe Mary? What was Mary's primary interest? What do you think Jesus means in verse 42? How can work make you "worried and upset about many things"? What do you think this passage says about work?

● Read Ephesians 4:28. Who should go to work? What kind of work is prescribed? How are earnings to be used? Does work create a greater desire to share or be selfish with your possessions? Explain. What do you think this verse says about work?

● Read Thessalonians 3:6-12. What sin is mentioned? Why is this sin so deadly among God's people? What example should be followed? Why? What would happen if Paul's instruction in verse 10 was applied in your city? in your state? across the nation? "Idle" people become "busybodies" (verse 11). What does this mean? What does Paul prescribe? If all Christians adopted this teaching as their own "work ethic," what do you think would happen in the workplaces of our nation? Do you agree or disagree that the Christian should be the best worker on the job? Why or why not? What do you think this passage says about work?

Summarize the discussion by asking young people to list the advantages of working. Write advantages on the overhead. Next, call for a list of the disadvantages of working. Finally, ask what principles regarding work were discovered in the Bible study. Conclude your study with these questions:

● Why should you work?
● What should you want to accomplish by working?
● Whom can you influence at work?
● How can you influence them?
● In your personal list of priorities, where should work fit in? Is it there right now? If not, why not? What do you need to do to "get work in its place"?

Have the kids read Proverbs for timely advice about work. Close your meeting with prayer.

—Doug Newhouse

Variations

1. Plan a progressive visit to each of the youth group member's place of employment. For example, car pool to McDonald's—eat some French fries, travel on to Dairy Queen—enjoy an ice cream cone, onward to an office building—tour around the grounds, etc.

2. Ask several church members to speak about their jobs. Invite a wide variety of people such as an artist, doctor, editor, football coach, travel agent, etc.

Your Ideas and Variations

_____

_____

_____

_____

ROBES

199

A Robe of Righteousness
TOPIC: CLOTHING/VALUES

How does our everyday clothing relate to a robe of righteousness? Discuss this topic with the youth group members; all you'll need is a choir robe.

Gather everyone in a circle, then open the discussion with these questions:

● Why are clothes important to us?

● What is your first memory of a favorite outfit? How old were you? Describe the outfit.

● What do today's styles say about our culture?

● Does how we dress make a statement about who we are? Explain.

● What perspective does Jesus give us when he says, "Do not be anxious about what you shall put on"?

● What does it mean to "put on Christ"?

● Read Isaiah 61:10. Describe a "robe of righteousness."

Bring out the choir robe and say that robes symbolize spirituality. Have each person put on the robe and say how he or she "wears" Christ in his or her daily life. For example, "I try to be helpful to others." "I pray every morning." "I help round up my little brother and sisters to take them to church on Sunday mornings."

Give everyone a chance to put on the robe, then close with this prayer: "God, cover us with a

robe of righteousness. Help us always to wear Christ and show your love to others. Amen."
—Lynn Potter

Variations

1. Gather the youth group members and practice a song such as "Open Our Eyes" or "They That Wait Upon the Lord" (**Songs**, by Yohann Anderson, Songs and Creations, Inc.). Wear choir robes and joyfully sing the song during a church service—let everyone see Jesus' love shine through the singers' eyes and smiles.

2. Play a dress-up relay. Make two piles of clothing. In each pile place a large shirt, pair of pants, pair of shoes and a hat. Form two teams of kids. Have the first person in each team run to a pile of clothes, put every item on, then take every item off, run back to the line, tag the next person, and so on. All members must participate— first team done wins.

Your Ideas and Variations

_____
_____
_____
_____
_____
_____
_____
_____
_____
_____

ROCKS

200

Casting Lots
TOPIC: GOD'S GUIDANCE/BIBLE STUDY

The call of the disciples is familiar to all of us—how Jesus told them they would, from now on, be fishers of men, how Matthew left his worldly job of tax collector, etc. But the method in which Matthias was chosen to replace Judas often comes as a surprise. This exercise illustrating that choice, gives the students a feeling of how Matthias might have felt.

Gather smooth, round pebbles, large enough to write a name on, and distribute one to each of the youth. You'll also need markers, white paper and a box. The box should be big enough to hold the rocks and sturdy enough to endure some shaking. After covering the box with white paper, draw Christian symbols on it, such as crosses, fish and rainbows.

Tell the group members, "When the disciples had to choose someone to replace Judas, they decided upon a method called 'casting lots.' All of the offices and duties in the temple were settled this way. The names of the candidates were written on stones, the stones were put into a box and the box was then shaken until a single stone fell out. The person whose name was on the stone was duly elected. As we begin our study of Acts 1:21-26, we will follow the same procedure."

Distribute the stones and markers and have the kids each write their name on one. Collect the stones in the box, pray for God's guidance, and then shake the box until one stone falls out. The person whose name is on the stone is the chosen "Matthias." Read Acts 1:21-26, then discuss these questions:

● How did you feel as the box was being shaken? Did you want your pebble to be the one that fell?

● (Ask Matthias) What was your first thought when you saw your name on the pebble that fell out?

● Were the rest of you disappointed? Why or why not?

● Was it just "by chance" that this group member was cast our Matthias? Explain.

● Did you like the idea of praying before casting lots?

● Can you think of another Bible story in which casting lots played a part? (The story of Jonah; how they knew he was the reason for the storm.)

● What does the biblical practice of "casting lots" tell us about God's role in the way things come about . . . the idea of "chance" or "accident"?

● Would you like to use this method to choose next year's officers (if your group has officers)? Why or why not?

Close by rereading the passage and offering a prayer of thanks for God's guidance in all our lives—even guidance we receive in surprising ways.

—Walter Mees

Variations

1. Cast lots to choose a person to celebrate. Ask the young people to, one at a time, affirm the chosen person with comments such as, "You always liven up a discussion" or "You are a positive person. I never hear you gossip or say anything bad."

2. Cast lots to choose a person to bring refreshments for the next meeting.

Your Ideas and Variations

_____
_____
_____
_____
_____
_____
_____
_____
_____
_____
_____
_____

201

Living Stones
TOPIC: DEVOTIONS/CHURCH

This is a 10- to 15-minute object lesson that can be used at a regular youth group meeting or at a retreat. The message involves each member's daily relationship with God. It is easy to act "religious" at church or in youth group meetings, but what about at school and when friends are around? Just what is involved in being a Christian?

Prepare for this lesson by thinking of several words or phrases that include the words "stone" or "rock." For example, a rolling stone, stone cold, cornerstone, stone fish, rock concert, rock band, rock of ages, etc.

Next collect rocks of various shapes and sizes to illustrate these phrases. A rolling stone could be illustrated by rolling a round stone down the aisle. To illustrate the rock of ages, I used a flat stone. I glued three toothpicks to it. Then, at the end of each toothpick, I glued slips of paper that said, "13 years old," "15 years old," "17 years old." The more detail you use, the more the kids enjoy it.

Begin the devotion by telling the youth group members that there are many kinds of rocks or stones in the world. Start with your objects hidden, then one by one present them to the teenagers. Have them guess what word or phrase each rock represents. You'll be surprised at how many they guess correctly.

When you are through with your rock presentation, call one of the counselors or teenagers up front. Ask the youth group members what kind of stone or rock the person represents. Tell them that the person is a "living stone," and explain that the Bible calls all of us "living stones."

Read 1 Peter 2:4-6 and explain, "As Christians we are all part of God's house. The church is not simply a building that we go to on Sunday, but it is a spiritual makeup of all Christians assembled together. The church is spread all over the world. Wherever Christians go, the church goes with them."

Give everyone a small stone to take home. Say that the stones are reminders that we take the church with us to school, to our homes, wherever we go.

Paul says, "We always carry around in our body the death of Jesus, so that the life of Jesus may also be revealed in our body" (2 Corinthians 4:10). It's the same idea. If we are Christians and "living stones" we cannot help but incorporate the church into every part of our lives.

—Thomas F. Bronson

Variations

1. Ask the youth group members to create their own representations of rock phrases.

2. Use this idea at a church fellowship activity. Let the church members guess what each rock represents. When a person guesses correctly, give him or her a piece of rock candy.

Your Ideas and Variations

_____
_____
_____
_____
_____
_____
_____
_____
_____
_____
_____
_____

202

Personalized Stones
TOPIC: OUTREACH

Have your young people personalize stones to give to shut-ins as tokens of their friendship. Pair each group member to a

shut-in. The shut-in can be a church member or a patient in a nursing home. The stone is delivered and a friendship begun. Here's how.

Gather a fist-size, smooth stone for each person, acrylic paints, paintbrushes, glue, plastic eyes, cotton, 3×5 cards, markers, boxes, and various odds and ends.

Have each youth group member choose a stone, decorate and name it. They can use cotton for the hair, plastic eyes and paint for the face.

Distribute 3×5 cards and markers. Have the kids write on each card, "I (the stone) am a stand-in for your new friend. I am here to keep you company and remind you every so often your teenage friend _____
(group member)

349

will return and visit you . . . I am a token of your new friendship."

Place each stone in a box along with the cards. Assign each youth group member to a shut-in and encourage the kids to deliver the gifts. Ask them to make regular visits or phone calls—help ease the loneliness of an elderly or handicapped person with this idea.

—Steve Newton

Variations

1. Buy inexpensive, plain-colored coffee mugs. Decorate them with paints or symbols and letters cut from colorful contact paper. Give these to the shut-ins as reminders of future conversations over steamy cups of coffee or hot chocolate.

2. Instead of personalizing stones, personalize Styrofoam cups. Glue on yarn, ribbon or strips of construction paper for hair; construction paper for eyes and mouth, etc.

Your Ideas and Variations

_____
_____
_____
_____
_____
_____
_____
_____
_____

203

Solid As a Rock
TOPIC: PEER INFLUENCE

With this meeting, youth group members will learn the difference between conformity and transformation. They'll be challenged to be transformed by Christ and to resist conforming to the world.

You'll need several clear containers of various shapes. Fill one with water. Find a smooth, nicely shaped stone that will fit into some of your containers, but not all of them. You also will need several versions of the Bible, a chalkboard, piece of chalk and eraser. Study Romans 12:1-2 and 1 Peter 2:4-5. Read the following on the life of Peter: Matthew 16:13-28; 26:30-45, 69-75; Acts 2—5.

Ask several young people to read Romans 12:1-2 from different versions. Ask for definitions of "transformed" and "conformed."

Bring out your containers. Hold up the one with water in it and ask the group members to describe the shape of the water. Wait until they say it's the shape of its container. Pour the water into another container and ask them to describe its shape. Again, it is the shape of its new container. Repeat until all containers are used.

Now ask for a revised definition of conformity: Accepting the mold; taking the shape of a container. See if the kids can suggest other things that change with the environment, such as chameleons or mood rings. Ask the young people to call out situations in which people must adapt such as school, work, clubs, parties. Have a volunteer write these situations on the chalkboard. Next, ask the kids to call out reasons for conformity such as fear of failure, peer pressure, pain. Have the volunteer write these reasons on newsprint.

See how much the young people can tell you about Peter. What were his strengths and weaknesses? Was he a conformer? Discuss Peter's denial of Christ as an act of conformity. Then ask what happened to Peter in the early days of the church.

Have someone read 1 Peter 2:4-5. Say, "Christians are not like water, but like rocks or living stones." Take the stone and place it in a container. Request comments on the rock's shape. Move it to the other containers. Notice that it is always the same shape, regardless of the container. Also note that it doesn't fit into some containers.

Say, "Once transformed by Christ, the Christian is the same in all environments. In some environments the Christian isn't welcome because, like Christ, he or she is too different and refuses to conform."

Have the youth group members think of one area in their lives where they conform to society. Encourage them to commit themselves to letting Christ transform them in that area.

Challenge the kids to carefully and prayerfully consider conforming situations. Have them visualize being firm as a rock and keeping their eyes on Jesus—focusing on how he would like them to act. Close with a silent prayer. Have each person pray for one other group member. Ask God to help the members remain solid as a rock and firm in their faith in compromising situations.

—Mark Reed

Variations

1. Ask a couple of the youth group members to present this object lesson for a children's sermon.

2. Place a clear glass of warm water in front of the group. Drop in a sugar cube and ask the young people to observe as it dissovles. Discuss how this illustrates conformity. Then drop in a small stone. Follow the same discussion as presented in Solid As a Rock.

ROCKS

Your Ideas and Variations

_____

_____

_____

_____

_____

_____

_____

_____

_____

_____

_____

_____

ROLLER SKATES

204

Outreach on Wheels
TOPIC: OUTREACH

Here's a new twist to an idea that works best in a small community. Have the youth group sponsor a skate-a-thon to help meet the needs of the hungry within the community. The public supports the skaters by cheering them on and by donating nonperishable food items. The townspeople can also supply the names of needy families. After the skate-a-thon, the young people will have a lot of fun delivering the food on their skates. Here's what you'll need to do:

● Find a suitable location to skate with a restroom nearby (parking lot, school yard).

● Set the date and time of the skate-a-thon.

● Make posters to advertise the skate-a-thon and post them throughout town. Make colorful banners to hang at the skate-a-thon. Use Matthew 25:40 as a theme.

● Have the young people rent or borrow roller skates.

● The day of the skate-a-thon, mark the course with ropes or cones.

● Enlist adult volunteers to help set up; collect food donations; write down the names and addresses of the needy; divide the food and put it into boxes for later deliveries.

● Gather supplies such as a tape player and Christian music tapes; boxes for food collection; tables; paper, pencils and a box to put names in; first-aid supplies; beverages and cups (ask stores to donate).

Begin the skate-a-thon with prayer. Ask the skaters to skate in shifts and to be careful not to overexert themselves. Enjoy a sack lunch together after the event.

Your next youth group meeting time could be spent delivering the food. When the skaters deliver the food, suggest that they invite the families to attend church.

—Gloria Menke

352

Variations

1. Have the participants collect pledges from neighbors, family and friends; for example, $1 for every hour of skating. Donate the money to community-help agencies or to needy families.

2. Rather than a skate-a-thon, the youth group could sponsor a rock-a-thon and use rocking chairs, a walk-a-thon, a jog-a-thon, a swim-a-thon or a volleyball marathon. Or the kids could plan a teeter-totter marathon. Make teeter-totters for every two people out of a sawhorse and a long plank. Make sure the participants bring pillows to sit on. The longer the time spent on the teeter-totters, the harder the boards feel!

Your Ideas and Variations

_____

_____

_____

_____

_____

_____

_____

_____

_____

_____

_____

_____

_____

_____

_____

_____

_____

_____

_____

205

Bound for Glory
TOPIC: FREEDOM/GOD'S WILL

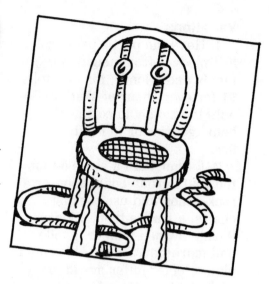

The youth group members will learn that being bound or tied to Christ is not stifling; it's freeing.

You'll need a chair, a short rope, a long rope, execution-style music (go to the library and check out a sound-effects record), a record player and songbooks.

As the kids enter the room, have the execution-style music playing in the background. Ask for a volunteer and tie up him or her like in the Old West: to a chair with hands behind his or her back (be gentle so nobody gets hurt). Discuss the meaning of being bound to sin—the ways we are all enslaved by negative habits and attitudes. Carefully cut or untie the ropes and discuss our freedom in Christ—freedom from anxiety, fear, sin and death. Ask volunteers to read: Psalm 118:5; John 8:31-32; Romans 6:17-18; Galatians 5:1.

Gather in a circle and ask the kids to grasp the long rope so it forms a loop. Say, "There is freedom—our choice to accept Christ and our bond to one another in him. Freedom doesn't necessarily mean unattachment; in fact, there is freedom in commitment and belonging. Here we experience a liberating way of being bound." Close by singing the hymn "Blessed Be the Tie That Binds" or "We Are One in the Spirit" (**Songs** by Yohann Anderson, Songs and Creations, Inc.).

—Lynn Potter

Variations

1. Gather the youth group members in pairs; have the partners stand side by side. Tie their adjoining wrists together and ankles together.

Have the pairs do various activities such as walk up and down the stairs, prepare the refreshments, clean the youth room, straighten a bookshelf.

Compare this experience to the binding nature of sin in our lives. Then cut the ties and have the kids do various activities. Compare this experience to Jesus' freeing forgiveness.

2. Gather a 50-foot rope and enough food to feed the entire group. The lunch should be one requiring some preparation by the students during the activity; for example, mix the juice, make the peanut butter and jelly sandwiches, cut the cake, etc. You also will need paper plates, cups, napkins and utensils to prepare the food.

Ask the group members to show how little space they can jam together in while sitting on the floor. As soon as they've crammed together, put the cord on the floor closely around the perimeter of the group.

Give the students the following instructions:

● Everyone must help prepare lunch.

● Everyone must stay within the confines of the cord until all people are finished eating lunch.

● No one can communicate verbally or nonverbally for the first 10 minutes.

Distribute the ingredients for lunch and have the participants prepare and eat the food. Be prepared for a lively discussion after the lunch (**Building Community in Youth Groups**, by Denny Rydberg, Group Books).

Your Ideas and Variations

_____
_____
_____
_____
_____
_____
_____
_____
_____
_____
_____
_____
_____

SEEDS

206

A Spring Worship
TOPIC: SPRING/WORSHIP/
SPIRITUAL GROWTH

Plan a spring worship service around Matthew 13—seeds that are sown in our lives.

You'll need a flower for each person, a bowl of flower seeds, and one or more planter boxes (depending on the size of the group) filled with good soil. You'll also need a watering can, and mellow-mood music to play in the background.

Focus the sermon on these portions of Matthew 13: Verses

3-9 raise questions about the condition of our inner soil, and ability or willingness to hear and receive. Verses 24-30 caution against premature judgment of good and evil. Verses 31-32 speak of the mustard seed, the small that becomes great. Also, seeds remind us of our co-creation with God—we till, plant, cultivate and harvest; but the Creator provides the seed, soil, rain and sun.

After the message is shared, pass the bowl of seeds and ask the group members each to take one, hold it to their heart, and think of areas in their lives where growth is needed (spiritually, love for an "unlovable" person, patience).

Ask each person to offer a silent prayer about that growth. Play soft background music. Ask everyone to step forward, poke a hole in the soil and plant his or her seed. After all the seeds have been planted, have somebody water the soil as you read, "As for what was sown on good soil, this is he who hears the word and understands it; he indeed bears fruit, and yields, in one case a hundredfold, in another sixty, and in another thirty" (Matthew 13:23).

Close the service by giving everyone a flower as a symbol of God's blossoming love and presence in their lives.

Assign someone to care for the flowers in the planter box so that eventually the group can enjoy a beautiful harvest.

—Lynn Potter

Variations

1. When the flowers bloom, arrange a bouquet and set it by the church altar—a colorful reminder of God's blossoming love.

2. Give each participant a bean seed and a small paper drinking cup filled with potting

soil. Have the kids plant their seed in their cup and label the cup, "God has 'bean' thinking of me." Have the kids keep their cup, water the seed and watch it grow.

Your Ideas and Variations

_____
_____
_____
_____
_____
_____
_____
_____
_____
_____
_____
_____
_____

SHOES

207

Shoe Renew
TOPIC: SERVANTHOOD/WORSHIP

How would your group members react to a foot washing service? Would they take it seriously, or would they make fun of the whole idea? Young people are sometimes so self-conscious about their feet that a foot washing service does not always

convey the message of servanthood that you want them to receive. One way to convey the same point in a contemporary way is to have a Shoe Renew. Here's how it's done.

For the next meeting, ask each young person to wear a pair of shoes that needs renewing—either dress shoes which need a shine or tennis shoes in need of new laces. Ask the group members to wear shoes they don't mind having "touched up." Have on hand different kinds and colors of shoe polish, rags and brushes, as well as several pairs of brightly colored shoelaces.

Begin by reading the story of Jesus washing the feet of the disciples (John 13:1-17). Tell the kids that, in Jesus' day when guests entered a home after walking about on dusty paths, they would have their feet washed by the servants of that

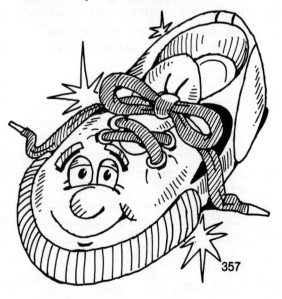

357

house. Jesus washed his disciples' feet to show them that they should be servants to one another.

After discussing the meaning of servanthood, let the kids serve one another by renewing the shoes of a partner, either with a glowing shoe shine or with a new pair of colorful laces. Not only the shoes, but the whole group will feel renewed through serving one another.

—Mark Killingsworth

Variations

1. Renew old shoes, then sell them at a garage sale or donate them to a mission.

2. During the Christmas season, renew old mittens and hats as well as shoes. Hang the mittens and hats on a tree and place the shoes at the base. Encourage congregation members to add to the collection. Give the items to a children's home, nursing home, or agency that assists needy people in the community.

Your Ideas and Variations

_____
_____
_____
_____
_____
_____
_____
_____
_____

208

Shoes-and-Jacket Scramble
TOPIC: CROWDBREAKER/
INDIVIDUALITY

Use this mixer to open a wintertime session on individuality.

Divide the youth group into two teams. Have members pile their shoes and jackets in the center of the room. Mix them up! Have the groups line up.

At the word "go" the first person from each team runs up to the pile, puts on a jacket and shoes other than his or her own; then they run back and tag the next person in line. The first team to finish wins.

After the race have everyone wear the different outfits. Discuss individuality and specify that it's okay to be different. God loves us no matter what.

—Maribeth Olson

Variations

1. Plan a sensational Shoe-Find Relay. Ask the youth group members to throw their shoes in one big pile in the center of the room. Divide the kids into two groups. Have them, one at a time, run up to the pile, find their shoes, put them on, then run back and tag the next person in line. First team done wins. For prizes, give away

shoestring potatoes or shoestring pieces of licorice.

Your Ideas and Variations

_____
_____
_____
_____
_____
_____
_____
_____
_____
_____
_____
_____

SHOWER CURTAIN

209

Rear-Projection Screen
TOPIC: MEDIA/PROJECTION SCREENS

A rear-projection screen is effective stuff to reduce the noise
and obstruction regular equipment can create for an audience. This is especially the case
for multimedia productions,
which use several projectors, recorders and a multitude of tangled wires. Also, it is sometimes
difficult to shoot over the heads
of the audience without the
screen being blacked out by

someone's shadow. Rear screens
eliminate these problems.

Professionally manufactured
rear-projection screens are very
expensive. But plastic shower
curtain liners are cheap, yet
serve very well as effective
rear-projection screens.

There are several types of
plastic shower curtain liners, so
here's what to look for: It must
be plain—no pattern printed on
it. The plastic should be a trans-
lucent, dull grey; you should be
able to see your finger through
one layer. There are white ones
with one shiny side, but these
don't work as well as the duller-
finished ones. They should meas-
ure 6 feet by 6 feet. You will
need to make a wooden frame;
1×2 lumber works well. Secure
the screen on the frame with
thumbtacks.

To avoid "hot spots" on the
screen, caused by bright projector bulbs, place the projectors
so that the beams from the lens
are slanting slightly upward as
they strike the screen. Also, remember to load your slides
backward so that any printed
material will appear correctly to
the audience. To reverse a
movie film, aim the projector to
the rear so that the light beam
hits a mirror. Angle the mirror
so that the image is reflected
back to the rear screen in the
place that you desire.

For a few dollars your group

can create a system that will prove very effective in keeping projection equipment out of the way of the audience.

—Ed McNulty

Variations

1. Use the shower curtain as a stage curtain for a puppet show.

2. Draw scenery on the curtain and use it as a backdrop for a puppet show.

3. On a rainy day, use the shower curtain for an affirmation activity. Give the kids each a marker and ask them to write positive graffiti on the curtain about others in the group. For example, "Karen and Joani shower happiness on the youth group" or "Tom and Rick are saturated with smiles and enthusiasm."

Your Ideas and Variations

_____
_____
_____
_____
_____
_____
_____
_____
_____
_____
_____
_____
_____
_____
_____
_____
_____

SKIS

210

Ski Trip Freeze-In
TOPIC: PUBLICITY

If you are trying to organize a ski trip, turn the thermostat down as far as it will go . . . low, low! Ask the youth group members to wear ski jackets, hats and mittens. Serve hot chocolate and show a movie on skiing. You can get the movie from a travel agency or order one directly from a ski resort.

Invite an experienced skier to bring his or her equipment and talk about skiing. Ask him or her to demonstrate how to ski (on the carpet). If any youth group members have skied before, have them share their experiences on the slopes.

This idea will not only promote the ski trip, it also will promote fellowship!

—J.B. Collingsworth

Variations

1. Divide into small groups and give each one a situation to pantomime. Allow the kids to guess what each group is miming. Let the young people create their own situations or use these: riding a chairlift; losing a ski pole; skiing during a blizzard; relaxing at the ski lodge.

2. Organize a ski fashion show and sell tickets to the congregation and community. Talk with the managers of different sport shops in town. Tell them that your group is going on a ski trip, and you want to sponsor a fashion show to raise money. Have each person in your group choose a ski outfit to model during the show. Ask a youth group member to announce each model, describe each outfit, and tell the audience where it can be purchased. After the fashion show, serve hot chocolate, hot cider, popcorn and trail mix.

Your Ideas and Variations

_____
_____
_____
_____
_____
_____
_____
_____
_____

SLIDES

211

He Has Risen!
TOPIC: EASTER/WORSHIP

Would you like an excellent way to create "atmosphere" for a youth group sunrise service? Here is an idea that really brings meaning to the Easter celebration!

Pick an empty room in your church that is somewhat dark and cool. This room will symbolize the tomb. Inside the room, project a slide on the wall that reads, "Why do you look for the living among the dead? He has risen." Carefully stack concrete blocks in front of the door to symbolize the stone used to seal the tomb.

When the youth group members arrive, have them move the stones that block the opening. This then opens the door to the tomb-like worship area. What a meaningful setting to celebrate and worship the risen Christ.

—Steven J. Bolda

Variations

1. By the door, pile several small stones (one for each person). At the end of the service, give each person a stone to carry in their pockets or purses, or to place in a prominent place at home. The stone is a reminder that Jesus overcame death. He rose from the dead and lives for us (**Dennis Benson's Creative Bible Studies**, Group Books).

2. Place an old white sheet in the "tomb." At the end of the service, cut the cloth into strips and give a piece to each person. Ask the students to tie the strips on their wrists as a reminder that Christ has risen and he walks with them. Ask the young people to pray for each other at a certain time each day. The cloth also can be a symbol of this act of mutual care (**Dennis Benson's Creative Bible Studies**, Group Books).

Your Ideas and Variations

_____
_____
_____
_____
_____
_____
_____
_____
_____
_____
_____
_____
_____
_____

212

Low-Cost Slide Shows
TOPIC: MEDIA/SLIDE SHOWS

Many churches and resource centers have old or partially damaged filmstrips that they no longer use. Too often these are just tossed out, which is unfortunate since they usually contain many frames that could be used again in slide shows. They might offer scenes of foreign missions, churches, crowds, nature and close-ups of people's faces. Filmstrips such as these are useful for a group that enjoys putting together slide and tape presentations. Many church resource center directors would gladly donate these old filmstrips to your youth group.

To reuse the filmstrip you will need a pair of scissors, a box of cardboard slide frames and an iron or slide press. The cardboard slide frames are sold by most photo supply stores. (Or write to Spiratone, 185-06 Northern Blvd., Flushing, NY 11354.) Ask for the "half-frame" size, which refers to the size of the opening in the frame. It is just big enough for the small frame of a filmstrip. Carefully cut out the filmstrip frames you want to save. Place the transparency in the cardboard frame,

fold it over, and run a medium-hot iron over the cardboard only. Be careful that the transparency doesn't slip down when you fold the frame. Press down firmly on the iron around all four sides of the cardboard frame. To prevent bowing, turn the slide over, and iron the other side. The heat-sensitive glue on the frame should bond to the transparency. No gaps should be visible along the edges of the slide. If there is a gap, re-iron the slide at that spot. It's possible that you didn't press down firmly enough, or the iron wasn't hot enough.

If you or your group produce a lot of slide shows, you might want to spend the extra money to purchase a slide press, which is an electronic appliance that quickly and efficiently mounts slides. Many photo supply stores sell them. A slide press saves many hours of precious time over the cumbersome iron method.

Plastic slide frames with the "half-frame" openings are also available. They usually come in a box of 100. The small transparency slips into a slot on one side of the frame. Plastic frames are more expensive than cardboard frames but they are easier and quicker to use because you bypass the heat process.

Whichever type of frame you use, this simple process can pro-

vide your group with hundreds of imaginative slides at a very low cost.

—Ed McNulty

Variations

1. Make an intergenerational slide show from old filmstrips. Cut out frames that depict people of all ages and nationalities, then title the show "God's Children."

2. Plan an intergenerational potluck. Invite people from the congregation and community to come and enjoy the food and the slide show. Sing songs such as "Children of the Heavenly Father," "Jesus Loves the Little Children" and "We Are the Family of God" (**Songs**, by Yohann Anderson, Songs and Creations, Inc.).

Your Ideas and Variations

_____
_____
_____
_____
_____
_____
_____
_____
_____
_____
_____
_____
_____

SOAP

213

The Great Shaving Cream War
TOPIC: GAMES

Rather than being surprised when kids have a shaving cream fight at a retreat or lock-in—plan for one!

Ask each group member to bring a can of plain shaving cream, not mentholated or scented. Ask each person to also bring an old aerosol spray can of any product.

Gather everyone outside in an open field. Show the kids how to pop off the top of the shaving cream (the one the cream comes out). Then have them remove the spray nozzle from the aerosol spray can. The aerosol nozzle should fit nicely onto the shaving cream can. (Experiment ahead of time to acquaint yourself with the procedure.) The result is a shaving cream "gun" that has a range of about 12 feet!

Now you're ready for the shaving cream war. Divide into teams or have an everyone-for-yourself war. When all of the shaving cream has been sprayed, award a prize for the messiest and the cleanest person. Perhaps a water war to end the day wouldn't be a bad idea!

—Thomas F. Bronson

Variations

1. Change a couple of volunteers' appearances. Give them new shaving cream hairstyles, mustaches or beards.

2. Host a shaving-cream sculpture contest. Have the kids sculpt snowmen, miniature buildings, people or symbols. Award a full can of shaving cream to the artist with the most original creation.

Your Ideas and Variations

_____
_____
_____
_____
_____
_____
_____
_____

214

Important Jobs
TOPIC: SERVANTHOOD/OUTREACH

Help your youth group members decide what is important in life by thinking about different occupations. You'll need a dust cloth, broom, cleaning supplies, flowers, vase, plate of cookies and beverages.

Tell the members, "We are expecting visitors today and I want the meeting room to look as attractive as possible."

Ask the young people to number off, "One, two, three . . ." Allow 10 minutes for all odd numbers to clean the room; all even numbers to arrange the flowers in a vase and the cookies on a plate.

After a while, discuss how fairly the work was divided. Which group did the more important work? Why? What if the room were clean, but there were no flowers, no refreshments? What if there were refreshments and flowers, but the room was dirty?

Allow time for a discussion on what vocations the kids think are more important. Why do we think some jobs are more important than others?

Take the youth group members to where the cleaning supplies are stored. Explain the church custodian's job. Next, move to the church office and explain the church secretary's job.

Return to the classroom and talk about what the church would look like if there were no custodian. Ask what would happen if there were no church secretary. Why are these jobs important?

Close by reading Luke 10:38-42. Why did Martha worry about the food? Why did Mary want to listen to Jesus? Both are important, but listening to Jesus should be a priority. Have a time of silence for each person to think of ways to do the work he or she is called to do, yet at the same time keep his or her eyes on Jesus.

Bring out the beverages and enjoy the cookies on the plate that the kids have arranged so beautifully.

—E. Jane Mall

Variations

1. The last verse of 1 John 4 tells us to love others even as we love God. Have the youth group members read 1 Corinthians 13:4-8 and choose characteristics of love that apply to people they know.

Ask the kids each to write a note of appreciation to the custodian, secretary or another church worker. Have the young people include two of the "Corinthians characteristics" in each of their notes. Deliver the notes when they are completed. Here's an example:

> Dear Mrs. Sands,
> Thank you for all of the hard work you do as the church secretary.
> Thank you for being kind in helping the youth group with our activities and patient when we ask you for last-minute favors.
> Love,
> Cheryl

2. Host a "Vocation Conversation" night. Invite several church members to come to a youth group meeting, discuss their jobs, and answer questions from the youth group members. Arrange for times to visit the various places of employment.

Your Ideas and Variations

_____
_____
_____
_____
_____
_____
_____
_____
_____
_____

215

Saturday Servants
TOPIC: OUTREACH

Saturday Servants is a service-oriented, outreach ministry designed to give youth group members an opportunity to fulfill Jesus' challenge to us to serve others.

We set aside one Saturday morning each month to perform this service. The needy people in our congregation (elderly, widowed, single parents) request our help with tasks such as housecleaning, window washing, caring for children, mowing lawns, raking leaves, washing/waxing cars, etc. Each youth group member is assigned to a specific task. The people are asked to supply us with the necessary equipment, or to let us know if they can't. Although this work is done as a service, if some people insist on paying us, we let them know that the money will be donated to the church or to another helping organization. This is not a fund raiser for the youth ministry—it is a service project.

Through their participation in Saturday Servants, the kids learn to "serve the Lord with gladness" and they gain a good feeling from helping those in need.

—Gary P. Wrisberg

Variations

1. Use this idea as a fund raiser.

2. Broaden your scope—use Saturday Servants to help needy people in your community.

3. Focus on one cleaning task. For example, host a "Window-Washing Wednesday" or a "Floor-Scrubbing Saturday."

Your Ideas and Variations

_____
_____
_____
_____
_____
_____
_____
_____
_____
_____
_____

SOFT DRINKS

216

The Lord's Taste Test
TOPIC: DISCUSSION STARTER

Should Christians be lukewarm in their faith? cold? hot? To initiate a discussion on this topic, start by filling three large containers with your favorite soft drink. Next:

● Label one "H" for hot; heat the drink to at least 150 degrees.

● Label another "C" for cold; cool the drink to approximately 32 degrees.

● Label another "L" for lukewarm; it should be at room temperature.

Give each of the youth group members a Styrofoam cup with a sample from each container for them to taste and evaluate on a scale of 1 to 10; 10 being high. Begin with "L" and end with "C."

Most of the kids will agree that the cold drink is the best. If any wisecrackers pick "L" just to throw you off, offer them the rest and present them with a prestigious "No Taste" award.

Break into groups according to the kids' favorite soft drinks. Ask each group to discuss Revelation 3:15-22, focusing on verses 15-16, "I know your works: you are neither cold nor hot. Would that you were cold or hot! So, because you are lukewarm, and neither cold nor hot, I will spew you out of my mouth." Have the kids think of ways they can make a noticeable difference in the world.

Close the session with ice-cold cans of pop to quench everyone's thirst.

—Donald W. Hendrick

Variations

1. Do the Lord's Taste Test with foods such as baked potatoes or hot chocolate.

2. Have a "spewing" contest with watermelon seeds or cherry pits!

Your Ideas and Variations

_____
_____
_____
_____
_____
_____
_____
_____
_____
_____
_____

217

You're a Star!
TOPIC: SELF-IMAGE

As a worship or Bible study theme, focus on how valuable and precious we are in God's sight—created in his image. Use this idea to close a youth group meeting.

Say to the kids, "There are many forces in our world that dehumanize and degrade, that make us feel inadequate. But to God, we are unique and deeply loved. Not only actors and actresses are stars; we all are stars in our own special way. We need to confess our sins, and claim our greatness in Christ." To accentuate this, give a gold or silver star to each person as a symbol of his or her "stardom." Read 1 Peter 2:9, which tells us we are chosen by God—we are very special to him. Have the kids stick the stars on their hand or forehead. Or they could take the stars home and stick them on a mirror as a daily reminder of their inner beauty and light.

Usually such stars are used to reward good behavior, but these

stars are reminders that we are loved—unconditionally—simply for who we are!

—Lynn Potter

Variations

1. Greet worshipers on Sunday morning with a hug or handshake, then stick the star on their hand and say, "You are chosen by God—you're a star!"

2. At a church service during the Christmas season give out the stars as reminders of the Bethlehem star that pointed the way to Jesus' birthplace.

Your Ideas and Variations

_____
_____
_____
_____
_____
_____
_____
_____
_____

STETHOSCOPES

218

The Heart
TOPIC: EMOTIONS

Is the heart's main function to pump blood through the body? Are there other functions? In this meeting, the kids will answer these questions and listen to their heartbeats. Use this idea on Valentine's Day or for a communion service.

Borrow a stethoscope from a doctor, nurse, or someone who has a home blood pressure kit. Give each young person a chance to listen to his or her heartbeat. Talk about the heart as a pump that circulates the blood. Compare that definition to the biblical understanding. The heart was thought to be the central, unifying organ of a person's life. The heart was considered the source of all physical, emotional and intellectual energy. Through the heart, humans talked with God (**The Interpreter's Dictionary**, Abingdon).

Ask the kids to remember the biblical meaning of "heart" and apply it to these verses. Read the following verses and discuss the questions:

● Exodus 7:3—What does it mean to harden one's heart?

● Psalm 51:10—What does it mean to have a clean heart?

● Jeremiah 29:13—What does it mean to seek God with all your heart?

● Jeremiah 31:33—What does it mean to write the law upon the heart?

● Matthew 5:8—What does it mean to have a pure heart?

Expand the theme by discussing how each person (heart, blood, circulation) is combined with others to form the Christian body. Conclude the study with communion—celebrate the body and blood of Jesus and his forgiveness.

—Lynn Potter

Variations

1. For refreshments, eat heart-shaped candy, cookies or cake and drink cherry Kool-Aid.

2. Tell group members to bring their favorite pizza ingredients (mozzarella cheese, pepperoni, mushrooms, etc.). Provide a batch of homemade pizza dough, tomato sauce and baking pans. Pair up group members and have partners shape pizza dough into a heart, then add their favorite pizza toppings. While the pizzas are baking, have a group Bible study on 1 Corinthians 13 or John 15:11-17.

3. On Valentine's Day, have young people sneak into their parents' bedroom or bathroom and write "I love you" on the mirror. They can use soap (if they promise to wash it off after Mom and Dad have been pleasantly surprised).

Your Ideas and Variations

_____
_____
_____
_____
_____
_____
_____
_____
_____
_____
_____
_____
_____

STICKS

219

The Power Stick
TOPIC: DISCUSSION STARTERS

In a group discussion when more focus is needed on an important issue, try the Native American practice of The Power Stick. A stick is passed around the circle in a clockwise direction—the direction of the sun's movement. The person holding the stick is asked to share from the heart and to be very focused. For example, "We're talking about the need for love and support in a family. My mom has been very supportive of me lately. My best friend unloaded a lot of her problems on me last week, and I talked to my mom about it. Mom listened and gave me a hug—just what I needed."

Everyone else is to be silent and respect the person who is sharing by listening attentively. The Power Stick noticeably deepens the quality of sharing in a group.

—Lynn Potter

Variations

1. Another way to facilitate a discussion is by throwing a ball from person to person. The teenager who holds the ball offers an opinion on the given topic. He or she tosses the ball to another person who states his or her opinion, and so on.

2. Use a ball of yarn or spool of thread to make sure every group member participates in the discussion. Begin by telling your opinion or answering a question on the given topic. Hold the end of the yarn, then toss the ball to another person. That person answers the question, holds onto a part of the yarn and tosses the ball to another,

and so on. Continue until everyone is holding the yarn. Notice the intricate web of discussion that has been formed.

Your Ideas and Variations

_____
_____
_____
_____
_____
_____
_____
_____
_____
_____
_____
_____

220

The Simple Things in Life
TOPIC: GOD'S LOVE

When Jesus said, "Consider the lilies of the field . . ." he was encouraging us to notice and appreciate the simple things in life. Sticks are good examples of simple things that we not only ignore, but that we try to dispose of.

Give the youth group members each a stick and a copy of the handout, Consider the Stick. Tell them to put the stick somewhere in their house where they will be certain to notice it every day

for one week. Encourage the participants to complete the specified part of the handout each day:

> **Consider the Stick**
> **Monday:** The stick reminds me of God's _____.
> **Tuesday:** Like the stick, life is sometimes _____.
> **Wednesday:** The stick is like me because _____.
> **Thursday:** If God cares about this stick then God must _____ me.
> **Friday:** The stick can break but God _____.
> **Saturday:** The stick says God's kingdom is _____.
>
> (A copyrighted resource from **Youth Ministry Cargo**. Permission granted to copy this handout for local church use only.)

Ask the youth group members to bring their sticks and handouts to the next meeting. Build a fire using the sticks; ask the young people to share what they learned.

Through this reflective exercise, the kids will learn that God truly cares for them—he loves them above all other things.

—Arlo R. Reichter

Variations

1. Instead of building a fire with the sticks, form a cross by

binding the sticks with string and wire.

2. Use this activity for a retreat. Give the participants 15 minutes to search for a stick. Have them meditate on the first sentence in the handout, "This stick reminds me of God's . . ." Tell the young people to keep their sticks. Throughout the rest of the retreat, plan five more meditation times for the kids to think of the five remaining sentences in the handout.

Your Ideas and Variations

_____
_____
_____
_____
_____
_____
_____
_____
_____
_____

STRING

221

The String Game
TOPIC: RELATIONSHIPS/FRIENDSHIP

Relationships, friendships, a sense of belonging and community are all essential dynamics for a healthy group. But we must work (or should we say play?) at developing community.

Tie community into the Christian tradition by creating a cross out of posterboard and placing it in the center of the room. Gather the members in a fairly large circle around the cross. For each member, cut one 6-foot piece of string. Tie one end of the string to each person and tape the other end to the cross.

After each person is tied to the cross, share feelings and reactions to the experience. Ask the kids to move around, but remain attached to the cross. See what things can be done: shake hands, talk to someone across the circle, walk around the cross merry-go-round style, sit on the floor, get tangled.

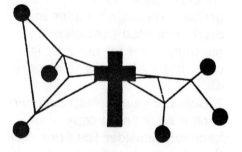

Untangle the web and return to the original positions. Untie one person and ask him or her to leave the room. Dream up an initiation ritual for the "outsider" and then invite him or her into the room and into the community. Demand that he or she follow the ritual before his or her full membership is granted. For example, walk around the circle and give everyone a back rub. When the task if finished, tie the member to the cross.

Talk about the experience. Allow the newly-admitted member to share his or her thoughts and feelings. Discuss the reasons for initiation rites and membership responsibilities. Discuss the new-member rites of your church.

Untie everyone from the cross and divide them into two groups. Give each group a piece of posterboard and scissors. Send each group to opposite ends of the room. Give each group five minutes to think of a central symbol or object to which they will attach their loyalty, allegiance and string. For example, money or a heart. Have them cut the symbol out of posterboard and connect themselves to their symbol.

Give the groups 10 minutes to recruit new members from the other group. Use whatever method is necessary to secure new members.

After a few minutes, discuss

feelings and reactions. See which methods worked the best. Find out why some did not wish to join the new group, and why others did join. Share ideas and feelings about competition.

● What happens when two groups compete for our loyalty?

● What happens when more than two groups compete?

● Why do we join certain groups and not join others?

Bring the two groups back together into one large group. Select a commonly agreed-upon object or symbol to represent the new group loyalty. Cut this symbol out of posterboard and place it in the center of the room. Tie everyone to that object.

As each person is tied into the community, ask the person to make one commitment to the group. For example, "I will support the total group by participating in every meeting." Allow each person to be as creative as he or she can in his or her commitment. These statements will personalize the activity and help build community and support from every group member.

—Wesley Taylor

Variations

1. Tie a piece of string to each person's finger and say, "Remember—you are a member of the family of God."

2. Gather one 3×5 card for each youth group member. Punch a hole in the corner of each card and attach a piece of yarn. On the cards write, "You are a special child of God." Tie a card to one finger of each youth group member.

Your Ideas and Variations

_____
_____
_____
_____
_____
_____
_____
_____
_____
_____
_____

STUFFED ANIMALS

222

Cuddly Creatures
TOPIC: GOD'S LOVE

Many teenagers still have stuffed animals lying around the house or on display in their bedrooms. Use these cuddly creatures at your next retreat.

On a list of things to bring, add "your favorite stuffed animal." Set up a table and exhibit the stuffed treasures. Plan to do these activities at the retreat:

1. Pin a number to each ani-

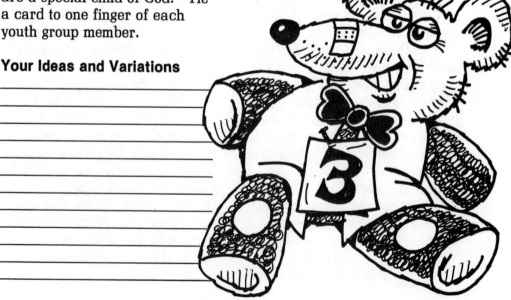

mal. Think of categories such as most lovable, most "used," most look alike of camp director, most look alike of youth sponsor, etc. Give the kids paper and pencils and have them vote for their favorite stuffed animal in each of the categories.

2. Have a cabin competition. The cabin with the most unique stuffed animals wins. Or, the cabin with the most colorful stuffed animals wins. Don't allow the young people to vote for their own, or their cabin's, animals.

3. Ask each cabin to choose a mascot from among the animals brought by their cabin members.

4. Plan a Bible study on "God's Love." Ask questions such as:

● Why do kids like stuffed animals? What makes them special?

● How does God's love compare to our love for the stuffed animals?

● Does God love us no matter how old or "worn out" we are? Explain.

● Does God ever put us in a closet and forget about us? Explain.

● Close the Bible study by having everyone shout in unison, "See what love the Father has given us, that we should be called the children of God" (1 John 3:1).

—Leonard Kageler

Variations

1. Plan a "Stuffed Animal Make Over" meeting. Ask the youth group members to bring an old stuffed animal or doll that they wouldn't mind giving away. If they don't have one, they could purchase one inexpensively at a garage sale or at a Salvation Army store. Renovate the toys using soap, rags, ribbons, brushes, etc. For Christmas, the youth group can donate the renovated treasures to a children's home. Or they could sell the toys to raise money for the youth group fund.

Your Ideas and Variations

_____
_____
_____
_____
_____
_____
_____
_____
_____
_____

SWIMMING POOLS

223

Swimming Party
TOPIC: SUMMER/PROGRESSIVE EVENTS

Instead of a progressive dinner party, plan a progressive swimming party. It's a refreshing way to cool down your kids on a hot summer day.

Contact a number of city swimming pools or congregational members who own pools. Set a time with each of them for your youth group members to swim for 15 to 20 minutes.

Have your kids meet at the church wearing their bathing suits. Board the church bus or vans and keep the windows closed tight to create a sauna effect. Then drive around the city and swim at each pool for the set amount of time. At the last pool, serve watermelon and talk about favorite swimming memories. For example:

● Describe the first time you can remember swimming.

● How old were you when you first began swimming lessons? How did you feel?

● How many of you water-ski? Describe your first time.

Take the plunge—dive into this fun idea!

—Tim Pontius

Variations

1. Plan a Bible study around the theme of water; use these ideas:

● Jesus turning water into wine—John 2:1-11.

● Peter walking on the water—Matthew 14:22-33.

● The woman at the well—

John 4:1-42.

Your Ideas and Variations

_____
_____
_____
_____
_____
_____
_____
_____
_____
_____
_____
_____
_____

TAPE RECORDERS

224

God's Unexplainable Love
TOPIC: GOD'S HOLINESS

Many people wonder not only why they are alive, but why God has chosen them for faith in Jesus Christ. This question has been posed in song, in poetry, and in casual conversation between friends. Ultimately, we may just have to lie back and marvel at God's unexplainable love for us. Scripture gives us insight regarding the value of our "holiness"—our having been set apart for discipleship. Through this scripture study, students may learn not only how holiness can benefit them, but also how by being holy, they can serve God and others.

Gather several tape recorders, tapes and microphones. Provide scratch paper, pencils and 3×5 cards. The following scripture references, which will be used later in the lesson, should be written on the cards.

Card 1. Ephesians 6:10-17 "Armor of God"
Psalm 29:2 "Holy array"

Card 2. 1 Timothy 3:8-13 "Rules for deacons"

Card 3. 1 Peter 2:9-10 "What can chosen people do?"

Card 4. Matthew 20:20-28 "Not to rule but to serve"

Card 5. Hebrews 12:1-11 "The value of discipline"

Tell the youth group members that Christians are to be holy. Say, "Webster provides a number of definitions of 'holy.' The following four are particularly useful for our purposes: set apart to the service of God or a god; characterized by perfection and transcendence; being awesome, frightening or beyond belief; filled with superhuman and potentially fatal power.

"Let's discuss each of these definitions. The first one emphasizes the differentness of Christians, as God intends them to be. How are you different from kids who aren't Christians?" Allow time for discussion, then say, "In the second definition of 'holy' we discover that God has standards for the people he considers holy. He wants us to strive for perfection, and to end our preoccupation with the things of this life. Certainly this is a challenge for all of us.

"The third and fourth definitions turn our attention to the source of our holiness, for they are references to God's awesome power and total otherness from us."

Move into the next part of the study by discussing popular commercials. What do the commercials try to get the consumer to believe about the products? What techniques do they use?

Tell the kids that they'll get to write a commercial about a Christian product or purpose which should relate to the scripture written on their 3×5 card. Distribute the cards, scratch paper and pencils. Give the young people 30 minutes to come up with a commercial. Then distribute the tape recorders, tapes and microphones, and have the kids record the commercials. Play them back for all to hear.

The group with Card 1 might think of a commercial similar to this: "You can be covered and protected with God's armor. This shiny covering will guard and protect you through life's trials and temptations. You will be doubly strengthened as you go through life's ups and downs. This armor is yours for the asking. Yes . . . that's right! FREE. All you have to do is pray for the armor. Ask God, and you will receive!"

Gather for a circle prayer. Give thanks to God for making us holy, not only for our own good, but for the good we can offer to others.

—Walter Mees

Variations

1. Tape sounds to go along with the commercial. For example, a person could mention God's protective armor then pound on an aluminum trash can. It sounds like a person is hitting a "breastplate of righteousness!"

2. Act out the commercials, then videotape the action.

Your Ideas and Variations

_____
_____
_____
_____
_____
_____
_____
_____
_____
_____
_____
_____
_____

225

Monthly Tape Magazine
TOPIC: OUTREACH/SHUT-INS

Inspire your young people to minister to your church's shut-ins by producing a monthly tape magazine for them.

Assign different members to record the following:

● The president of the women's group, one of the elders, a representative of the church school, or another congregational leader, relating an interesting activity the church has sponsored during the past month.

● A high school student reporting "school news." What fun things have happened this past month at school?

● Organ music, the church choir, or the congregation singing a favorite hymn.

● The pastor giving a short message.

● A popular book, record or tape review. Offer to lend the reviewed material to those who are interested.

Get a person to splice the interviews, music and news together into one tape. Make copies and distribute them to the shut-ins. Make sure the people have access to a tape player. They'll love the contact with the kids, as well as being kept up-to-date with church news.

—Mardie H.C. MacDonald

Variations

1. Make a Christmas tape. Record Christmas hymns and carols; the Christmas story (Luke 2:1-20); Christmas wishes such as, "Have a wonderful holiday season." End the tape with the youth group singing, "We Wish You a Merry Christmas." At the end of the song shout, "God bless you!" Make copies of the tape. Place them in separate boxes, decorate with wrapping paper and ribbons, then deliver them to special people.

2. Tape the weekly church services for those who can't come. Make copies and deliver

them each Sunday. Check with your local radio station and try to schedule a weekly spot to broadcast your church services.

Your Ideas and Variations

_____
_____
_____
_____
_____
_____
_____
_____
_____
_____
_____
_____
_____

TOILET PAPER

226

Toilet Paper Torches
TOPIC: FUN

Light the way on a dark night with Toilet Paper Torches. Use these torches for lighting snow-tubing runs or nighttime snow sculpture contests.

Make a torch by cutting out the front of a #10 tin can; nail the can to the top of an 8-foot pole. Place a roll of toilet paper in the can and soak it with kero-

sene. The lighted torch will burn for about 15 to 20 minutes.

Use several of the torches to light up an outside area for youth group events. Let your lights shine for all to see!

—Tim Pontius

Variations

1. Have your group sit in a circle and pass a roll of toilet paper from person to person. Instruct the young people to each take as much as they would need to blow their nose.

After everyone has taken some toilet paper, go around the circle and ask each person to tell one interesting fact about

himself or herself for each square torn off (**The Return of Try This One**, Group Books).

Your Ideas and Variations

_____

_____

_____

_____

_____

_____

_____

_____

_____

_____

_____

_____

TOILET PLUNGER

227

Taking the Plunge
TOPIC: GAMES

Has your group tried plunging? Yes—you guessed it—you use a toilet plunger to play! The game can be played individually or in teams of any number of people.

The object of this game is to stick the plunger cup in the middle of a target. Here's how it works:

On the tile or wood floor of a large room with a high ceiling, use masking tape to outline a 7-inch square within a 12-inch square. Twenty feet away, make a similar target. Then stand behind one target, throw the plunger and try to make it stick in the opposite target.

Rules may be varied any number of ways: outlaw underhand throws or overhand throws; agree on point values for hits within the 7-inch or the 12-inch square; play like darts in that each turn is taken freely, or like horseshoes in that the second player could destroy the points of the first player; if the plunger doesn't remain upright, it can be considered a complete miss. Use your imagination for other "plunging" variables.

—Walter Mees

Variations

1. Ask all youth group members to decorate a "personal

plunger." Award prizes for most original, most useful and most elaborate.

2. Challenge other youth groups to form a "Plunger League" and sponsor this crazy tournament in your church.

Your Ideas and Variations

_____
_____
_____
_____
_____
_____
_____
_____
_____
_____
_____
_____
_____

TOOLS

228

Talents
TOPIC: TALENTS/GIFTS

Help the youth group members recognize and appreciate their talents with this brief, yet effective lesson.

Gather several hand tools such as a hammer, screwdriver, wrench, scissors, paintbrush, magnet, crochet hook, spatula, paring knife and knitting needles. Try to find tools that aren't too easily recognized. Place all of these in a heavy canvas bag or wrap them in a small blanket; tie securely so they don't fall out. You also will need paper and pencils.

When the group members arrive, ask them to sit in a circle. Pass the bundle around and see how many tools the young people can identify by feeling through the cloth. After all have had a turn, open the bag and display the tools. Then discuss these questions:

● Are we aware of the talents and abilities with which we were born? Explain.

● Who knows our potential?

● How and when do we recognize and learn to use these talents?

● How do our talents compare with the tools in the bag?

● Why can't we recognize some of our talents?

● Do responsibilities and opportunities help develop our talents? Why or why not?

● Where do we get our talents and abilities? Did our heavenly Father have anything to do with these gifts?

Give the group members each a piece of paper and pencil and have them write their name at the top of their paper. Next, have them pass the papers to

the right. Ask the members to write one talent or gift that they appreciate in the person whose paper they are holding. Follow this process and keep passing the papers until they reach their original owners.

Ask the group members to keep the papers and use the talents that God has given them. Close with a prayer asking God to help us recognize our talents and then use them.

—Janet R. Balmforth

Variations

1. Divide the youth group members into small groups; give each group two tools. Have the kids develop role plays about the talents and abilities associated with the tools. For example, a person could use a hammer and pretend he or she is building a wall. Another person could use a paintbrush and paint the wall. They both could stand side by side, admiring their creation.

2. Form a circle and pass around each tool. Have the teenagers think of different uses for

each one. For example, a tweezers could be used to pluck feathers off of chickens, repair tiny watches, pull splinters out of tiny fingers, etc. Try to think of many, many uses for the different tools!

Your Ideas and Variations

_____
_____
_____
_____
_____
_____
_____
_____
_____
_____
_____
_____
_____
_____

TOYS

229

Adventures in the Christian Life
TOPIC: CHRISTIAN LIVING

Yo-yos are a fascinating pastime, especially if you can do tricks with them. During an object lesson with my youth group, I wanted to share that the Christian life was not easy; it had its ups and downs, but it was fulfilling to be a child of God.

Everyone received a yo-yo and they practiced the basic up-and-down motion. "Pretty easy," they said. Then we tried doing some tricks: Around the World, Walking the Dog, Rock the Cradle and Loop-to-Loop. The tricks were a lot harder. (For more information on tricks write Flambeau Midwest Corporation, 801 Lynn Ave., Baraboo, WI 53913, or call (608) 356-5551.)

I told the kids, "When we begin our Christian life we have days when we feel really close to God; and we have days when we feel far away from him. If we stop growing with God, it will be easy to go up and down in our Christian faith. But when we strive to please God, and do as he asks, he will bless us. Yes, it will be hard at times, just as the yo-yo tricks were, but it will be worth the effort.

Young people catch on to the idea that Christian life is a life of growth, not just "ups and downs."

—Bob Hicks

Variations

1. Gather at a nearby playground and use the equipment for this meeting. Ask the youth group members to ride the merry-go-round and discuss the "merry-go-round of life." Ride swings and teeter-totters and talk about life's ups and downs.

2. Bring a Slinky to a youth group meeting. Compare this toy to several topics such as:

● God helps us spring back into shape after we are stretched by life's difficulties.

● Life is like a Slinky—sometimes we go round and round in a spiral wondering about our purpose and goals.

● Sometimes we think we can do only a few things well. Then God surprises us by showing us a talent we never knew we had. Just as a Slinky goes back and forth from hand to hand—ho hum—yet it also can walk down stairs!

Your Ideas and Variations

_____
_____
_____
_____
_____
_____
_____
_____
_____
_____

230

Childlike Faith
TOPIC: JOY/FAITH

A famous cliche states that children should be seen and not

heard. However, children in Jesus' time came to him without pretense and without fear. They had complete, open faith. Jesus said that we are to be like children and come to him with childlike faith. This study allows youth group members to discuss what it means to be childlike.

You'll need several kinds of baby toys such as rattles, dolls and blocks (one toy for each person). Beforehand, ask the students to bring one of their baby pictures and not to show it to anyone. (Bring one yourself!) Post the baby pictures on a bulletin board. You'll also need cookies or candy.

Give each student a baby toy as they enter the room. Say, "We have an hour for this class and I'm going to let you play with your toys." After five minutes stop the play and ask, "Were you bored? Did you feel silly?"

Collect the toys and sing a song such as "Twinkle, Twinkle, Little Star." Read and discuss Luke 18:15-17. Ask what Jesus meant when he said the kingdom of heaven belongs to people who are "like a child." What does it mean "to become like children"?

Give the youth group members a few minutes to look at the bulletin board of baby pictures. See who can identify the most pictures and then say, "Each of you have changed. You're not the same now as you were then. So how can you become like a child again?"

Give each person a cookie or piece of candy and tell the students to enjoy it. When they have eaten the treat say, "Maybe I poisoned those cookies or candy. You didn't even hesitate to eat them. Why? You had a childlike faith and trust in me. You know me. You trust me. So you accepted what I offered you. That's how we are to become childlike in our faith. We go to Jesus without fear. We know what he says and promises is true. But you must temper this childlike faith and trust. If a stranger on the street offers you a cookie or a piece of candy you won't eat it. At the very least, you would question it. When you are on sure ground you can have this childlike faith. It's difficult to have childlike faith in this world where there are so many dangers and pitfalls. But with Jesus you can be open and childlike and go to him in confidence. You can enjoy your faith. What a comforting thing this is!"

—E. Jane Mall

Variations

1. Assign the youth group members to help with the elementary-age Sunday school classes, or to assist in the nursery. Have them notice the spe-

cial qualities of the young children. After all have worked with the little kids, discuss what it means to have a childlike faith.

2. Ask the young people to bring a gift-wrapped toy from home. At the meeting, unwrap the toys and play with them. Discuss this study and the gift of childlikeness. Afterward, rewrap the toys and give them to the church nursery or to a children's home.

Your Ideas and Variations

_____
_____
_____
_____
_____
_____
_____
_____
_____
_____
_____
_____
_____
_____

231

From Hostility to Hospitality
TOPIC: RECONCILIATION/OUTREACH

Human nature causes us to build walls that separate; Jesus' love causes us to build bridges that connect.

Illustrate this concept by using wooden blocks. Borrow several boxes of blocks from the church nursery or a local preschool.

Divide the young people into two groups. Have the two groups use the blocks to build a wall between them. Talk about the ways we alienate ourselves as individuals and as nations through jealousy, resentment, pride, fear, nationalism, etc. Have each group turn their backs on the other—talk about how this isolation feels.

During this discussion, quietly dismantle the wall of blocks. Ask the groups to face each other and experience a new pos-

sibility—breaking down the dividing wall of hostility.

Read Ephesians 2:14, "For he is our peace, who has made us both one, and has broken down the dividing wall of hostility." Ask the group members to demonstrate this concept in a different way—perhaps build a bridge with the blocks, walk across and then shake hands or hug. Discuss the difference between the two feelings—separateness and togetherness.

Truly Jesus enables us to cross the great divides to form a land of unity and love.

—Lynn Potter

Variations

1. Instruct the youth group members to use the blocks to form a symbol of unity and love; for example, a heart, circle, cross, etc.

2. Instead of blocks, build walls from newspaper and masking tape. Divide the young people into small groups; give each group a stack of newspapers, a roll of masking tape and a garbage bag. Tell the groups to each build a wall with the material so they can't see others and others can't see them. Leave the groups within their "confines" for several minutes, then read Ephesians 2:14. When the kids hear the words ". . . broken down the dividing wall of hostility" have them tear down their walls and stuff them in their garbage bags.

Your Ideas and Variations

_____

_____

_____

_____

_____

_____

_____

_____

_____

_____

_____

_____

232

Sodom and Gomorrah
TOPIC: GOD'S JUDGMENT/BIBLE STUDY

This is a fun and crazy way to reenact the story of Sodom and Gomorrah. Build a scale model of the two cities. Find some old doll houses to create your towns. Go to a Salvation Army store, Good Will store or to garage sales. Make the townspeople out of clay by using this recipe:

Clay
1 cup table salt
⅔ cup water
1 cup cornstarch
½ cup cold water

Mix the salt and water over medium heat until it boils. Remove from heat; add the other ingredients. Mixture will thicken. Add blue food coloring to signify males and red coloring to signify females.

This demonstration should be done in the church parking lot, where nothing can catch fire. Set up with lighter fluid, matches, stones and lots of water.

Arrange the people in your model cities. Relate the story of Sodom and Gomorrah to the youth group (Genesis 18:16—19:29). When you get to the judgment part, spray lighter fluid on the town and ignite it. Throw a few stones at the model to represent brimstone. Afterward, thoroughly douse the model with water.

Your youth group members will never forget the story of Sodom and Gomorrah after this fiery reenactment.

—Tom Franks

Variations

1. Create a slide show of Sodom and Gomorrah before, during and after destruction.

2. Have the kids dress in appropriate costumes and act out the story. Illustrate "fire and brimstone" by flicking on and off the lights and playing thun-

der sounds from a sound-effects record (check your local library). Place a white sheet over Lot's wife when she is turned to a pillar of salt!

Your Ideas and Variations

_____
_____
_____
_____
_____
_____
_____
_____
_____
_____
_____
_____
_____
_____

TREES

233

A Tree-mendous Faith
TOPIC: FAITH/SPIRITUAL GROWTH

Use this Bible study to focus on faith as a living, growing thing in need of care and nourishment.

Gather Bibles, pencils and cross sections of wood (found at a local craft store); or assemble the group around a tree stump.

Begin by saying, "Today we

will learn something about ourselves. To do that we will look at how a tree grows. Events that happen in the life of a tree affect the tree's core and growth. It is the same for us."

Gather around the tree stump, or give each person a cross section of wood. Describe different parts of the cross section: the outside bark; cracks that develop when the wood dries; rings that are shaped as a "V" indicating branches growing at that position; scars indicating damage; the heartwood or core of the tree.

Divide the youth group members into small groups called "growth rings." Have the members discuss these items:

● When were you born? That date is your heartwood—the beginning of your life.

● What is your earliest memory of church? What's the first prayer you were taught? the first Sunday school song? Do you remember your baptism? Do you know your baptismal date?

● What scars or problems are you dealing with right now?

● Notice the "V" markings that indicate growth. How have you grown in the past year? What do you feel best about in your life?

Read Colossians 2:6-7 to the group, "As therefore you received Christ Jesus the Lord, so live in him, rooted and built up in him and established in the faith, just as you were taught, abounding in thanksgiving."
Then close with these points:

● **We need roots.** We need to be firmly anchored in Christ.

● **Growth comes from doing.** Unless the roots of the tree are receiving nourishment, and that nourishment is moving throughout the tree's system, there will be no growth. It is the same for us. Prayer, worship, a daily sharing with God of concerns and celebrations keeps us growing and strong as Christians.

● **The tree knows how to grow.** Built into the tree is the blueprint for growth—the need for sunlight, water, nourishment and a strong root system. It is the same for our life in Christ. We need to trust that God has created, deep within us, a need to love, serve and obey him, and to grow as Christians.

● **Growth takes time.** A tree

does not grow strong in one year. Rather it builds upon itself—layer upon layer, ring upon ring, year after year. Slow, consistent growth and understanding are important.

—Bill Zieche

Variations

1. Give the kids each a marker and have them write in their cross section the answer to this question: "What do you need to do to develop a deeper relationship with God?" Have them take the cross sections home as reminders to grow stronger in their faith.

2. On the outer edge of the cross section, close to the strong bark, have the kids write a way their faith has been strengthened in the past year.

3. Use this idea in conjunction with a nature hike, camp or retreat.

Your Ideas and Variations

_____
_____
_____
_____
_____
_____
_____
_____
_____
_____
_____
_____
_____

TROPHIES

234

Using Old Trophies
TOPIC: AWARDS

Every church or home storage area contains at least one, old, forgotten trophy. Gather several of these castaways, dust them off, unscrew the parts, then reassemble them to make a superhuge trophy. Use the trophy several ways:

● Label it as a "traveling trophy." Give it to each week's winning church team (whatever the sport).

● Make it a "real winner" award. At each youth group

meeting, award the trophy to someone who helped out a lot, participated the most or shared a great insight. Let the winner take the trophy home and return it the next week. Award it to another "real winner" at the end of that meeting, and so on.

● Let the youth group members build trophies too. They love to get in on the creative reassembly work.

Everyone saves money with this idea and it also helps clean out old closets.

—Mitchell M. Olson

Variations

1. Affix a golf ball to the top of an old trophy and label it "Best Sport."

2. Affix a pencil to the top of an old trophy and label it "Most Scholarly."

3. Roll up a piece of paper and secure it with a bright piece of yarn. Affix the "scroll" to the top of an old trophy and label it "Best Bible Memorization."

Your Ideas and Variations

_____
_____
_____
_____
_____
_____
_____
_____
_____
_____

TUBS

235

Polar Bear Bob
TOPIC: GAMES

After a hot-summer game of softball or volleyball, cool the players off with Polar Bear Bob. It's definitely a unique game your group members will never forget.

Fill a large washtub with water and a block of ice. For a special effect, add blue food coloring and then throw in gummy fish, worms or dolphins (Swedish candy). Have extra candy on hand to "restock the pond" during the game. Set up the pond outside or in an uncarpeted area that can easily be cleaned.

Ask the youth group members to wear old clothes. You also will need lots of towels for this activity!

Ask for volunteers to "dive" for fish like polar bears do. Give them 30 seconds to get as many fish as they can.

Polar Bear Bob is truly an eye-opening, bracing activity.

—Tim Smith

Variations

1. Bob for apples in the cold, clear water!

2. Award prizes such as fish crackers, a pack of fishhooks or an old fishing pole.

3. Top off the "arctic" experience by eating Popsicles or ice-cold ice cream sundaes.

Your Ideas and Variations

_____
_____
_____
_____
_____
_____
_____
_____
_____
_____
_____
_____
_____
_____
_____
_____
_____
_____

TULIPS

236

God's Love
TOPIC: GOD'S LOVE

Tulip bulbs and a blooming tulip provide an object lesson on how God's love transforms our lives.

Give each young person a bulb. Have them notice how ugly the bulbs look. Next compare the bulbs with a blooming tulip. Say to the kids, "This is how God often works in our lives— taking ugly things such as faults,

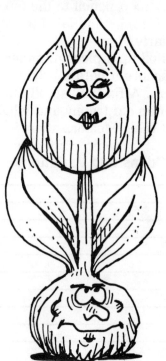

mistakes, problems and crises and transforming them into learning experiences and growth. If we are willing and co-operative, God will use us in his service."

Let the participants take the bulbs home and plant them as an ongoing reminder of God's transforming love.

—Lynn Potter

Variations

1. Ask the property-management board for permission to plant a flower garden on your church property. Let every member enjoy the bright, blooming, colorful, sweet-smelling reminders of God's love.

2. Label a bottle of hand lotion "God's Love—Rub It In." Ask everybody to apply the lotion to their hands (**Clown Ministry**, by Floyd Shaffer and Penne Sewall, Group Books).

Your Ideas and Variations

_____
_____
_____
_____
_____
_____
_____
_____
_____
_____
_____
_____
_____

TURKEYS

237

Tom Turkey Hunt
TOPIC: THANKSGIVING/PROGRESSIVE EVENTS

Interested in a new idea to try with your youth group before Thanksgiving? The Tom Turkey Hunt was a real success and crowd pleaser for us.

Several days before the hunt, I contacted different merchants and vendors and arranged to leave some clues at their business locations. I made up a set of simple, rhyming clues. For example, "Drive through the land of the Irish; ask for something cold; when you have it in your grasp; another clue will be told." This clue led a group of kids to the drive-up window of McDonald's. The next clue was found in an ice cream cone! I made a copy of the clues so I could divide the kids into two groups for the hunt.

I borrowed a live turkey for the event from a family in our church. The turkey was quite large, so I had to secure a large pet cage which, incidentally, would not fit into my car. But it did fit in one of our church vans. I taped to the side of the

van a large sign that said, "Turkey Transporter." I took the van and hid it at a spot known only to myself and one other person.

On the night of the hunt, I split our group into two separate teams, gave them each a set of clues, and sent them throughout our city to find the turkey.

The winning team received a 25-pound frozen turkey; everybody received cookies that were decorated like turkeys. This is a "funtastic" way to celebrate Thanksgiving!

—Randy Gross

Variations

1. Have the kids brainstorm for needy families who could use a frozen turkey for Thanksgiving. Choose one family and deliver the frozen turkey to them. When you deliver it, sing the following song to the tune of "Happy Birthday":

Happy Thanksgiving to you,
Happy Thanksgiving to you,
Happy Thanksgiving,
God Bless thee,
Enjoy your turkey!

Your Ideas and Variations

_____
_____
_____
_____
_____
_____
_____
_____
_____
_____
_____

TYPEWRITER RIBBONS

238

Sin
TOPIC: SIN/REPENTANCE

Stimulate a discussion on sin with a used, disposable ribbon cartridge from a typewriter.

Begin by holding up the used ribbon cassette or cartridge. Talk about how neatly the ribbon is wound inside and how much simpler these are than the messy, old-fashioned ribbons you had to rewind.

Then ask the young people to take hold of a piece of the ribbon and begin to gently pull it out. Keep pulling gently until the ribbon is completely pulled out of the encasement. When this is done, have everyone pull simultaneously. This will break the ribbon into many pieces.

Restore order, then talk about how in the Garden of Eden our lives started out neat and orderly, like the ribbon. Through sin, our lives run increasingly out of control. Note that no person could possibly put this ribbon back together, or our lives, for that matter. Throw away all the scraps; bring out a new cartridge and say, "Jesus can restore our lives and make them better than new because of his death on the cross and his grace."

—Dave Mahoney

Variations

1. As each person holds the ribbon, have him or her think of an area in his or her life that needs improvement or forgiveness. Have the kids pull simultaneously and break the ribbon to pieces. Gather the bits of ribbon in a sack and say, "God forgives all of our sins. He gathers the

bits and pieces of our broken lives and makes us whole."

2. Bring two typewriters and two pieces of typing paper. Divide the young people into two groups. Say that each team will type a story about forgiveness. The first person in each team is to run up to the typewriter, put the paper in it, then begin the story—typing only one sentence. When the typist is finished, he or she tags the next person who then runs to the typewriter, reads what has just been typed, and continues with the story— typing only one sentence. The process continues until everyone has added one sentence to the story. Give prizes for the most creative story, the most meaningful message, the first team done, and the story with the fewest typing errors.

Your Ideas and Variations

_____
_____
_____
_____
_____
_____
_____
_____
_____
_____
_____
_____
_____
_____

VALUABLES

239

Forever Treasures
TOPIC: VALUES/CHRISTIAN LIVING

Use this meeting to help your youth group members discover what they most value in life. They will compare earthly treasures to heavenly ones.

On a table in front of the room place several items, or symbols, that represent earthly treasures: 14k gold ring; bank book; diploma; graduation cap; designer jeans; model of a sports car; gold coin; corsage; radio; travel brochure; report card showing all A's; the word "love" printed on a red, heart-shaped piece of construction paper; and pictures of a television, handshake, beautiful person, successful businessman or businesswoman, choir, one person receiving admiring glances from others, a nurse or doctor at the bedside of a patient. (Be sure each picture clearly depicts what you are intending it to.) You also will need a chalkboard, piece of chalk, eraser, pencils, Bibles, and copies of the worksheet.

As the session begins, write

this question on the board: What do you have that you value most? Allow the young people to give several answers as you, or someone else, writes them on the board. Discuss whether or not each item mentioned has equal value for everyone. Erase the answers, but leave the question.

Explain that each student will choose from the display on the table, 10 treasures he or she would most like to have. Allow the young people to get a closer look at the display items. Give them the option of adding any item not on display. Distribute pencils and copies of the following chart.

Ten Treasures	Meets specifications of Matthew 6:20	Makes John 15:11 come true	Results from the practice of Romans 12:11	Promotes 1 Corinthians 10:31	Encourages obedience to Ephesians 6:18	Allows practice of 1 Thessalonians 5:22	Is described in James 1:17	Makes it possible to practice 1 John 3:17	Fulfills the promise of 1 John 5:13
1.									
2.									
3.									
4.									
5.									
6.									
7.									
8.									
9.									
10.									

Ask the students to write down their 10 most-desired items. Have them look up each scripture and mark an X by the items it applies to. Explain that every item will not have a clear-cut rating. For example, in regard to spiritual growth, a 14k gold ring inherited from a godly grandmother might serve as a reminder to read the Bible and pray. However, if the ring was a gift from a high school boyfriend, it may not be appropriate to check Ephesians 6:18. Encourage the young people to use their imaginations as they check the blocks that apply. Help the students to realize that education and a bank account *can* have spiritual values, if used in the right way.

After all items have been rated, ask the students to count the number of X's. Any student who has at least one X under each of the scriptures should re-ceive an extra 10 points. See who has the highest score. Ask the students if they would have made different choices had they read the scriptures first. Discuss how this exercise can help in setting goals.

Close the session by praying for "forever treasures" such as joy, forgiveness and love.

—Esther M. Bailey

Variations

1. Divide the young people into small groups; give each group one of the "earthly treasures." Have the kids create a two-part skit around their treasure. The first part of the skit is a person wanting this treasure for "earthly" reasons; the second part of the skit is a person wanting this treasure for "heavenly" reasons. For example, a person with a bank book could jump up and down, shouting with joy, "Oh yea! I have a fat, full bank account! Money! Money! Money! I can buy a red sports car with black interior and all the extra goodies. I can travel around the world and buy all kinds of souvenirs. There's no end to what I can buy with this money."

In the second part of the skit a person could say, "God is good. He has blessed me with this bank account. What should I do with it? I could give 10 percent to my church, or I could donate to a world relief program. I know of a needy family in my church. I could buy them a gift certificate to a local grocery store and give it to them anonymously.''

Your Ideas and Variations

_____
_____
_____
_____
_____
_____
_____
_____
_____
_____
_____
_____
_____
_____
_____

WATER

240

A Healing Ceremony
TOPIC: HEALING/FAITH

Center a meaningful worship service around the theme of water and healing. Share the biblical significance of water as it demonstrates the miraculous power of faith. Ask different youth group members to read these verses out loud: Deuteronomy 11:4; Psalms 105:41; 107:35; Matthew 14:29; Luke 8:25.

Place a bowl of water on the altar, and ask participants to

meditate on a part of their body that needs healing. Invite them, one at a time, to move to the bowl, dip their hand in the water and place it on that area. Ask the other worshipers to pray silently for that person. Conclude by singing together a song such as "Kum Ba Yah." For special verses sing, "Heal our hurts, Lord"; "Your will be done, Lord"; and "Thank you, Father."

—Lynn Potter

Variations

1. Divide the group members into pairs, then pass the bowl from pair to pair. Have the kids dip their finger in the water, use that finger to form a cross on their partner's forehead, and say, "Jesus died for you; he forgives all of your sins."

2. Place a Band-Aid on each person's hand and say, "God heals all of your hurts and disappointments."

Your Ideas and Variations

_____
_____
_____
_____
_____
_____
_____
_____
_____
_____

241

Ripples of Water
TOPIC: MEDITATION

Meditation has added depth and inspiration to our youth ministry. Use this idea to enable your young people to consider how their actions affect others.

If meditation is new to your group, explain, "Meditation is a discipline that teaches us to concentrate on one thing at a time. Unlike hypnosis, the participant is always in control and can stop at any time. Meditation has been practiced by Christians since the beginning of the church. It is a way to calm and still ourselves in order to get in touch with the Spirit of God within us. As we practice meditation, we learn to push aside the many distractions within so that we might hear God more clearly!"

Gather your group around a large bowl of water, or beside a swimming pool or lake. Toss a stone into the water and watch for a minute or two in silence. Then lead the group in this guided meditation. Pauses are indicated by an ellipsis (. . .). Be sure to allow sufficient time for each pause.

"Sit in a comfortable position and close your eyes . . . Take five deep breaths, breathing in relaxation and exhaling tension and worry . . . See yourself standing in the center of the pool of water of your life . . . It is misty and still here . . . There is a sense of mystery and wonder . . . This is the very center of you . . . Parts you know and parts still to be discovered . . . The water is warm and peaceful.

"Now become aware that each of your words and actions cause ripples to extend beyond you . . . Affecting whatever and whoever they touch . . . Realize that you have great power over the kind of ripples you make and the affect you have on others . . . You alone control this power . . . No one can take it from you.

"Now as the mist clears see the people in your life standing around you in your pool . . . Those you know best are standing very near to you . . . Others are standing close or farther away depending on your relationship to them . . . You realize that those standing the closest will be most affected by the ripples you make with your words and actions . . . You now realize with great clarity the power you have to affect the persons closest to you.

"How will you choose to affect these persons? See the ripples of your negative words and actions becoming cold water and slapping against others and hurting them . . . Even knocking them down . . . How do you feel? . . . Now see the ripples of your positive words and actions gently caressing others as warm water . . . Enabling them to feel good and to enjoy playing and splashing . . . How do you feel?

"As the bright sunlight surrounds you and the others in your pool, know that the light of God's love is with you . . . Know that this light and warmth are always available to you . . . God will always be there to warm the water of your life's pool and enable you to affect others in positive ways . . . When you feel ready, open your eyes and come back to this place."

After the meditation, allow time for verbal sharing. Meditation is very personal, so don't force anybody to share. Questions to guide sharing are:
- How do you feel about this meditation?
- Did you discover anything new about yourself? Explain.
- Will you act any differently? Why or why not?

Our youth group members enjoyed this so much that they always ask for guided meditations, especially on retreats and before going to sleep on trips.

—Kathi B. Finnell

Variations

1. After the meditation, reaffirm each other's baptisms. Dip your finger in the water and draw a cross on each person's forehead. Say, "Remember that you are a child of God. He loves you very much."

2. Ask the youth group members to plan a daily time and place where they can meditate quietly on God's Word. Have them meditate each day for two weeks, then evaluate their feelings. Do they feel calm? secure? stronger spiritually? Have the teenagers continue this quiet time with God throughout the year.

Your Ideas and Variations

_____
_____
_____
_____
_____
_____
_____
_____
_____
_____
_____
_____
_____
_____
_____
_____
_____
_____

YARN

242

Promises for You
TOPIC: FRIENDSHIP/AFFIRMATION

God's Word promises many things. This activity offers special promises for everyone involved. It works best at a retreat.

After morning worship, give the participants each a small slip of paper and ask them to write their name. Collect the slips, mix them up and redistribute them. Tell the kids that the person named on their slip of paper will be their partner for the day. Explain, "Keep the name of your partner a secret. Observe your partner throughout the day and choose a scripture promise you feel will bless him or her. At the end of the day, we'll make a special gift for our secret partners." List on a piece of paper at least 10 Bible promises for the kids to choose from: Daniel 12:3; John 3:16; 11:25; 15:10-11; 1 John 1:7, etc.

At the end of the day, gather everyone and distribute paper, markers and yarn. Have the kids write in big letters on the paper the scripture reference they

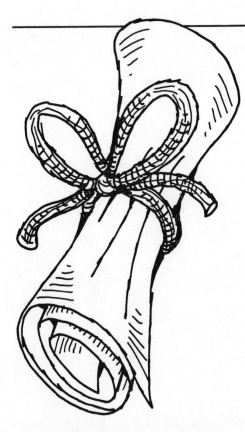

Variations

1. Have the young people do this activity during a school day. Who says secret partners can only be used during meetings and retreats?

2. Assign the youth group members to a visitor or a new member—surprise the new people with scripture-scrolls.

3. Give inexpensive gifts that represent the scripture; for example, a candle could represent God's light and a person's shiny smile, a bottle of bubble soap could represent God's love and a person's enthusiasm, etc.

Your Ideas and Variations

_____
_____
_____
_____
_____
_____
_____
_____
_____
_____
_____
_____
_____
_____
_____

chose. Then have the participants roll the paper like a scroll, tie a piece of yarn around it, and present it as a gift to their partner.

Each person may say something like, "After observing you all day, I feel this scripture would bless you. You are bright, shiny and bubbly so I chose Daniel 12:3: 'And those who are wise shall shine like the brightness of the firmament; and those who turn many to righteousness, like the stars for ever and ever.'"

Close with partner prayers; have them thank God for fulfilling his promises to us.

—Debbie Valleau

YOUTH MINISTRY CARGO PERSONNEL

The Contributors

Mary E. Albert
Gail Alston
L. Jim Anthis
Esther M. Bailey
Tommy Baker
Janet R. Balmforth
Steven J. Bolda
Susan Bonjour
Walter John Boris
Brethren House Ministries
Thomas F. Bronson
Therese Caouette
Rick Chromey
J.B. Collingsworth
Jeffrey A. Collins
Karen Darling
Beth Dewey
Jim Farrer
Linda Ferree
Kathi B. Finnell
Mary Kay Fitzpatrick
Tom Franks
Sue Fries
Nancy Going
Randy Gross
Linda R. Hazzard
Donald W. Hendrick
Bob Hicks
Gary G. Jenkins
Russ Jolly
Leonard Kageler
Margaret Kelchner
Mark Killingsworth
Mardie H.C. MacDonald
Dave Mahoney

E. Jane Mall
Ed McNulty
Walter Mees
Gloria Menke
John Miller
Karen Musitano
Doug Newhouse
Steve Newton
Bruce M. Nichols
Chris Oehrlein
David Olshine
Rhonda Olshine
Maribeth Olson
Mitchell M. Olson
Tim Pontius
Mary Joyce Porcelli
Lynn Potter
Lissa Pressley
Mark Reed
Arlo R. Reichter
Steve Roberts
Julie Sevig
Rickey Short
Tim Smith
Wesley Taylor
Denise Turner
Debbie Valleau
James D. Walton
David Washburn
Rich Weihing
Kerrie Weitzel
Sherry Westergard
Gary Wheeler
Gary P. Wrisberg
Bill Zieche

■ Controversial Topics for Youth Groups

by Edward N. McNulty

Get essential tools for teaching teenagers how to deal with tough issues. Help young people develop the skills they'll need to make ethical decisions. Plus, get 40 creative program ideas for examining thought-provoking topics, such as . . .

- Reincarnation
- AIDS: Punishment for immorality?
- Loyalty to a friend who cheats
- Christians and politics
- Abortion, and 35 other hot topics

Teach your young people how to think through hard issues, apply scriptural values, then make their own faith-based decisions.

You'll get loads of current background information. Ready-to-use program ideas. Plus, dozens of creative approaches for handling life's hot topics.

ISBN 0931-529-51-4
360 pages, $13.95

■ GROUP Magazine's Best Youth Group Programs, Volume 1

edited by Cindy S. Hansen

Now you can have 79 proven, ready-to-use youth group programs right at your fingertips. Each complete meeting plan is easy to follow, so each meeting can be ready in a snap. Time-saving programs cover loads of topics, such as spiritual growth. Self-image. Relationships, and more.

So, meet the needs of your young people. Make your ministry more effective with this super collection of creative, ready-to-use youth group programs.

ISBN 0931-529-11-5
224 pages, $17.95

■ Group's Best Jr. High Meetings, Volume 1

edited by Cindy Parolini

You'll discover more than a year's supply of complete, ready-to-use meetings. Meetings to help your junior high young people develop self-esteem. Build strong, positive relationships. Communicate better with their parents. And strengthen their emerging faith.

Give your junior highers the positive, Christian support they need. Create a caring, encouraging time of growth with **Group's Best Jr. High Meetings, Volume 1**.

ISBN 0931-529-58-1
324 pages, $18.95

Recharge Your Ministry With Fresh Ideas

■ Determining Needs in Your Youth Ministry

by Dr. Peter L. Benson and Dorothy L. Williams
foreword by George Gallup Jr.

Discover what your young people are most deeply concerned about. **Determining Needs in Your Youth Ministry** helps you get honest answers to important questions. Plus, you get loads of practical suggestions for creating dynamic programs to fill those needs.

This easy-to-use research kit helps you zero in on the real issues facing your young people. The complete kit includes . . .

- 20 ready-to-use questionnaires and answer sheets
- Tally and summary sheets
- Detailed "How-to-use" information
- Interpretation guidelines
- Plus, practical suggestions for using survey results to build programming to meet those needs.

Open new lines of communication with your kids. And plan programs that really meet the needs of your young people with this effective ministry tool.

ISBN 0931-529-56-5
240 pages, $19.95

■ Instant Programs for Youth Groups (Volumes 1, 2 and 3)

from the editors of Group Publishing

Get loads of quick-and-easy program ideas you can prepare in a flash.

Each book gives you 17 (or more) meeting ideas on topics important to teenagers . . .

1—Self-Image, Pressures, Living as a Christian
2—Me and God, Responsibility, Emotions
3—Friends, Parents, Dating and Sex

Each meeting idea gives you everything you need for a creative program. Step-by-step instructions. Material lists of easy-to-find items. Dynamic discussion starters. And ready-to-copy handouts to involve kids.

With all three books, you can keep a year's worth of program ideas at your fingertips—ready to tap instantly.

Instant Programs for Youth Groups 1
ISBN 0931-529-32-8
90 pages, $7.95

Instant Programs for Youth Groups 2
ISBN 0931-529-42-5
90 pages, $7.95

Instant Programs for Youth Groups 3
ISBN 0931-529-43-3
90 pages, $7.95

More Creative Programming Resources

■ Training Volunteers in Youth Ministry
Video kit

Give your volunteer youth workers a deeper understanding of youth ministry. You'll get expert, in-depth education with the **Training Volunteers in Youth Ministry** video kit. The nation's top authorities on teenagers and youth ministry provide solid, practical information.

Design a complete training program to meet your needs using helpful tips from the 128-page leaders guide and four 30-minute VHS videotapes . . .

Video 1: Youth Ministry Basics	Video 3: Building Relationships
Video 2: Understanding Teenagers	Video 4: Keys for Successful Meetings

You'll use this valuable resource again and again, sharpening the skills of your volunteer team. You'll discover how to find, motivate and keep volunteers. Plus, you'll strengthen your youth ministry team spirit with practical, affordable youth ministry training.

ISBN 0931-529-59-X, $98

■ Outrageous Clip Art for Youth Ministry

Discover off-the-wall cartoons to spice up your newsletters, handouts, brochures, posters and fliers . . .

Tickle the funny bone of teenagers with hundreds of ZANY clip art cartoons. Delight your young people with eye-catching newsletters. Announcements. Handouts. Grab attention fast with out-of-the-ordinary clip art.

Clip art is fast and easy—a cinch to choose, clip, paste and copy. A quick index helps you find a cartoon and the right headline—with many sizes to choose from.

Promote your events with not-so-typical invitations. Use preposterous pictures to boost interest in special occasions, service projects, meetings and much more. Plus, get 335 attention-grabbing ways to announce your events . . .

● Burger bash	● Pie party	● Bus brigade
● Roller derby	● Water war	● Frisbee fling
● Lunch munch	● Taco fiesta	● Pancake feed

● and a Bring Your Own Banana—Banana Split Night.

Add spark and spice to all your printed pieces. Boost attendance and excitement—with kid-pleasing cartoons straight from the bizarre imagination of artist Rand Kruback . . .

ISBN 0931-529-39-5
256 pages, $14.95

These and other Group resources are available at your local Christian bookstore or direct from the publisher. Group Books, Box 481, Loveland, CO 80539. Please add $2 postage/handling ($4 for video orders) when ordering direct. Colorado residents add 3% sales tax.